FLEEING HITLER

Hanna Diamond is Senior Lecturer in French History at the University of Bath. She lived and taught in Paris for many years and has spent her career researching the lives of the French people during the twentieth century. Her previous book, *Women and the Second World War in France 1939–48: Choices and Constraints*, is also based on personal narratives and oral history and was the first book to explore the range of women's experiences of the war.

GW00323249

Praise *for Fleeing Hitler*:

'A major contribution'
Modern and Contemporary France

'The strength of Diamond's book is to convey the poignancy, drama and ambiguity of an experience that directly touched the lives of many more people than the Resistance ever did ... her readable book superbly conveys the strange unreality of those hot summer days of 1940.'
Julian Jackson, *Times Higher Education Supplement*

'A fascinating story, rich in biblical drama, and one that has not been previously told in English. [Diamond] is excellent at describing the political machinations that culminated in Paul Reynaud's resignation ... [a] valuable book.'
Walter Cook, *Tribune*

'Hanna Diamond ... tells the story vividly and even-handedly. [The] book benefits greatly from the vast number of eyewitness memoirs.'
Allan Massie, *Literary Review*

'A vivid and poignant account ... a forgotten moment of the devastation of war brought to life.'
Robert Gildea, author of *Marianne in Chains*

'Diamond tells a compulsive and intricate story, making superb use of eyewitness accounts and individual testimony'
Rod Kedward, author of *La Vie en Bleu: France and the French since 1900*

'Diamond has an excellent eye for the striking detail ... as a work of history, this book is an invaluable account of the fall of France, seen through the lens of the sufferings of its citizens.'
Carmen Callil, *Financial Times*

'Readable and well-informed ... the first general account in English and one of the most satisfactory in any language.'
Robert O. Paxton, *The New York Review of Books*

'For many French people in 1940, the arrival of the German army meant the collapse of civilization. Seven decades later, the specifics of that collapse are largely forgotten; this book is the remedy ...'
Kirkus Reviews

FLEEING HITLER

FRANCE 1940

HANNA DIAMOND

OXFORD
UNIVERSITY PRESS

OXFORD
UNIVERSITY PRESS

Great Clarendon Street, Oxford OX2 6DP

Oxford University Press is a department of the University of Oxford.
It furthers the University's objective of excellence in research, scholarship,
and education by publishing worldwide in

Oxford New York

Auckland Cape Town Dar es Salaam Hong Kong Karachi
Kuala Lumpur Madrid Melbourne Mexico City Nairobi
New Delhi Shanghai Taipei Toronto

With offices in

Argentina Austria Brazil Chile Czech Republic France Greece
Guatemala Hungary Italy Japan Poland Portugal Singapore
South Korea Switzerland Thailand Turkey Ukraine Vietnam

Oxford is a registered trade mark of Oxford University Press
in the UK and in certain other countries

Published in the United States
by Oxford University Press Inc., New York

© Hanna Diamond 2007

British Library Cataloguing in Publication Data

Data available

Library of Congress Cataloging in Publication Data

Data available

Typeset by SPI Publisher Services, Pondicherry, India
Printed in Great Britain
on acid-free paper by
Ashford Colour Press Ltd, Gosport, Hampshire

ISBN 978-0-19-280618-5 (Hbk)
978-0-19-953259-9 (Pbk)

1 3 5 7 9 10 8 6 4 2

For Sam

Preface

My intention has been to write an accessible detailed account of the experiences of civilians and soldiers caught up in the events of spring–summer 1940 in France. It is informed by a wide range of sources including journals, memoirs, diaries, and interviews with those affected. I have wanted to portray what happens when ordinary people are faced with possible death and domination after invasion by a foreign power. At a time when refugees are a sadly familiar sight, it is difficult now to imagine how unprecedented this kind of population displacement was in 1940. Stories of migration, of people being uprooted from their homes in the wake of international wars, civil wars, and natural disasters are now commonplace. In 1940 the Parisians who left their homes were predominantly women and children. In attempting to flee the Nazi invasion, they became refugees in their own country.

Acknowledgements

I have very much enjoyed writing this book. I appreciated the help and support I received from friends and family too numerous to mention here. Thanks most especially go to Claire Gorrara whose invaluable help during the early stages gave the book coherence. Rod Kedward's detailed comments on a later draft of the manuscript were insightful and thorough; this is a better book as a result of them. Other colleagues helped me with translation, passed on wonderful material, read drafts, and most important of all cleared the decks so I would have time to write. My thanks go in particular to Bill Brooks, Anna Bull, Marion Demossier, Roger Eatwell, Ernie Hampson, Simon Kitson, Nina Parish, Chris Reynolds, Julian Swann, Steve Wharton, and Tim Brooks who gave me advice about maps. My GP Nicole Howse and Rob Slack at the RUH kept me healthy, Robin Leclercq and the Smith family distracted Sam. In the Tarn-et-Garonne, the Anglas family found me contacts, and fed and housed me on visits to La Française and Molières.

In Paris, Laura Downs and Francesca Trabacca offered unfailing encouragement, helpful tips, and material. Friends Roly and David Aknin let me use their spare room whenever I needed it. Solange Pierrat passed on family documents. She and Solange Bordier searched out witnesses for me to interview. David Fee and Olivier Belenfant allowed me to interview their relatives and friends. Those who were prepared to talk to me about their exodus experiences included: Madame Asquin, Madame Basselet, Madame Bertucat, Madame Bully, Madame Conrad, Monsieur Fee, Madame Fontanier, Monsieur Godin, Monsieur Ichbia, Madame Kerloch, Madame Leclercq, Madame Perrot, Madame Pierrat, and Madame Thouvenot.

My thanks also go to the staff at the National Archives in Kew and the Imperial War Museum. Patricia Gillet helped me at the Archives nationales de Paris, and Bruno Rambourg and Thérèse Blondet-Bisch at the Bibliothèque de documentation internationale contemporaine at Nanterre. I am also grateful to the archivists at the Archives départementales du Tarn-et-Garonne and staff at the University of Bath library, especially Felicity Nurdin at inter-library loans whom I worked very hard.

My publishers at Oxford University Press have been terrific. Thanks in particular to Katherine Reeve, Christopher Wheeler, Luciana O'Flaherty, Matthew Cotton, Deborah Protheroe, Emmanuelle Péri, Rowena Anketell, and Catherine Berry.

All translations from the French are my own.

H. D.

Contents

List of Maps

List of Illustrations

The Refugees

Since close to two million Parisians left their homes in June 1940, there could never be a single narrative of that experience. By bringing together the experiences and testimonies of a number of those affected, this book seeks to present a picture of that traumatic and confusing time. The refugees I have chosen to focus on wrote about their experiences in illuminating detail. They include the following:

GEORGES ADREY, son of shopkeepers, he was a militant socialist and syndicalist. His hundred-page account of his exodus experience is modestly subtitled *The Notes and Impressions of a Parisian Metalworker during the Exodus*. Published in 1941, he wrote it in the interests of pacifism.

SIMONE DE BEAUVOIR (1908–86), teacher and philosopher, is best known for writing *The Second Sex* (1949), a book which offers a detailed analysis of women's oppression and became a foundational document of contemporary feminism. De Beauvoir met the philosopher Jean-Paul Sartre in 1929 when they were both still students. Her autobiographical text *La Force de l'âge* (*The Prime of Life*) appeared in 1960, but was based on her war diaries which were published by Gallimard in 1990. Both texts offer detailed accounts of her experiences during the exodus and immediately after her return to Paris.

RUPERT DOWNING, born in England in 1901, was screenwriter and the composer of Boris Karloff's first British horror film, *The Ghoul* (1933). His lively and humorous account of his escape from Paris during the exodus, entitled *If I Laugh*, appeared in 1941.

ROLAND DORGELÈS (1885–1973) was a prolific novelist. He takes credit for inventing the French expression *drôle de guerre*, meaning phoney war, the period between the declaration of war in September 1939 and the German offensive in May 1940 during which time there was little evidence of hostilities. Posted to Lorraine in October 1939, he wrote a newspaper article entitled 'Drôle de guerre'. The French word *drôle* means both funny and strange. 'I did not anticipate the success this formula would meet with . . . It certainly was a *drôle de guerre*, not in the sense of cheerful—as there is nothing cheerful about death—but in the sense of bizarre and surprising, as indeed it was, especially for those of us who had participated in the previous war.' His book *La Drôle de guerre 1939–1940* which appeared in 1957, along with *Vacances forcés*, published in 1985, provide fascinating accounts of his life in 1940.

GEORGETTE GUILLOT was a secretary at the Ministry of Interior who kept a diary of her three-week exodus from Paris. Her ten-page handwritten diary is held at the Archives nationales de Paris.

SIMONE PERROT recounted her exodus experiences to the author in Paris in April 2005. Aged 16 in 1940, she lived at home with her recently widowed mother and sick brother. In June 1940, with a group of others from Montigny, their village situated just outside Paris, they travelled to a farm near Châteauroux. Their three-week exodus left vivid memories that she related with clarity and emotion.

GEORGES SADOUL (1904–67), former member of the surrealists and a communist, he made his reputation as a journalist of film in the 1930s. In 1940 he kept a journal of his period in the armed forces from September 1939 to July 1940. It was first published ten years after his death. His remarkable account lucidly depicts both his own experiences and those of the refugees he comes across and provides invaluable insights into the period.

LÉON WERTH (1878–1955), a Jew, was a novelist and also worked as a journalist, best known for his art criticism. He was a great friend of fellow writer Antoine de Saint-Exupéry, author of *The Little Prince*, which was dedicated to him. Werth and his family survived the war, unlike Saint-Exupéry. His book *33 jours* (33 Days), describes their difficult journey at a time when 'the Germans were still courteous'. In 1941 Werth, in hiding in Saint-Amour (Jura), was visited by Saint-Exupéry and entrusted him with this text. Saint-Exupéry then offered the manuscript to an American publishing house during a visit there but for reasons that have never been uncovered it was never published. It finally came to light again and was published in 1992.

Paris, June 1940

In June 1940, Paris was a city in mourning... Thick clouds of soot from the burning petrol reserves masked brilliant sunshine. People loaded furniture and knick-knacks on to vehicles of all kinds, as houses were cleared of their contents passengers, furniture and objects alike, took shelter under pyramids of mattresses. Dog owners killed their pets so they would not have to feed them. In this sad frenzy of departure people rescued whatever possessions they could save... Weeping women pushed old people who had been squashed into prams; their children followed behind, overpowered by the heat.

Marie-Madeleine. Fourcade, *L'Arche de Noé*

On 14 June 1940 Nazi tanks rolled into the French capital which had been deserted by the vast majority of its inhabitants. The previous day, the gates of the Gare d'Austerlitz swung shut for the last time as the final train south left. In the preceding two weeks, this station, like the city of Paris, had witnessed some of the most extraordinary scenes in its history. Suddenly, government ministries were left deserted as administrative officials and other staff left for the Tours area, anxious not to fall into German hands. Witnessing this departure made Parisians finally realize that the arrival of the Nazis in their city was imminent, leaving only one option if they did not want to find themselves under occupation: escape. In their panic to leave Paris, the train was their first thought and mainline stations were inundated. It immediately became clear that the railways could not cope with this unexpected demand for evacuation and the services struggled to keep up. Undeterred, and with one thought uppermost in their minds, Parisians continued their journey on foot rather than find themselves stranded in the capital. As they took to the roads, they encountered exhausted and frightened evacuees from Belgium, Holland, and Luxembourg along with fellow citizens from the north and east of the country who had fled the German armies just days before. Growing numbers of soldiers, retreating from the front, now mingled with civilians and attracted the attention of German aircraft. While those from Paris were at first unaware of the dangers they might face, refugees from other regions knew that they could find themselves under attack at any time. No one had planned for this exodus and the result was total chaos with an enormous price to pay in terms of human misery and suffering.

Invasion was by no means a new experience for the French people. The German armies had crossed the frontiers into France twice before: during the Franco-Prussian war of 1870, and once again in the early months of the Great War of 1914–18. Neither of these experiences had adequately prepared the nation for the events of May–June 1940 which affected the civilian population on a scale that had never been seen before. In the Paris region alone, close to four million people left their homes and fled south. By the time the Germans entered the city, just one-fifth of the normal population remained; mainly the elderly, the infirm, and those who could not afford to leave. This departure of the capital's inhabitants swelled the numbers of people who were displaced from their homes to such an extent that for these few weeks, more people were on the move than at any time in previously recorded history, probably since the Dark Ages. For the Parisian writer Camille Bourniquel, the events of June 1940 marked the collapse of civilization:

> Now it has been given a name, only an experience in the Bible could represent this surge of humanity, this shifting of one part of the country to another. It marks the return of chaos which marked the past, the historical wilderness when the jackals roamed! The exodus!
>
> An entire people of stragglers at the outposts of a civilization for whom the Middle Ages have been reinvented; with their feet blistered and bleeding, disputes over water, people crushing one another, dominated by fear, all this against a background of devastation.[1]

In similar terms, Jérôme Tharaud, another writer, described the exodus as a phenomenon unknown since the barbarian invasions of the fourth century.[2] And for the contemporary Fascist sympathizer and commentator Lucien Rebatet, 'In the space of four days, France had jumped backwards six centuries, finding itself at the gates of a medieval famine.'[3]

The dramatic spectacle moved those who witnessed it. Armand Lunel, writer and academic, was shocked by his first sight of peasant carts as he withdrew from the north of Reims:

> It was... five in the morning... when we caught sight of the first French peasant cart, these people were once again victims of invasion, these carts which might also have been present at the time of Callot or of 1814 with their four sad pieces of furniture loaded sideways on to some straw, the battery of kitchen utensils attached to the side rails, the chicks at the back in a salad bowl and all the family on foot, father, mother, and the little ones shivering... less with cold than with distress.[4]

The presence of these carts in the city brought back memories of their peasant origins that in moving to the capital many Parisians had sought to leave behind them. 'These wagons rolling across the tarmac seemed like a terrible image of war and made them feel as if they were back in the Middle Ages.'[5] A further witness, Georges Sadoul, a journalist whose diary offers many evocative descriptions of this period, also looked to the past as a way of expressing what he could see: 'the lines from a witness describing the flight of the population of Moscow in the face of Napoleon's advance seem to me to give an idea of the spectacle which I have been incapable of seeing clearly, its scale so defies human understanding'.[6] These were appalling sights, utterly unfamiliar to those who witnessed them.

Responses to these events ranged from anger and outrage to a sense of powerlessness and despondency. On Thursday 13 June, while participating in the organized retreat of the French army, Sadoul found himself passing through the deserted streets of the suburbs of Paris. His realization that the city would not be defended and that he was among the last troops to abandon it filled him with mixed emotions.

> The roads we pass through are those of a town infested with the plague. The six-floor façades of the houses in the centre of Bezons and Houilles are entirely shut up. Not a single shutter, domestic or commercial, is up. And no one on the road, no police or members of the military... Only from time to time do we see deserters in their khaki uniforms who stagger around the exits of pillaged bistros. Sometimes, old ladies make a friendly sign to us with their hands.
>
> 'They should not wave to soldiers who are running away!' I say to a friend, enraged.
>
> The Eiffel Tower passes by my left shoulder little by little... We are abandoning Paris, where, from the Eiffel Tower, tomorrow the swastika will fly...
> The street starts to fill with the first refugees. We have caught up with the rearguard of the civilian army fleeing Paris. A poorly dressed woman rapidly

walks along. Five children follow behind. The six of them have nothing with them. They carry nothing in their hands and have nothing in their pockets.[7]

As he found himself among these refugees,[8] he feared for the more vulnerable among them.

There are so many people, so much accumulated distress that we can't distinguish between them any more. Moreover, all these unhappy people are only a few kilometres from the gates of Paris. They still have all their strength and all their courage. But we wonder among ourselves what will become of all these women and children, as well as those who are sick and old, after two or three days of walking... it will be impossible for them to find food or even shelter.[9]

Some days before, Léon Werth, writer and art critic, had left Paris with his wife on the advice of friends who urged him to leave for his traditional holiday retreat somewhat earlier than normal, fearing that his Jewishness would make him vulnerable to persecution in the event of German occupation. People were aware of the anti-Semitic policies that had been introduced in Germany by the Nazis and it seemed probable that similar measures would be extended to all territories that came under German occupation. Like most others leaving the city, Werth soon found himself at the mercy of the 'interminable caravan' of traffic queues.

We are no more than a link in the chain which slowly spreads out along the road at a speed of 10, or even 5 km [7, or even 3 miles] an hour... We drive with a strangled engine in second gear, but more often in first, 20 m [66 feet] at a time. Then we stop for six or seven hours, I don't know any more. Six or seven hours in the sun.[10]

The novelist Roland Dorgelès who, like Sadoul, had followed orders to withdraw from the front, noticed, during his journey to Tours where he planned to join the exiled government: 'In spite of everything, a sort of order reigned over this dreadful crowd. No cries, no horns—anything like that would have been useless.'[11] Despite this apparent calmness in the early stages of their journeys, many would soon face the danger of bombing and particularly machine-gunning by the enemy. Georges Adrey, a metalworker who left Paris on foot, accompanied by his wife and some work colleagues, described how they were frequently obliged to take cover.

We start to cross an extremely dangerous area near to the railway line. The German aircraft are bombing the region in waves and this leaves us no respite. Several times we are obliged to leave our vehicle and lie flat on our stomachs in the ditch or on the grass or even to hide in the woods in order to escape death.[12]

Who were these people filling the roads out of Paris in June 1940? The majority of men who left the capital at this time were those who had not been mobilized, having been classed as specially designated workers assigned to industries considered vital to the war effort. When the arrival of the Germans in the city seemed inevitable, they too realized that the time had come for them to leave. They knew that they faced the very real possibility of being taken as prisoners of war or being sent to work in labour camps in Germany. Some were given explicit orders to leave. Others heard radio broadcasts which encouraged them to go. The Englishman Rupert Downing, who found himself in Paris at this time, heard a radio announcement and decided to get out of the capital straightaway.

> On June 12th, the German army was within 20 miles [32 km] of Paris, and I was still in my flat near Montparnasse . . . In my very bones I knew it: the incredible was about to happen. During the afternoon the French radio issued a Government decree that all male civilians, except the aged and the infirm, were to leave the capital. There seemed to be a desire not to leave Hitler with too many future munitions workers. Just how we were to escape was not specified; most of the cars had been commandeered by the military, and the trains had stopped running 48 hours previously.[13]

Rupert and his friend Dee agreed that it was not a time for bravado and that the best thing for them was to leave. He acquired a bike on which to wheel their luggage and that evening, after a good few drinks, they headed out into the night.

In Georges Adrey's factory, there had been talk of evacuation and departure for several days. Unlike his colleagues, Adrey was reluctant to accept the idea of leaving. But when the orders finally came, he accepted that he no longer had any choice, only to find that once again the orders were cancelled at the very last minute. After some considerable confusion, he and his wife decided to leave.

> Our decision taken, we put the luggage in the hand-cart and cover it with curtains and bags, we take a ewer, a tin dish, and a litre of cocoa and after having hoisted MM, who had a mutilated leg, on to the cart, in this far from brilliant way we headed towards the Porte d'Italie, already dark with people, where the refugees were pressing down the road in increasing numbers.[14]

While there were thousands of men and soldiers among those caught up in the exodus, the majority of Parisians who left home were women and it has been estimated that between a third and a quarter of those on the road were children.[15] In the absence of husbands who were at the front, women had to single-handedly get their children out of the city and organize their journey to the best of their abilities. Though many set off alone with their children, most preferred to try and travel with others and often teamed up with parents or parents-in-law. These family groups were rarely able to sustain travelling as a large group and invariably became separated in the crowds. Separation from loved ones would become a common experience in the exodus and was often one which remained unresolved until long after these dramatic weeks. Unfortunately, few women have left any record of their exodus.[16] The famous feminist writer Simone de Beauvoir, however, kept a detailed diary account which offers valuable insights into what she and other women were going through at this time. Already on 9 June, she was beginning to sense the imminence of the German arrival and wrote:

> I took the German advance as a personal threat; I had only one idea which was not to be cut off from Sartre, not to be taken like a rat in Occupied Paris.[17]

She learnt from her friend Vedrine that all school exams had been cancelled and that as a teacher she was released from her duties:

> that froze my soul, it was definitive and without hope, the Germans would be in Paris in two days, I had nothing else to do but leave with her for Angers—I went up to see my parents to tell them I was leaving, they could not leave for a couple of days because of financial worries . . . I packed but only took what was essential, I left all my books, papers, and old clothes. I took my manuscripts, notebooks, and clothes I was attached to.[18]

For other families, deciding who should stay and who should leave was the first and most difficult consideration. It was often impossible to imagine any realistic way of transferring elderly or sick relatives. Stanley Hoffmann, who later became a distinguished historian of France, was 11 in 1940: 'On the morning of 12 June, my mother pulled me out of bed, took out some very small cases, handed over charge of my uncle to the maid as he was in no fit state to travel . . . My mother was very unhappy to leave her sick brother, but her main concern was to "rescue" me.'[19] For those who did eventually decide that it was too dangerous to take the elderly with them, they left their homes feeling doubly tortured, terrified not only about their own unknown fate, but also about the fate of those they were leaving behind. Others went to extraordinary lengths to try and accommodate the sick and elderly in their travel arrangements: some were able to come up with ingenious solutions and it was not unusual to see elderly folk being pushed along in prams or even wheelbarrows.

1. This family leaving Paris at the very last minute have rigged up an old pram so that grandma can be wheeled along with the rest of the family.

What induced the people of Paris to indulge in this mass departure rather than remain in their own homes? Why did the invading army instil such terror in Parisians? What triggered these personal decisions that launched them into the unknown in such an uncompromising way? What persuaded women to leave with young children, often simply taking to the streets, convinced that the dangers they might meet on the road were nothing compared to the dangers that they would surely experience if they stayed in their homes in Paris? In the midst of the tumultuous events of the 1940 defeat most people felt that the decision to leave was imposed upon them and that staying was an impossible option. For some it was instinctive, and for others the possibility had already been considered and contingency plans put into place. Fear overwhelmed any other feelings and departure seemed the most rational course of action. The confidence in victory that the media and the government had projected until the very last minute meant that when they finally realized that the Germans were likely to reach Paris, people had a very long way to fall. Nothing had prepared people for the possibility of defeat, so no one had envisaged such an outcome. On the contrary, everything seemed to point to confidence in the invincibility of the French army. French people believed the propagandist assurances that the military superiority of the Allies over the Germans was unquestionable. The Allied populations were prepared exclusively for certain victory. 'We will win because we are the strongest', they were told. When the Germans finally attacked in May 1940, no one doubted the outcome.[20]

But in the event, the Germans surprised them, making incursions into French territory with astonishing rapidity. Parisians remained calm, remembering the battle of the Marne during the First World War when the Germans had appeared equally menacing. They comforted themselves with the thought that it would only be a question of time before the Germans were overwhelmed as they had been then. After all, the success of the Germans in Belgium, the north of France, and even their advance across the river Meuse seemed very much in line with what had taken place in August 1914 so surely this was no undue cause for worry. The French propaganda machine kept the full extent of the army's collapse out of the public domain, so most were able to pass off this apparently 'temporary' success of the Germans as a consequence of their superior military force in armaments and their willingness to resort to cruelty and uncivilized methods. Official communiqués reinforced this interpretation of events and on 24 May 1940 Prime Minister Paul Reynaud broadcast the following announcement: 'France has been invaded a hundred times and never beaten . . . our belief in victory is intact.'[21]

The sudden discovery that all was not as it had seemed influenced the precipitous nature of people's departure. There was so little reliable news coming from the normal channels of information like the radio or the newspapers that people were forced to look elsewhere for clues about how they should behave and interpret the situation. Even well into June, people found the apparent normality of what was going on around them to be reassuring. Léon Werth, for example, described a meeting with his friend on the Champs Élysées when they noted that the grass was still being watered: 'this jet of water from the hosepipe inspires childish thoughts and gives us confidence: "If the situation was serious they would not bother to water the grass".'[22] Similarly, Georgette Guillot, a secretary at the Ministry of the Interior, marvelled at the attitudes of her friends who also appeared unaware of the gravity of events. She met two of them on the Champs Élysées for lunch. He, a military dentist, had remained in Paris with his girlfriend. 'This couple represents a perfect lack of concern, they are at ease with their comfortable mobilization. There are many others like them, this is certainly a very *drôle de guerre*,' she remarked. Guillot makes

reference here to the period between September 1939 and May 1940—the
drôle de guerre—during which time virtually nothing appeared to be happening. She noticed lorries passing by from time to time loaded up with all
manner of things including saucepans, mattresses, boxes with sad and
grubby people sitting on them. 'We feel ashamed to be negligently sitting
at the terrace of a café. Before it was Belgians who were crossing Paris, but
these incessant sad convoys of people are no longer just Belgians but also
people from the north of France, and from the department of the Aisne.'[23]
Despite the fact that this was visible and tangible evidence that German
troops were gaining on Paris, such complacency continued until the communiqués charting the progress of the German invasion started to contain
the names of places that people recognized as being relatively close by.
For example, when Parisians were told that the Germans were at Forge-
des-Eaux, a small Normandy village just two hours away, 'this brought back
precise recollections evoked from memories of the distance travelled during
holidays and to have it mentioned in an official document made the defeat
appear more dangerous, and the immediate sense of danger was considerably increased'.[24]

A second factor which caused people to simply take off was blind panic
and fear. While the propaganda sought to reassure the population, once they
realized that the Germans would soon reach them, fear of aerial attack from
the Nazi war machine overcame them. People had seen and heard of new
bombing techniques in Barcelona and Guernica during the Spanish Civil
War which had been widely reported in new technicolor pictures in maga-
zines like *Paris-Match*. These images gave a new angle to understandings of
war. People imagined that if they became caught up in a bomb attack on the
capital, they risked the worst kind of experiences. Reports of the bombing of
Poland weighed heavily on their minds and their capacity to visualize themselves experiencing something similar often served to exaggerate the extent of
the danger they were really in. Marc Bloch, the historian, wrote in 1940:

> They did not hesitate to warn of the potential dangers on numerous occasions.
> Had we not had the atrocious images of the ruins of Spain frequently put
> before our eyes in cinemas? Had we not been repeatedly exposed to report
> after report on the martyred Polish villages? In a way we were too well
> informed and too well prepared, of this I remain convinced.[25]

As people learnt of the decision of one family to leave, it encouraged others
in their circle. Departure created its own dynamic. Witnessing the frenzied
departures of neighbours, friends, and other family members, people started

to feel that to stay would be foolhardy. Leaving home seemed the only solution for many—Guillot wondered why this was so:

> Why do they think that there is less danger elsewhere? In wartime a farm can become a strategic point, the front seems to move around very quickly. Surely living in a town where there are thousands of houses reduces the danger. If I was in charge of my own actions I think I would stay. But most people obey this need to leave in a way that is *contagious*.[26]

Being afraid of losing one's life because of German bombs was compounded by the historical legacy of Franco-German relations and people's understandings of events of the previous war. For those who were more reluctant to leave, reminders of the potential dangers they would face from the Germans were a persuasive reason for departure. Not only did fear of possible German occupation prey on many people's minds, but since the First World War, children had been conditioned to hate the German soldier. Many had learnt of this experience from stories grandparents told and this was reinforced by propaganda which dwelt on the terrible legacy left by the behaviour of the Germans during their occupation of northern France. Simone Perrot, at 16, was very reluctant to leave her village with her mother and invalid brother despite being urged to do so by the mayor. She recalls:

> During the phoney war, we were confident and it was calm. Things started to go wrong in June. When they invaded Belgium we knew that things were bad. We saw the other refugees arriving from the north. One of our neighbours had married and moved there so they came here to take refuge at their brother's home. They arrived with everything they could carry—carts, horses, furniture. Then they left again.
>
> The mayor of the village came to see us and told us that we had to leave. He said, 'listen—if it's going to be like it was in 1914, they rape the women and they cut the young girls' hands off. This is what had happened during the war in the north, you must leave. The former mayor has bought a very large farm in the Indre. I am going there and I am sure he will have room for you all.' So about eighteen of us left together in a convoy of four cars. I took my bike and at times I cycled along beside them.[27]

Such stories about German atrocities had been widely circulating since the previous war. It was indeed the case that between 1914 and 1918 the German army had occupied ten French departments, an area which represented 6 per cent of French territory and 12 per cent of the population.[28] During the invasion, real atrocities were committed by the Germans. Attacks were made on civilians and there was a high number of rapes in some areas. However, they were much exaggerated, both at the time and subsequently, as a way of mobilizing public opinion.[29] At the time stories emphasizing the cruelty of German soldiers were published in all the Allied countries, 'in government reports, pamphlets, newspapers, posters and cartoons—all of which portrayed German soldiers as brutes and sadists preying in particular on women and girls whom they not only raped but often mutilated'.[30] This image was embellished by rumours spread by soldiers and civilians and then carried even further afield by the frightened refugees who left the war zone. This in turn created a fear of atrocities which provoked the mass flight of hundreds of thousands of people in 1914. By autumn 1918 more than two million French refugees had left the occupied areas.[31] This reaction can be explained in part by their shock as civilians at finding themselves caught up in a war at a time when understanding about warfare was based on the assumption that there were clear rules of engagement. Until this time, there had been a recognized distinction between those who were fighting (soldiers) and those who were not meant to be involved (civilians). The apparent merging of these two categories and the notion that the civilians were now also targets and could therefore also find themselves victims of the battle was new and extremely frightening. These fears became so acute that they could have triggered a collapse of national morale and thereby sparked a similar exodus to the one under discussion here, some twenty-six years earlier, had the course of the war not taken a positive turn with the Allied victory at the Marne.[32] The German revaluation of the franc to their own advantage in the areas they occupied was seen as an added incentive for French people to try to ensure that they remained on the French side of the battle lines where their currency would still retain its 'proper' value. Able-bodied Frenchmen also wanted to avoid the prospect of finding themselves requisitioned to work in German labour camps as many had been during the previous occupation.

Throughout May and early June 1940, the papers deliberately kept alive the memory of what had happened in the previous war by recounting examples of horrific incidents allegedly inflicted by the Germans. Examples of German atrocities during the First World War were cited on a daily basis in the northern local press. *La Croix* (1 June 1940) spoke of extensive German barbarism and cruelty at that time. The inhabitants of these previously occupied areas were soon convinced that the invasion of the German forces in May would provoke a re-enactment of what had gone before. Leaving the area seemed the only solution. It would protect them from experiencing such hardship and it would allow people to remain in areas still under French administration and authority and escape the threat of deportation to unknown destinations. This desire to escape German occupation triggered the departures of many communities north of Paris. When these fleeing populations reached the capital they recounted stories which fed and brought alive this image of the viciousness of the German soldier. Such accounts were embroidered by terrified Dutch and Belgian refugees traumatized by their own experiences close to the battle front.

But, as far as Parisians were concerned, it was the departure of the government on the night of 10 June which was to prove the final trigger in persuading them that the time had come to leave. Even if there were to be no official orders to do so, it now seemed clear that the government was effectively demonstrating by example how people should behave. Loss of confidence in officials and the apparent absence of provision for their safety led people to decide to take responsibility for their own survival into their own hands.

Using the testimonies of Simone de Beauvoir, Roland Dorgelès, and Georges Sadoul—as well as of other contemporary witnesses, both British and French—this book tells the stories of how the exodus was experienced by the French people. The entire social fabric to which people were accustomed, all the points of reference upon which they had been socialized to depend, suddenly collapsed without warning in a way that they could not understand. In leaving their homes, many soon found themselves exposed to starvation and dehydration on the unseasonably hot roads and railways. What drove them on in the face of mortal danger and adversity? Their flight brought a message of total collapse to communities displaced from the fighting. As swamped towns farmed out refugees to far-flung rural areas, the repercussions of the exodus were felt across the nation. With few possessions and often reduced to destitution, these populations had become refugees in their own country, entirely dependent on the goodwill of these host communities who struggled to meet their needs in the face of diminishing supplies. This book will argue that the exodus was a pivotal moment for the people of France. It will show how the trauma of the exodus left the French vulnerable and confused. While the Germans took control of a country in collapse, by promising to bring the suffering of the refugees to an end, Pétain was able to overthrow the Third Republic and step into power unopposed. His subsequent government, established at Vichy, mobilized the exodus as the basis of its legitimacy and soon set about a policy of collaboration with the Germans.

PART I

Exodus

I

The Invasion of Paris

It seemed that a prodigious cloud of toxic, nervous, and paralysing gas had engulfed the country. Everything was unravelling, falling to pieces and being thrown into panic like a machine that was drunk, everything was taking place as if it was part of an indescribable nightmare.

André Morize, *France: Été 1940*

As reports of the German invasion reached the capital, Parisians at first remained calm. Populations from Belgium and the north of the country gradually began to arrive in the city. Their plight was increasingly visible as they camped out in railway stations and adjacent areas. Arrangements were quickly put into place for the majority to be transported to departments in the south and west but the widespread belief in victory had meant that there were no contingency plans in the event of invasion and defeat. As the military situation continued to deteriorate, the government prevaricated. Its uncertainty gave the impression that it was overwhelmed. Finally, the French Prime Minister Paul Reynaud took the decision to evacuate the government from the capital, a move which triggered a surge of departures of civilians from the city. Paris was left almost abandoned.

Outbreak of war

When the war was declared in September 1939, the French people were repeatedly told with great confidence that the Allies would triumph—and they believed it. The majority of civilians never imagined or even contemplated the possibility of defeat. Public confidence was high that the Germans would be swiftly overpowered. It was announced that the Maginot line of defence would protect the country and that any attack would be rapidly repelled. Mobilization was undertaken with less fervour than had been seen in 1914 at the beginning of the First World War when close to one and a half million men had been wiped out. In 1939 the absence of a generation of potential soldiers forced the French government to call up men across a wider age range than in Germany.[1] In this way, a correspondingly large proportion of French families found themselves forced to make do in the absence of a husband or father.[2]

The government struggled to balance the manpower needs of the military with what was required to keep the essential war industries going. At first the number of men exempted from mobilization and allocated the status of specially designated worker was overestimated. Georges Sadoul was working in an aviation factory at this time and explained: 'Until three months ago none of us were supposed to leave. We were all specially designated workers . . . Then two months ago, they changed all the mobilization statutes and now more than half the factory has left.'[3] Even so, the government still ended up mobilizing workers who were essential to the armaments industries and was soon forced to send large numbers of them back into civilian life to work in these factories.[4] The presence of all these workers of mobilizable age was confusing to Parisians who imagined that they would be more useful on the front. More importantly, it led to a concentration of male workers in the Paris region where the majority of these factories were situated and this would now have to factored in to any plans for evacuation of the capital.

Early departures

Evacuation, however, was not expected to be a serious concern since the French government had invested hugely in the Maginot line, a defence strategy which was strongly advocated by the Supreme Commander of the French armed forces, General Maurice Gamelin. This line, which ran from the Swiss border to Longwy, close to France's border with Luxembourg and Belgium, was fortified with military installations placed at regular intervals along it and was expected to prevent the German army from making any significant incursions on to French territory (see Map I). The area where the line would notionally have continued into Belgium was seen as being beyond the responsibility of the French. Any possibility that it might be extended

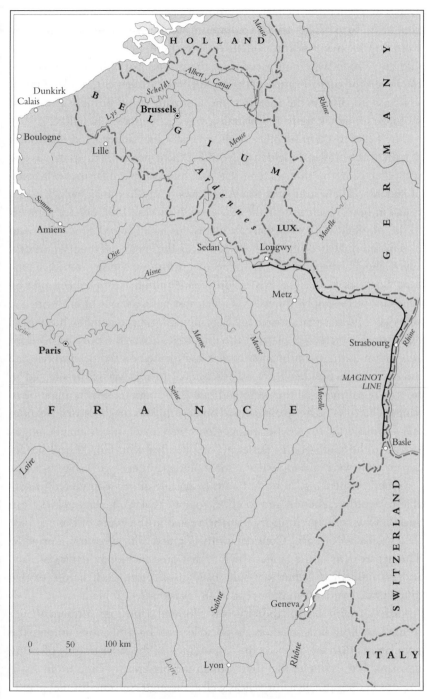

Map 1. The Maginot line

evaporated when the Belgian government declared its intention to remain neutral in 1936.[5] The original intention had been that the Maginot line would release manpower for offensives elsewhere. Belgian neutrality meant that the French were now faced with the prospect of fighting in this area. However, the rugged nature of the terrain of the Ardennes forest led French strategists to dismiss the idea that the Germans could possibly choose to mobilize for attack there and planning was concentrated elsewhere.

The belief in the infallibility of the Maginot line strategy and the notion that the war would be fought in more or less the same way as the previous one was reflected in the arrangements that were put into place for the well-being of civilians. The assumption that Allied superiority in the air, which was a reality in 1918, would remain the case some thirty years later, blinded planners to the possibility of any serious air incursions into France.[6] Since the main plan from a military point of view was to keep the enemy off French territory, any really effective and serious arrangements for evacuation seemed redundant. Suggestions that the evacuation of large numbers of people might be necessary were simply dismissed as a defeatist position, out of line with the aura of confidence that surrounded all planning for the impending hostilities.[7] Discussions which took place in the mid-1930s about the possible need for evacuation in the event of another war had focused on the need to relocate those civilians considered not to be essential to the war effort situated in frontier departments in the north and east of the country which might be in danger of attack. At first plans centred on departments neighbouring Belgium and Germany; in 1938 these arrangements were extended to include populations in the south-east in the event of a conflict with Italy. These border departments were all allocated a destination department (see Table 1).

Generally speaking, in the interests of morale, it was considered preferable to avoid evacuation and to endeavour to protect the large cities from attack. Thus, only preliminary plans were laid in the event of the need for the evacuation of Paris. Considerations of practicality were not a priority. The department of the Seine which at that time included the city of Paris and its immediate suburbs would have to disperse itself across twelve different departments in the event of an invasion (see Table 2).

Each *arrondissement* of the city was allocated a host department which seemed to bear little relation to possible existing affiliations among the population. Planners ignored the importance of the rural origins of many Parisians. For example, they overlooked the presence of high numbers of Bretons in the 14th *arrondissement* as well as the high concentration of people

Table 1. Departments of origin and their destination departments in the event of evacuation[8]

Department of origin	Destination department
Nord	Ille-et-Vilaine, Côtes-du-Nord, Manche
Pas-de-Calais	Finistère, Morbihan
Aisne	Mayenne
Ardennes	Vendée, Deux-Sèvres
Meurthe-et-Moselle	Gironde, Landes
Moselle	Vienne, Charente
Vosges	Indre, Creuse
Bas-Rhin	Haute-Vienne, Dordogne
Haut-Rhin	Lot-et-Garonne, Gers, Basses-Pyrénées
Territoire de Belfort	Corrèze
Haute-Saône	Lot, Tarn-et-Garonne
Doubs	Haute-Garonne, Hautes-Pyrénées
Jura	Tarn
Ain	Cantal
Haute-Savoie	Puy-de-Dôme
Savoie	Haute-Loire
Hautes-Alpes	Ardèche
Basses-Alpes (now Alpes-de-Haute-Provence)	Lozère
Isère	Aveyron
Var	Ariège
Alpes-Maritimes	Aude, Pyrénées-Orientales

from the Auvergne area who had recently come to live in the city. Quite how these Parisians could be prevented from returning to their homes and persuaded to follow instructions directing them elsewhere was never given any consideration. More realistic planning might have given these arrangements more coherence.[9] Blackboards were erected in the mainline stations and other key areas of the capital which advised Parisians how they should reach their destination departments (see Illustration 2). This gave the impression that the appropriate preparations were in place in the unlikely event that they would prove necessary.

In the months before the outbreak of the war, planners remained convinced that there was no real need to privilege the protection of civilians from possible threat from the air. Evacuation still remained a priority for

Table 2. Residents of Paris and their destination departments[10]

Destination departments	Paris *arrondissement*/suburb
Calvados	1st, 4th, 5th, Colombes, Puteaux, Vincennes
Cher	11th, Issy, Ivry
Eure	16th
Eure-et-Loire	2nd, 7th, La Courneuve, Pierrefitte, Pré-Saint-Gervais, Stains, Villemomble, Villetaneuse
Loir-et-Cher	3rd, Anthony, Asnières, Bobigny, Bondy, Bourg-la-Reine, Champigny, Châtillon, Fontenay-aux-Roses, Fresnes, Gentilly, Kremlin-Bicêtre, Montrouge, Nanterre, Pantin, Le Perreux, Saint-Denis
Loire-Inférieure (now Loire-Atlantique)	8th, 14th, 18th, Boulogne-Billancourt, Clamart
Loiret	10th, Alfortville, Arcueil, Bagneux, Cachan, Charenton, Fontenay-sous-Bois, Joinville, Maisons-Alfort, Malakoff, Montreuil, Saint-Mandé, Sceaux
Maine-et-Loire	13th, 15th
Nièvre	12th, Bagnolet, Bonneuil, Châtenay-Malabry, Choisy-le-Roi, Créteil, Drancy, Les Lilas, Orly, Saint-Maur, Saint-Maurice, Thiais, Villejuif
Orne	6th, Aubervilliers, Bois-Colombes, Clichy, Levallois, Rosny, Saint-Ouen
Sarthe	9th, 17th, 19th, Bourget, Courbevoie, Dugny, Épinay, La Garenne-Colombes, Suresnes
Yonne	20th, Noisy-le-Sec, Romainville, Vanves, Vitry, Bry-sur-Marne

those populations perceived to be potentially under direct threat of finding themselves in the thick of military operations. Concern focused particularly on the populations who lived in the close vicinity of the Maginot line and in particular those whose homes were in the much-contested areas of Alsace and Lorraine to the north-east. The geographic position of these areas, strategically placed along the frontier between France and Germany, and the historical claims that Germany had upon them, suggested that Hitler would certainly have his eye on regaining this territory in the event of a victory. Many of these long-suffering residents did not wait for the declaration of war to leave their homes. Whether they left of their own initiative

2. The blackboards which appeared in Paris provided detailed evacuation itineraries for departure in the event of evacuation. The capacity of particular populations easily to reach relevant train stations or appropriate main roads out of the
capital in order to follow these routes was not given consideration.

or as a result of official arrangements, most were transported to departments in the south of the country. Evacuation procedures were carried out calmly and efficiently as in the case of the 250,000 inhabitants of Strasbourg who were evacuated to Périgueux in just one day. By 3 September 1939, the city appeared deserted.[11] Other evacuees from these departments were not so lucky. Many experienced a difficult three- or four-day rail journey in goods carriages and on arrival expressed dissatisfaction with the arrangements they found had been put into place for them in the rural areas of Dordogne. Since the majority of those evacuated there were factory workers, they could not offer their services to replace badly needed agricultural workers who had been mobilized. Relations between the two populations often degenerated. Certain host populations resented the presence of these unwelcome guests whom they often perceived as being arrogant, useless, and lazy.[12]

As far as the capital was concerned, officials still hesitated to put together detailed plans for mass evacuation, fearing it would give out the wrong kind of signals to everyone. Government announcements presented a position of total confidence. On 2 July 1939, for example, General Weygand declared that, 'if we are obliged to ensure that we win again, we will certainly do so'.[13] It was feared that the circulation and publication in the press of detailed plans for population withdrawal would appear defeatist and could have a detrimental impact on morale. It was also felt to be important not to give the Germans any impression that the French lacked confidence.[14] In the light of all this, it was agreed in government circles that attempting to undertake mass evacuation would prove far too costly and, in all probability, unnecessary. The extent of danger that the city faced from possible bombing attacks was difficult to predict and there was considerable argument about how such a potential threat should be managed.[15] Some effort was made at building bomb shelters in Paris and care was taken to protect some of the more obvious monuments. None of these policies were implemented in a very sustained way and public discussion about them remained low key. Few precautionary measures were introduced which were not already familiar to Parisians from the past when the city had been under siege in 1870 by the Prussians and again when it was bombed during the Great War. People were conscious that there had never been cause for serious alarm on these occasions even if the capital had seemed close to the battlefield for a certain amount of time. These preparations were therefore not seen as a serious indication of threat.

In August 1939 close to fifteen thousand Parisian children were already absent from their homes participating in *colonies de vacances*. Since the beginning of the century, thousands of French children had left their homes and family each summer for six to eight weeks to spend time on one of the nation's dense network of organized holiday camps.[16] As the prospect of war became increasingly real, on 25 August 1940 the government ordered the municipalities of the department of the Seine to prolong their camps beyond the normal closing date of 15–20 September. Thus thousands of children were kept in safety at the seaside, in the mountains, or in the countryside. Subsequent orders at the end of August 1940 led schoolteachers and municipal councils in the Paris region to organize the evacuation of a further thirty thousand children aged between 6 and 14. The effectiveness of these measures is illustrated by the Paris suburb of Suresnes where at the end of October 1939, only 820 out of 4,600 schoolchildren remained.[17] These children, unaware of the reasons for the extended holiday, were delighted to benefit from the extra time away.[18] Parents whose children did not qualify for these official measures sometimes took the precaution of sending them to stay with family in the provinces. Others struggled to find schools prepared to accept their children, as fears about possible overcrowding led many schools in reception areas to limit available places to children from officially nominated departments.[19]

As far as the population in general was concerned, making arrangements for evacuation was largely left to their own discretion. Those who wished to find more secure situations were encouraged to try and find shelter with family or distant relatives. In the capital, the police distributed tracts recommending people to make their own arrangements to leave immediately in the event of air attack. They were urged to go to country homes or to find accommodation with extended family.[20] In 1940 many city dwellers were only one generation removed from the countryside. Relatively recent urbanization meant that most Parisian families still had relatives in the provinces. Those who wished to initiate their own evacuation arrangements found themselves at a disadvantage. While those who followed evacuation orders to leave their homes qualified for a benefit of 10 francs a week, and 6 francs for each child, those who chose to leave without orders to do so could not collect this allowance. The state only offered benefits to those who were evacuating under the official plans and then only if they went to their allocated department. Those who fell outside this framework were entirely dependent on their own financial resources. Inevitably, therefore, only the more affluent populations who could carry the financial burden of doing so were able to leave. Some such families had made advance arrangements for rentals in seaside resorts, villas, and houses, replying to small ads in the press which had promoted 'properties which were ideal for the purposes of evacuation'.[21] In a letter dated 2 March 1940, the prefect of Nièvre explained that 'a large number of Parisians . . . have rented properties before returning to Paris; at the first sign of an alert they will come back to occupy these places'.[22]

After the declaration of war, a wave of people who considered themselves under threat quickly took to the roads. At this time about 550,000 Parisians left the city. Stanley Hoffman was among them.

with the thousands of Parisians, we made up part of the first exodus[23] of which we hear so little, the one that took place in the first days following the declaration of the war which brought together (or rather dispersed) many of those residents who were convinced that the conflict would begin with bombings of the cities on a massive scale on the model of Guernica.[24]

This initial flurry of activity and panic reflected the fact that people did not really know what to expect. Parisian fears that the population would be immediately subject to serious bombing raids did not materialize, as Georgette Guillot explained: 'When the war broke out we thought that Paris would be pulverized the very next day, that clouds of gas would kill us, and none of that happened.'[25]

In these first weeks of the war there was no evidence of military activity and people began to wonder if the expected hostilities would ever take place. Life took on a new routine and the danger of bombing felt increasingly remote. People began to accommodate themselves to the situation. As the distinguished politician Pierre Mendès France, government minister under the Popular Front, who later also held office during de Gaulle's post-war provisional government, recounted: 'Everyone, civilians and military alike, sought only to arrange their personal life as well as possible, so as to get through this seemingly indefinite period without too much loss or discomfort.'[26] Families developed strategies which enabled them to cope without their men whom they believed safe on the Maginot line. Many of those who had been evacuated decided that remaining in the uncomfortable conditions they had been allocated seemed unnecessary and they trickled back home, seeing no reason to stay away from their families and jobs. The authorities were soon overwhelmed by demands for repatriation to be arranged at state expense. Furthermore, state-sponsored evacuation schemes had not always met with success. The publicized scandal relating to the chateau of Pommeraie in Calvados organized to look after the orphans from the department of the Seine where 350 children were neglected and barely fed, led many parents of children who had left on such schemes to bring them home.[27] The people of the exclusive bourgeois Parisian suburb of Neuilly-sur-Seine organized a petition against the 'scandalous mixing' of their children with those of the nearby predominantly working-class Levallois-Perret.[28] By mid-October most of the children who had been evacuated from the city had been collected by parents who became increasingly convinced that the potential danger had been exaggerated.

Throughout the winter of 1939, the uncanny lack of activity on the front continued. Despite publicity about German bombing raids in Poland, officials still baulked at the idea of implementing extensive evacuation plans. The notion that such a policy would undermine public confidence in the ability of the army to defend them was an added concern.[29] Indeed, the circumstances of the war had left the army struggling to maintain the morale of the often bored and anxious soldiers who felt that they had abandoned their families and left them exposed to potential risk and danger. Aware of these anxieties, the army sought to comfort them by explaining that by defending the nation they would be fulfilling both their patriotic duty and protecting their own families as well as those of others. In this context, as a measure of the government's confidence in their ultimate success, the need for evacuation had to be seen to be unnecessary. The decision to place a higher priority on the protection of the morale of the soldiers was an added reason for the general reluctance to elaborate extensive evacuation plans, paradoxically just at the same time as support for such a policy was beginning to grow.[30]

Officials now realized that the limited arrangements that had been put into place were unlikely to prove adequate in the event of a need to evacuate large groups of people from the capital. It now seemed that the only solution was to actively discourage people from leaving, quite the opposite position from earlier tracts which had been distributed urging people to 'Leave before the rush'. On 12 December 1939 the president of the council for the prefecture of the department of the Seine explained that 'there is no point in encouraging a massive exodus of adults which would ruin the Parisian economy and add to the difficulties already being experienced by the country'.[31] To reinforce this message the press put out reassuring advice such as this notice which appeared in L'Œuvre, a daily Parisian newspaper, on 21 February 1940: 'Able-bodied adults have a duty to stay at home. The massive human departures of people to departments which are already inundated will create more risks and inconveniencies than keeping an able-bodied population in place. Paris is the best protected town in France, the one where the shelters are the most effective and the most numerous.' The only real targets for evacuation were reduced to the category of children under 14 and pregnant women, people that the population at large could easily identify as being the most vulnerable. In Paris, this meant that more children were targeted and the government now actively encouraged Parisians whose children still remained in the capital to remove them from the city. From February 1940 free travel tickets were made available to them for this purpose, but most schools were not actually closed until 8 June in the wake of the first serious bombing raid on the city.[32]

By March 1940, it was clear that the departments that had been lined up to receive the refugees and provide them with shelter were already struggling to meet the needs of those who had arrived thus far. Within government circles, warnings were circulated to the effect that there could be problems should evacuation prove necessary on a mass scale. Robert Schumann, appointed Director of Refugee Services in April 1940, realized that current arrangements had to be expanded but still refused to plan for total evacuation.[33] His move to extend the category of women who could qualify for refugee benefits to include all those who were accompanying children, as well as mothers and pregnant women, enabled many more women to leave the capital with their children.[34] Nonetheless, departure remained impossible for the majority of working people who had no private income and could not afford to leave their jobs. This suited the authorities who had decided that they did not want to encourage people to leave. Any further disruption was to be avoided. In any case, most Parisians were reluctant to move from their homes when the military situation did not really seem to require it.[35]

During this period of military inactivity, in an effort to keep the population focused on the war, French people were bombarded with propaganda warning them to be vigilant about possible underground and spy organizations operating from within the country on behalf of the Germans.[36] The idea of the enemy within had first gained currency during the Great War, but it was only during the Spanish Civil War that it was labelled the 'fifth column'. Propaganda posters appeared across the country especially in public places like cafés where soldiers and civilians might meet, warning people that the enemy could be present, collecting information which might later be used against them. In line with these requests, initially, the whereabouts of mobilized soldiers remained shrouded in secrecy. Soldiers were forbidden to inform their families where they were and censorship was fierce; inappropriate information was obscured with a black marker pen. The acronym QQPEF (*quelque part en France*, somewhere in France) which soldiers were instructed to write in letters home, entered common parlance. However, as the months went by, men started coming home on leave and this added to a growing sense of normality. While at home, they talked to everyone about their postings and their positions soon became an open secret.[37] In this way the phoney war was marked by an atmosphere of false security for most French people who continued their lives as best they could in the circumstances. In the absence of any military activity they wondered if the German offensive would ever take place. If it did, most assumed that the enemy armies would be immediately stopped in their tracks by the superior military forces of the French.

The First Exodus

On 10 May the Germans finally attacked. In the early hours of the morning air raid sirens awoke the populations of thirty French cities. At 7.30 a.m. the Minister of Propaganda, Ludovic-Oscar Frossard, announced to the French people that the war had begun and that the Germans had invaded Holland, Belgium, and Luxembourg. Despite this dramatic news, for the most part, people were not motivated to change their plans for the forthcoming bank holiday weekend, believing that it was a mere reversal that would later be overcome.[38] When more detailed news of the attack finally filtered through, it first appeared to be concentrated in northern Belgium and southern Holland, a move which had been more or less anticipated. What was less expected was the second thrust in the region of the Ardennes which had been written off by military strategists as areas that the Germans would never consider broaching because of the difficult terrain and forests. It had been noticed that this area appeared particularly weak, but recommendations to improve defences in the area were not followed up.[39] By 13 May, however, German panzer tank divisions had set up a bridgehead on French territory at Sedan: the impenetrable Ardennes had been well and truly penetrated.

It was the Dutch, Belgian, and Luxembourg populations who were the first to flee this German onslaught. The bombing of Rotterdam met virtually no Allied resistance and pushed the first Dutch people on to the roads who then passed into Belgium and from there into France. The terror of the air raids was probably almost entirely responsible for these first movements of the population.[40] No contingency plans had been put into place to deal with the eventuality that large numbers of civilians would take flight in this way. All these populations fled towards France and were allowed through the frontiers behind the lines to escape the enemy raids and find shelter. Allied soldiers soon found themselves moving up to the front in the opposite direction to this improvised departure of civilians desperate to escape danger. 'No one really knew the reason for their journey, but everyone had just one desire which was to leave.'[41] The Belgian government was fast overwhelmed by the unexpected turn of events. It became extremely difficult to organize any serious defence and the situation was aggravated by the need to deal with the mass of refugees who obstructed the Belgian armies soon obliged to retreat. By 12 May Brussels was in chaos and any hope of controlled evacuation was abandoned. No one anticipated the

3. The Belgian refugees who flooded across the frontier into France were channelled down certain roads by the military. Here the crowds are brought to a standstill by a passing military convoy.

4. In rural areas, peasants saddled up their farm horses, loaded up their carts with family members, and set off in the opposite direction from the sounds of battle. They look on as they are overtaken by tanks heading for the front.

enormous number of refugees that flooded into France. Most simply wanted to escape the bombs.[42]

For their part, the French had not anticipated attack in the region of Sedan close to the Franco-Belgian border, despite its notorious position as the site of German victory in 1870. The focus of strategic thinking was centred on defence along the Maginot line and confidence was high that this would hold firm in the face of a German offensive. General Charles Huntziger, Commanding Officer in this area, held this view until the very last minute. On 7 May he assured the mayor of Sedan that he did 'not consider that the Germans will think of attacking in the region of Sedan'.[43] But even when the arrival of Germans there appeared imminent, Huntziger remained reluctant to declare the evacuation of the town. This was not only because he still simply could not believe that the Germans would really attack there, but because he was also concerned that a civilian retreat might interfere with the troop movements that would become necessary if such an attack were to take place. The prefect, on the other hand, repeatedly pressed Huntziger to allow civilians to leave.

By the end of 10 May, it had become clear that the Germans were indeed targeting the Sedan area for attack. At 9 p.m., it was finally agreed that the town should be evacuated in as orderly a manner as possible. But although arrangements were put into place for the departure of the townspeople and trains were lined up at the stations to take them south, officials had not anticipated the impact this departure would have on nearby rural inhabitants. These people, learning of the evacuation of Sedan and conscious that the battle front was fast approaching, started to leave of their own initiative although they had no orders to do so. At first these French rural communities watched the sad columns of people without much concern for their own safety as the passage of Belgians fleeing the battle conformed to past experience. Then the military authorities finally agreed that evacuation had to be extended to include all civilians in the combat zones. The inhabitants of these areas were ordered to leave their homes immediately. The sight of these departing peasants with all their worldly possessions piled high on their farm carts bore witness to the scale of the disaster. As these populations withdrew, their neighbours to whom it had endlessly been repeated that the Germans would 'never penetrate the Ardennes', now began to realize that these passing refugees were no longer 'foreign' Belgians but hailed from nearby. This was a clear indication that the Germans were approaching and that they could not be far away. In the absence of clear instructions many now chose to take flight.

Huntziger struggled to combat the German attack but French reinforcements were hampered and delayed by the hordes of fleeing refugees. In the absence of the arrival of military or air back-up, the German advance continued apparently unchallenged. Air attacks on the towns and villages along and behind the battle lines terrified local populations and quickly persuaded those who were not already on the road that they should be. People fled from their homes when they heard the piercing sirens of the German Stuka planes which announced bomb attacks. In the ensuing chaos, many soldiers joined the civilians in flight. The sad spectacle of often unarmed retreating soldiers carried with them a powerful message of military collapse. The accounts these men gave of their experiences on the battlefield, often exaggerating stories of German invincibility in an effort to justify their escape, could only add to these already disastrous impressions.

It was the presence of Allied soldiers (mostly French) caught up amongst the civilians which drew the Germans to bomb and machine-gun the columns of fleeing civilians. These soldiers and refugees on the open roads were easy targets, allowing the Germans to create panic with maximum effect. As fleeing populations found themselves surrounded by strangers, it occurred to them that the enemy might also be among them as propaganda had repeatedly warned. As they tried to make sense of the sudden and unexpected rout they found themselves a part of, the notion that France had been betrayed from within made sense. Stories about German spies infiltrating the country might be a way of explaining the disaster. In this way, fears of possible fifth column activity grew and refugees regarded those around them with suspicion.

So the exodus began. The evacuation of Sedan with its prevarication and confusion between the positions of the military and civilian authorities was to become the common experience of the mass exodus in northern France. It started the process whereby the power of rumour, coupled with the sense that the authorities could not be relied upon to help, led populations to decide to leave home without any official orders or advice to do so. The first precipitated departures were an effort to escape German bombing. In the wake of the breakthrough at Sedan, many towns in the Ardennes found themselves at the heart of the fighting. False rumours of betrayal and fifth column activity, combined with widespread bombing and machine-gunning of refugees, made the Germans appear all-powerful and the only way to escape death seemed to be to flee. Panic pushed people on to the roads as soon as they started to make out the ominous sounds of the approaching battle. Fear for their own safety gradually increased at the sight of other fleeing refugees passing by. The first flux left, provoking the departures of their neighbours, and so the cycle continued. The distances covered by these displaced families varied. Some did not manage to get very far. They took shelter in the surrounding countryside, at times only for a matter of hours. Certain communities remained in hiding for a few days until lack of food brought them back to their villages. The experience of these refugees was short-lived: they returned to their homes when the enemy arrived and the battle appeared to have moved on.[44] One woman who was 14 in 1940 recounts her exodus from Amiens.

We left because we saw the others leaving and we were afraid of the Germans. My mother had lived through 1914–18 and was very afraid: 'we can't stay here', 'we can't stay here'. We did not take much, just what we could carry. We just dropped everything and took off. We were so scared. We did not know where to go. We just walked and walked. We did not get far because there was my sister's baby and we had nothing to eat. Luckily I knew how to milk cows, so I slipped across the pastures and milked the cows for the baby and we all drank it.
   Then we came upon a man who cried out to us, 'It is not worth carrying on. They are in front of us.' So we decided not to go any further. We came to a large farm which was deserted and pillaged but we decided that we would

settle ourselves there for a bit and see what happened. The next day the
Germans came and told us to go home.[45]

Other refugees continued their exodus for several days. Those who found
themselves on the roads were at first to some extent organized and their
movements were confined to certain routes. The military authorities endea-
voured to maintain some degree of control over these fleeing populations.
Certain roads and itineraries were kept free to enable armies to put their
increasingly beleaguered defence strategies into place. Care was taken to
leave the way clear for retreating and regrouping military convoys. Refugees
were channelled along routes which were signposted clearly by the military
authorities. Mistakes were made. Refugees were directed towards Reims and
thence to Paris, rather than orienting them towards the empty, open countryside of Champagne and Burgundy. This kind of error certainly added to the
scale of the overcrowding which later ensued.[46] As the authorities lost control
of the situation, those on foot were particularly vulnerable. Lack of organization, the absence of the police or any other officials to direct the growing
columns of fleeing civilians, meant that successful escape was often a question
of chance. Less fortunate refugees found themselves caught in a pocket and
travelled round in an immense circle, often eventually to find that they were
surrounded by the Germans. Others walked many miles before they found
shelter, only to be forced to move on almost immediately as the Germans
continued to gain on them, so rapid was their advance.

Pierre Mendès France wrote of how in his role as mayor of Louviers,
30 km (19 miles) south of Rouen, he organized the authorities to provide
shelter and comfort for the interminable columns of Dutch, Belgian, and
French refugees who passed through the town. Their order of arrival
corresponded to a certain hierarchy of those whose degrees of wealth gave
them access to different means of transport:

> In the first days we saw the sumptuous and fast American cars go by, driven by
> uniformed chauffeurs, their passengers were elegant women clutching their
> jewellery boxes and their husbands studying maps of the region... Then came
> the less fancy older cars... whose drivers were members of the middle classes
> and they were generally accompanied by their families and they often needed
> our help. One or two days later came the most incredible bangers passed
> through... then came the cyclists, mostly young people... There were also
> pedestrians, sometimes entire families...
>
> Lastly, came the heavy carts belonging to the peasants of the Nord depart-
> ment, they advanced at foot pace loaded up with the sick, children, the elderly,
> agricultural machinery and furniture... Several of these carts followed one

another ... they were generally a village undertaking a collective move, with the mayor, the priest, the elderly schoolmaster, and the local policeman. It was a colossal uprooting, the avalanche of one entire region onto another.[47]

Families continued walking until they were able to reach a town where some might have been lucky enough to get a place on a train. In this way, on 18 May a group of women turned up in the department of the Yonne in Burgundy. They had come from Vouziers in the Ardennes, just south of Sedan, carrying only the useless satchels of the children they had picked up from school. Overcome by panic at the school gates, they had made for the station and jumped aboard the first available train without even returning to their homes.[48] However, catching a train was not always a guarantee of escape. The Germans mercilessly bombed stations and main railway lines in an effort to disable transport and spread terror. At best progress was slow and unpredictable. Train passengers who were the targets of bomb attacks were forced to continue on foot as damage to railway lines left trains stranded in the open countryside. Nonetheless, the French train system did manage to evacuate many hundreds of people to safety. Many of these confused and traumatized refugees ended up in the railway stations of the capital with few possessions, little money, no place to go, and no idea of what they should do next but comforted by the thought that they had now reached safety.

Repercussions in Paris

Throughout the month of May, Parisians remained largely ignorant of the situation which was unravelling in the north and east of the country where events were moving with dramatic speed. Their access to information was strictly controlled and censored. News reports indicated that all was not entirely well but gave a relatively benign view of what was happening. The people of Paris remained quietly confident and few interpreted the reversals in the north as evidence of serious setbacks. It had all happened before. Benoîte Groult reported her father's reaction on Tuesday 13 May when news of the German offensive had reached the French public: 'Let them withdraw ... it doesn't matter. We will win the war at Clermont Ferrand.'[49] There were also other signs which people recognized from past experience. Buses and taxis disappeared from the avenues of Paris and the explanation that they were being used to help deal with the multitude of refugees who had now arrived in Paris or to help the troops at the front seemed plausible.[50] It chimed in with popular memory of the triumphant battle of Marne in September 1914 when six hundred taxicabs were commandeered by the military governor of Paris, Joseph Gallieni, to transport over six thousand French reserve infantry troops. Just when the Allies appeared to be threatened with the defeat, these reinforcements helped win this decisive Franco-British victory. In 1940 Parisians could still rely on the Metro to get about and these moves seemed to suggest that the situation augured well.[51]

On 16 May news came through from the communiqués that the Germans had broken through the front and were approaching Laon. The realization that the way was open to Paris provoked fears in government circles that the capital might fall that very evening. General Pierre Hering, the aged military governor of Paris, advised the government to leave the city without delay. It was unclear exactly how effectively the military would be able to mobilize to defend the capital. So at 11 a.m. orders were given to the various ministries to evacuate their archives and government members were told to prepare their staff to be ready to leave at a moment's notice.[52] Some of those in the know now took it upon themselves to notify those whom they considered to be in the greatest danger from the German invasion. Jews were expected to be potential targets of racial persecution in the event that Germans established control. Pierre Mendès France noted in his memoirs, 'I know of a Minister who literally spent the whole of the morning telephoning all his friends to advise them to leave the threatened capital. He was particularly concerned to give this advice to Jews, explaining to them the risks that they were running.'[53]

Prime Minister Paul Reynaud now had to manage the country and assess the seriousness of the army's apparent collapse in the face of the German offensive. In office since March 1940 when he had been elected by the Chamber of Deputies to take over from Édouard Daladier with a majority of just one vote, Reynaud's sense of isolation may help to explain the hesitancy which marked his leadership. His unstable government was now facing an enormous national crisis. Since taking power he had singularly failed to appoint enough of his supporters to create an effective team around him. This lack of allies within the cabinet would eventually undermine his capacity to implement his preferred course of action. At this stage, however, he was still in control and had to decide whether the government should remain in the capital or evacuate immediately.

At a meeting held late in the morning of 16 May to discuss the possibility that the Parisian population should be invited to leave, Reynaud finally determined that such a step would be premature. Orders for evacuations of the ministries were also cancelled when it became clear that they would struggle to function adequately outside Paris.[54] Alexis Léger, Secretary General of the Ministry for Foreign Affairs, acting immediately in response to the evacuation orders before they were rescinded, ordered his staff to throw official papers out of the windows on to the lawns of the Quai d'Orsay, the location of the Foreign Office on the banks of the river Seine, where they were piled up and unceremoniously burnt. Winston Churchill who was present in Paris for a meeting of the War Council, concluded, like most Parisians who could see it, that 'the evacuation of Paris was being prepared'.[55] This massive bonfire in the gardens of keyside ministerial departments was visible to all who passed through the administrative centre of the city on both sides of the river Seine. Coupled with the loading up of the archives of some of the main ministries in convoys of large lorries—an undertaking which could not be carried out discreetly—this fire was a clear signal that the government was now seriously entertaining the possibility of German invasion of the capital and its own departure from it. Later in the day, however, Reynaud took action to quash rumours and offset panic, massaging the truth a little in his address to the Chamber when he declared:

> There are some absolutely absurd rumours going around. People are saying that the government wanted to leave Paris, this is not true! People are saying that the enemy has new irresistible weapons when our aviators are covering themselves with glory, and our tanks outclass those of the Germans in the same category.[56]

If this apparent frankness served to reassure people, the growing numbers of refugees arriving in the city suggested a rather different interpretation of events.

Those who were evacuated and those who were fleeing the German invasion from the north were mostly channelled through Paris on their way to their official destination departments. The two million Belgians (about one in three) who had left their homes were now flooding into the French capital.[57] The French Minister for Refugees had never planned for the arrival of such volumes of displaced people. Worst case scenario estimates had put the figure of possible arrivals at 800,000, of which it had been hoped that 200,000 might be sent to Britain.[58] Arrangements were now hurriedly put into place for these populations to leave the city. Trains were laid on to conduct them to their destination departments in the south.

> The life of the city is concentrated around the stations. The first train of refugees arrived on 10 May. Most are too exhausted to even leave the train. Other refugees arrive on foot. Some were able to cover some of the distance in

5. By 15 May 1940, regular convoys of Belgian refugees were arriving at the Gare du Nord in Paris. These women, children, and elderly refugees were ferried on to buses by boy scouts and taken to overnight reception centres. They were then quickly sent to destinations in the centre and south of the country.

> a lorry or a train. Everyone is placed in shelters. These unhappy refugees thought that they had escaped.
>
> Many separated families tried to meet up again in the capital. At the Gare de l'Est a 'Meeting point for lost people' was arranged.
>
> They have brought with them an illness from which they would like to recover but which they only pass on.[59]

Officials in the rapidly organized makeshift shelters in stadiums, schools, hospitals, and military facilities were anxious to move them on quickly and urged refugees to remain discreet about the exact nature of their experiences, fearing that their accounts would spread demoralization.

In the face of these massive arrivals, efforts were made to organize the populations into various groups as Belgians were quickly followed by other nationalities which included those from Luxembourg and Holland. Then came Polish miners and rural workers from the bombed departments of the Pas-de-Calais and Nord. This growing refugee presence also provoked fears that spies or fifth columnists could have made their way to Paris hidden amongst them. Roger Langeron, prefect of the Paris police, had established a 'protective cordon' around the city on 17 May for fear that refugees might flood into the capital in an uncontrolled way and to prevent the infiltration of spies.[60]

The prefecture of police kept a watchful eye on suspicious travellers, held back factory workers and specially designated workers who could be recovered to work in the armament factories, and delegated local police stations to round up any refugees who were wandering around who had arrived by road and thereby avoided being checked through the reception centres that had been established in the stations. These authorities sorted out the transfer of refugees to their allocated departments in the south, and according to possibilities which changed hourly took them to Austerlitz or Montparnasse to board trains for the south or held them in centres or allowed those with the financial means to do so to stay in the city.[61]

Here, once again, the French railways came to the rescue, organizing extra trains to transport refugees to their destination departments. Most were taken first to Poitiers and then on to the south-west to towns like Montauban and Toulouse, sometimes even as far as Tarbes.

Parisians who remembered the refugees who had arrived in the capital during the First World War were moved by the often miserable state of these displaced people. Many had left their homes in such precipitous circumstances that they had been able to bring little with them and now found themselves virtually destitute. Paris had not yet been bombed and the stories of the air raids told by the Belgians and those from the north moved and incited compassion on the part of the capital's inhabitants. Once again, memory of the previous conflict was reassuring. As long as the presence of the refugees appeared to conform to the pattern of what had happened before, they did not provoke undue concern. Eugène Dépigny, an administrator in the *mairie* of Paris, wrote the following in his account of the period:

In May we saw refugees mainly who arrived by car at first and then by train where they were looked after in the stations of Paris and then sent on to the provinces. Factory workers from Longwy travelled through the city by bike, grouped together in an orderly way. Peasant families streamed through the capital with their workers, their animals were kept under control, and their carts were tidy and clean. Superbly reassuring orders offset the anxiety we were feeling and inspired confidence... In spite of their destitution, their evident anxiety and suffering, these lonely individuals did not look hunted in May.[62]

Only those whose families were directly involved were likely to take immediate action and plan for departure. For the time being, most Parisians themselves did not follow.

Furthermore, by 18 May, despite the worst fears that the Germans would soon arrive in Paris, they did not appear to be marching on the city, preferring to turn their attention to the Channel ports. If Paris now appeared spared, this was less good news for the Allies in military terms. The British Expeditionary Forces (BEF) as well as what remained of the Belgian armies, were attempting to join forces with the main bulk of the French troops in an effort to concentrate their remaining resources. This strategy now appeared to be directly threatened by the Germans. Lord John Gort, the Commander-in-Chief of the BEF, reported that they were struggling to change their position and complained that the situation was aggravated by roads which were 'very badly congested with refugees'.[63] The French army was facing similar problems in its ongoing retreat from Belgium. Reports of this now reached the French government who deduced that the military situation appeared to have reached catastrophic proportions. These military difficulties persuaded Reynaud that the time had come to make some changes to his government. In this reshuffle, Reynaud ousted former Prime Minister Daladier from the Ministry of Defence where he had been since Reynand had taken over as premier and sent him to the Foreign Ministry. Thereafter Reynaud held both positions, acting as Defence Minister as well as Prime Minister. Georges Mandel, right-hand man to former wartime premier Georges Clemenceau, who had held office as Minister of Colonies since 1938, was promoted to the Ministry of the Interior. Most significantly, Reynaud called on Marshal Pétain to take on the position of Deputy Prime Minister and also replaced General Maurice Gamelin with General Maxime Weygand.

Of all these men, Marshal Pétain was the most familiar to the French public. His credentials were clear. At 84, he was a national hero of the previous war with enormous prestige. Reynaud presented him as the man who had a record of manufacturing victory from an apparently cataclysmic disaster. Reynaud's hope was that Pétain's glorious military past would help raise the army to victory after losing this first important battle. His appointment was designed to reassure public opinion and it paid off. He was very well received and it was widely believed that if France was to be saved, he was surely the one who could do it. The press enthusiastically reproduced Reynaud's words:

the victor of Verdun, thanks to whom those who attacked us in 1916 did not pass through, thanks to whom the morale of the French army was bolstered for victory in 1917... He is from now on at my side as Minister of State, Deputy Prime Minister, putting all his wisdom and strength at the service of our country. He will remain there until we are victorious.[64]

Weygand's reputation also emanated from his record during the previous war and centred around the fact that he had been closely associated with General (later Marshal) Foch, Supreme Commander of all the Allied armies in France during the final Allied offensive in the summer of 1918.[65] Both men had to be recalled from posts abroad. Weygand was serving in the Near East, coordinating the French forces there, and his journey from Beirut took a couple of days. When he arrived in the capital, Marshal Pétain had already arrived from Spain where he had been ambassador.[66] Both men appeared less convinced than Reynaud that they would be able to provide the outcome he seemed to be asking of them. Weygand's first comments on the military situation were less than encouraging. He reported to Reynaud on 19 May upon taking up his post, 'You will not be surprised if I cannot answer for victory, nor even give you the hope of victory.'[67] For his part, Pétain, whose position in government was that of a politician rather than a military commander, had long made it known that he disapproved of the war—indeed he was well known as a defeatist in London.[68]

While Reynaud seemed convinced that the presence of these well-respected military men would mark a change in the situation, he evidently also believed that the time had come to announce publicly the current state of events. On 19 May he thus gave an extraordinary speech in the Senate which finally suggested something of the looming disaster. The British journalist Alexander Werth offered an eyewitness account of the reactions to Reynaud's speech to the Senate: '"*La patrie est en danger*," says Reynaud. He talks about the Weygand appointment. Voices on the right: "*Trop tard*"... But a deadly gloom hangs over the assembly; and when Reynaud suddenly declares that Arras and Amiens have fallen, a gasp of bewilderment rises from the senators' benches.'[69] Reynaud ended his speech with the following: 'If I was told that a miracle would be needed to save France, I would answer, I believe in miracles because I believe in France.'

It was now clear to those on the scene that the growing scale of the exodus in the north was having a seriously detrimental impact on efforts to organize the military. The government now sought to stem the numbers of people who were leaving their homes. One of Weygand's first moves on

19 May was to finally pass an order forbidding the evacuation of civilians. A communiqué was put out which urged people to stay put and resist the temptation to leave.

> The Germans are putting out false news using communiqués, agents provocateurs, and several other means: in this way they wish to create panic among populations to incite them to leave towns and villages—even those which are situated far from the combat zones. Their aim is in this way to block the roads and hinder the manoeuvres of the Allied forces. Our military operations are being slowed down as a result. German planes are taking advantage of this to bomb and gun down both military personnel and civilian evacuees indiscriminately. Such bomb attacks are considerably aggravating the sense of panic in the population.
>
> The population is strongly urged not to withdraw without orders from the civil or military authorities . . .
>
> In cases where, in spite of these orders, population movements become too significant, the command will be obliged to take rigorous measures to protect its strategic routes from becoming blocked.
>
> The civil and military authorities have put together plans to organize the withdrawal of populations from the exposed areas in a controlled way. By acting on their own initiative, inhabitants are bringing considerable confusion to the good functioning of these plans and are thereby bringing about their own woes.[70]

The communiqué went on to say that those who lent themselves to the spreading of enemy propaganda of this nature and who thus contributed to premature evacuation would be liable to very severe penalties. This effort to stem the departure of civilians from their homes was long overdue, but its impact was undermined by the momentum the exodus had already gained. By this time it had taken on a life of its own. It seems probable that the Germans were instrumental in this attempt to frighten civilians into unnecessary departure.[71] First, they intended to add to the disorder and complicate the job of the military command by rendering it difficult for the retreating armies to organize a regrouping. Secondly, they were aware that bringing about the hasty evacuation of certain industrial centres which were in no immediate danger of attack would disrupt production and paralyse industry to their advantage.

Although the news reaching government circles about the course of the war could not be construed as positive, at the War Cabinet meeting on 23 May, there was still reluctance to order full evacuation. The intensity of armaments production in the Paris area and the concentration of workers meant that large-scale evacuation measures would both hinder important production and could provoke panic in the population.

M. Chautemps . . . depicted the consequences of any such evacuation on the part of the ministries and showed how dangerously contagious it might become where the population of Paris was concerned. It was his opinion that the Civil Servants ought not to be the first to leave Paris or they would appear to be specially favoured by the existing regime. There had been a good deal of comment on the evacuation of certain public bodies as this seemed in flat contradiction of the declarations of Government. He gave an account of the cautious efforts that had been made during the past few days, though without much success, to persuade families to send their children away.[72]

Weygand, among others, was particularly reluctant to agree to the departure of the government, fearing that the resulting power vacuum would leave the way open for some kind of communist takeover. Fear of communism was never far from the minds of the ministers when they were trying to decide what was the best way to proceed in terms of departing from Paris. One diplomat confided to a senator that the soldiers fleeing from the 71st and 76th divisions, inspired by communism, were marching on the capital to proclaim a revolution. In order to offset any possibility of this nature, in the short term, then, remaining in the capital was decided upon.[73] Once the first shock of the news of the German breakthrough had been absorbed and the arrival of the first wave of refugees had been organized, everything seemed to point towards the need to wait and see how the situation would develop in order to safeguard industrial production which was recognized as a priority from everyone's point of view.

The Collapse of the Second Front

In the meantime, Weygand had established a second front, seeking to implement his plan to establish a defence line from the Somme to the Maginot line (see Map 2). Under this strategy Weygand wanted to create an offensive by pushing the French army north from its position south of the Somme and in a joint defence initiative meet with the British troops and halt the advance of the Germans. The British, and especially Churchill, had thrown their weight behind the Weygand plan, but communication problems between the British and the French High Commands eventually undermined its enactment.

By 23 May, the French armies still seemed unable to organize an offensive and the Germans were pursuing their advance towards the Channel with such success that the British feared their forces might be cut off from the sea and stranded on the French mainland. In order to prevent this happening, Lord Gort abandoned efforts to advance to meet the French and ordered withdrawal to the Channel ports, thus sabotaging the plan. Despite Reynaud's accusation that the British were sacrificing Weygand's plan to protect their own interests, Churchill had come to believe that the plan had become impracticable and sent orders for as many army forces as possible to be evacuated from Dunkirk. Weygand's desperate efforts to organize some small-scale operations for the regrouped French troops to retake Abbeville, Amiens, Laon, and Rethel failed, and by early June the new second front was in collapse. The line struggled to hold under German attack and was finally penetrated by the Germans on 6 June and soon disintegrated. This defeat, as well as isolating the troops stationed in the fortresses of the Maginot line, triggered a further mass exodus of those civilians immediately in the line of progress of the German army which had now arrived at the Chemin des Dames. This infamous ridge high above the valleys of the rivers Aisne and Ailette had been the scene of the failed Nivelle offensive in 1917 which had led to the first mutinies.

The news of the collapse of Weygand's front, combined with the presence of this new wave of refugees from less distant areas of the north whose stories of the battle now seemed more relevant to those that heard them, contributed to a mounting sense of malaise in Paris. Stories of attack by German machine-gunners flying low over the columns of escaping civilians, lost children often orphaned by these very actions, enemy agents disguised as nuns or even French officers, were very unsettling. But most frightening of all were their accounts of the French troops retreating in shambolic disarray, pillaging homes in the villages they passed through to assuage their hunger (so much so that in some cases they left little for the German troops who were not so very far behind them). In this atmosphere of growing tension and increasing paranoia about fifth columnists, where the refugees had recently provoked sympathy and compassion, they were now anxiously viewed as potential spies. The Belgian capitulation on 28 May was seen as a treacherous move and provoked many French people to express overt hostility towards the Belgians in their midst. This was aggravated by the fact that the authorities seemed to have become overwhelmed and no longer properly equipped to deal with the relentless numbers of arrivals. Parisians began to wonder if all was as well as they were being led to believe. Were the authorities beginning to lose control of the situation?

Despite press efforts to present Dunkirk in a positive light, Parisians were starting to draw their own conclusion that there was little to prevent the Germans from reaching their city. The appearance of soldiers in Paris and the suburbs was also becoming more frequent. At Versailles, the first soldiers who appeared were treated as deserters who had abandoned their posts. Before the order for them to be shot could be carried out, the continual arrival of more routed soldiers alerted the military authorities to the fact that the situation was more significant than that of a few stragglers.[74] Wary of the impact the growing numbers of miserable soldiers might have on morale, the military subsequently tried to introduce measures to prevent them from gaining access to the city and set up camps for them in the suburbs.[75] They did not fully succeed and these tired, hungry, and demoralized men indicated that the army was no longer in a position to cater to their needs. It was now clear to the people of Paris who had the freedom and the means to do so that they should try and get away. People from some of the wealthier *arrondissements* therefore started to leave and these areas of the city, notably the 16th and 8th, rapidly emptied. The bulk of Parisians, however, still stayed put.

It was the bombings of Monday 3 June which were to be a crucial marker in the realization for many Parisians that they were not to be immune from the effects of the war and invasion. This first air raid on the Paris region, which destroyed the airports of Orly, Villacourbly, Bourget, and a number of buildings in the 15th and 16th *arrondissements*—although relatively minor compared with what was to be experienced later in the war—was a warning to Parisians. Of the 906 people affected, 254 were killed, 195 of them civilians. In addition to the news of these deaths, a decree passed on 3 June now officially designated certain parts of the Seine department, including areas of the capital, as being part of the battle zone. This included restrictions on the use of telephones, making it impossible to use them in certain public areas. This direct manifestation of the war led many people to choose this moment to leave as Eugène Dépigny recalled:

> The bombing of the factories in the Paris area on Monday 3 June by the German airforce accelerated and extended the scope of the exodus. From that same evening packed trains from the suburbs arrived at Saint-Lazare and Montparnasse stations. . . . Population movements increased hourly. The obsessiveness of the exodus developed and a sort of pathological panic-filled nervous anxiety overtook the crowds. People left, abandoning everything, more concerned to escape their fear of war than to escape the war itself.[76]

In the light of this manifestation of panic, official communiqués sought to play down the impact of the bombing. Parisians had been trained to expect some level of attack and the majority of them still hung on to finding explanations which justified staying.

The murderous bombing of Billancourt had increased people's fears; there were more people in the stations and cars packed with cases had started to pass by again, but this fever did not last. 'There is no danger' the cleverest amongst us assured us. 'They will only bomb the factories in the suburbs.' And life had continued to take its course.[77]

Throughout June, the Parisian press appeared reassuring and on the whole the papers were unanimous in their advice to the population that they should wait and see how the situation was going to develop. People were urged to resist temptation to flee and running away was presented as giving in to fears propagated by the fifth column. At the same time, even if they did not encourage people to leave, neither did they tell them explicitly that they should stay put. They were simply told to wait for the order to evacuate.[78] But as this order to evacuate failed to materialize, frightening rumours continued, relating to the government's increasing readiness to leave the capital, and many decided that the time had now come to bring their uncertain wait to an end and take action into their own hands. The government's decision to close all schools in the Paris area from 8 June released many families and provoked another substantial wave of departures from the capital.[79] Numerous factory workers no doubt would have liked to make similar plans but simply could not afford to abandon their jobs and were obliged to stay put until they were given official instructions otherwise. Many were forced to watch while others fled the city, as Alexander Werth remarked on 8 June: 'I hear that there is terrible dissatisfaction among the Paris working class. They have been given the strictest orders to stay where they are; if they leave Paris they'll be treated as deserters. Naturally they don't like to see other people buzz off like this.'[80]

On 5 June Reynaud had announced a further cabinet reshuffle in response to the growing sense of crisis. He finally sacked former Prime Minister Daladier, now Minister for Foreign Affairs, who was held responsible for the current failure of National Defence. It seemed important to demonstrate that someone was to blame. Reynaud added this portfolio to those he was already holding as Prime Minister and Defence Minister. De Gaulle joined the government as Under-Secretary of State for National Defence and thus began his political career. He was immediately charged with liaising with

Churchill to explore the possibility of continuing the battle from North Africa in the event of the occupation of Paris, although both Pétain and Weygand immediately declared themselves fiercely against the idea. Churchill himself immediately rather took to the young officer. He remarked on meeting de Gaulle: 'He was young and energetic and made a very favourable impression on me. I thought it probable that if the present line collapsed, Reynaud would ask him to take command.'[81]

In the meantime, extraordinary rumours of fifth column activity were circulating in the capital. Enemy agents had allegedly been parachuted into the centre of Paris only a stone's throw from the National Assembly buildings.[82] Paul Léautaud, who lived in the leafy suburbs of Fontenay, feared that his area would provide numerous opportunities for potential parachute landings and wondered anxiously how he was supposed to distinguish between a genuine French person and a potential enemy agent if one came ringing on his doorbell dressed as a gendarme.[83] In a symbolic effort to counter this 'threat', policemen in the city were armed with old-fashioned rifles. The effectiveness of this move seems to have been questionable and in fact may have done more to alarm the population that reassure them. Such concerns were further aggravated when on 6 June the people of Paris woke up to find that measures had been taken to prevent enemy planes from landing on any of the open areas of Paris, namely the Champs Élysées, the Place de la Concorde, and the Champ de Mars where the Eiffel Tower is situated.

By this time discussions were once again underway as to whether the government should leave the capital. Apart from provoking panic, fear that departure would be exploited by extremists on the left or the right once again dominated these deliberations. Particular concerns were voiced about the possibility of communists stepping in subsequent to the disappearance of the government. Efforts to repress communist activity had followed the banning of the Communist Party in September 1939 amidst fears that the Nazi-Soviet pact would encourage French communists to indulge in defeatist behaviour. This policy had been a high priority for the government since the outbreak of the war and many individuals had been arrested. Mandel had carefully reinforced these measures on taking up his position as Minister of the Interior. While Reynaud and Daladier shared these concerns, Weygand was obsessed with them. In 1870 the defeat of the French armies by the Germans had been followed by a revolutionary commune which established itself in the capital. Many conservatives feared such a situation might recur. Weygand was haunted

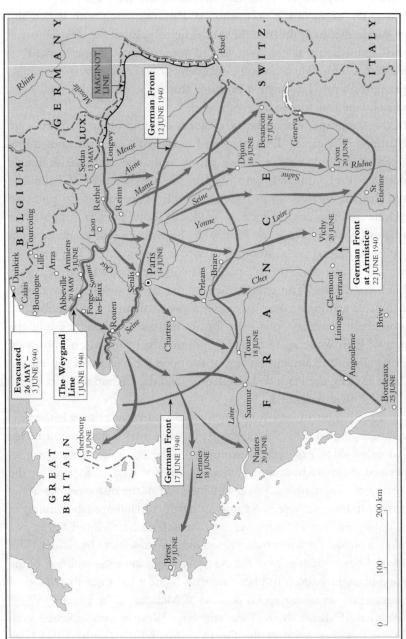

Map 2. The German advance, May–June 1940

by this possibility: 'if the government wants to avoid the development of a revolutionary movement in the capital, it must affirm that it will stay in the capital whatever the situation', he claimed.[84] It was therefore agreed that, should the government eventually depart, the Parisian police would have to stay in place to offset any possibility of popular unrest and communist upheaval. Such arguments were in no way based on fact. Since the September ban communist activity had been undermined and the communists were in no position to organize any such step at this point.

On the evening of Saturday 8 June, the Germans reached the town of Forges-les-Eaux, 120 km (75 miles) north of Paris. Paul Reynaud finally ordered that ministers whose activity was not considered indispensable to national defence should evacuate the city the following day. He would stay in the capital along with the Ministers of the Interior, Marine, and Air, but he conceded that the two Presidents (of the Chamber of Deputies and the Senate) and other cabinet members should leave. Thus, departure of the government from Paris was finally decided after weeks of announcing and then rescinding such a move. Several government departments hurriedly started the evacuation of the greatest part of their staff, leaving only a nucleus in place. The next day, on Sunday 9 June, with the Germans only 30 km (19 miles) from Notre-Dame, the bulk of the government evacuated Paris.

These decisions coincided with a growing wave of civilian departures. Georgette Guillot left the capital with her colleagues at the Ministry of the Interior:

> In the ante-chambers the officials hammered down the lids on boxes containing Ministry archives ... Our line manager told us to be ready for anything. Knowing that the worst could happen, I went home to collect a few clothes. It was difficult to choose.
>
> I could not find a taxi to get back to the office, there was not a free car to be found in Paris. The roads filled with cars loaded up beyond any imagination. The whole city was escaping. I walked back to work. Everyone seemed to have left except the concierges.

Once at work again, she met a senior civil servant who said to her,

> 'Don't take this fleeing as a tragedy—we will soon be back: in 1914 we left for Bordeaux and we were back a month later...'. I believed him. We did not discuss military events, our own situation was all that concerned us. We did not appear to be in immediate danger.

At 11 we heard echoes of what was going on in the Council of Ministers, that there could be a surrender and that there might be a change of government, the defence of the country was pointless . . .
At midnight the order came to leave. We thought that Paris would be defended after all. We still had hope. It was only at about 1 a.m. that the cars silently moved along the Avenue de Marigny, then down the banks of the Seine. We were abandoning Paris the capital.[85]

This discreet departure of the government was interpreted by the remaining population as abandonment and tangible proof of military defeat. The agitation around the ministerial buildings, the activity of lorries being loaded up and moving off in convoys towards the south of the city, all this was noticed by the locals. Meanwhile, the Germans appeared to encircle rather than head directly for the capital. French troops, lacking clear instructions, assumed that it was their duty to organize some kind of defence though they had no explicit orders to do so. For those inhabitants left in Paris, it was still unclear whether the city would soon find itself at the centre of the fighting. The heavily censored papers failed to provide any clear information enabling the people to evaluate the levels of risk they might face. People were simply told to 'hold their own', organize the defence of Paris, and remain vigilant. Official communiqués said little to offset the possibility that the capital might become a centre of the fighting and people started to imagine scenes like those which had filled the black and white newsreels and double-page spreads of *Paris-Match* relating to Warsaw. Most still believed that Paris would be defended and that the city was soon likely to become a battleground.

This was by no means the assumption made by government. The military had already declared several of the cities in the north of the country 'open cities'. In doing so they had indicated to the Germans that they had abandoned all efforts at defence. This move was designed to prevent bombing and destruction and to avoid excessive civilian casualties. With the government now on the move, Weygand had to decide what action to take in relation to the defence of Paris. He had suggested to Reynaud that Paris should also be declared an open city. This move essentially meant surrender to the Germans in the hope that the city would be spared. The population, however, remained unaware of this possibility. The Military High Command left Vincennes, situated in the east suburbs of Paris, for Briare, further south near Tours. A communiqué explained that 'The government has been obliged to leave the capital for compelling military reasons. The President of the Council is with the armies.' Parisians had little time to assimilate this news before a further announcement called on all men from 18 to 50 to depart. The burning of the petrol reserves to prevent them from falling into German hands was widely interpreted to mean that Paris was under attack and was a further incitement for people to leave. 'It is horribly hot and close. Large clouds of petrol smoke from the west are not breaking up. The air carries fine molecules of greasy coal which lands everywhere and blackens everything including our hands and faces. The walls of our homes as well as the furniture is covered in it.'[86] As Parisians flooded out of the city on 11 June, no officials remained to oversee evacuation or organize the departure of the population.

By 12 June those Parisians toying with the idea of leaving could hear the noise of distant cannon fire and had to weigh up the possibility that they might find themselves caught in the front as the German army appeared to be rapidly moving towards the city. Pockets of French soldiers who still had no orders continued rather hopelessly to fire in improvised attempts to slow the now inevitable German advance. This apparent resistance led the Germans to satisfy themselves with surrounding the city until they were given orders to occupy it. It was not until midday that Weygand's orders finally reached the French generals Hering and Dentz, informing them that Paris was to be declared an open city which would therefore not be defended. When Colonel Groussard learnt this news he asked to be relieved of his duties but was told by his superior officer Dentz that he must follow orders, however difficult they might seem. Not to do so would be desertion.

We were left responsible for the capital and for my part, I have never felt so humiliated and so full of anger. The military should fight not to hand itself over. I sincerely believe that I would have given my life to save myself from having to obey these orders.[87]

Interior Minister Mandel had arranged for very few officials to remain in the capital, fearing that any remaining politicians might take it upon themselves to 'represent' the government in some way.

All those elected to parliament and local government in Paris and the Seine department should leave Paris. They will be officially informed that they should have no contact at all with the enemy. Only the two prefects should stay in place. The municipal council will have no role to play, no responsibility to take on.[88]

He did not want anyone to be in place who could possibly claim that they had the status to negotiate with the enemy now that the government had evacuated. Only members of the military, and the prefect of the police, Roger Langeron, were left in Paris. His main concern was to prevent the emergence of a sort of provisional government like those that had emerged in other occupied countries.[89] Other than these individuals, few other administrative structures were present after 10 June. Those authorities who remained had to set about dealing with the needs of the civilians who were still left in the city.

Day and night from 11 June, I was bombarded with telephone calls and visits from panic-stricken individuals. The administrations, the communes, complained about the departure of their bosses and simply asked that they be given a minimum of guidance. My reply was always the same of course: 'Stay in place and keep your department going.' But how few of them obeyed![90]

The French government feebly tried to oversee what was happening at a distance from its sprawling position spread across the numerous chateaux of the Touraine. In the absence of clear instructions and lacking any kind of precedent, Hering, Dentz, and Langeron were left to improvise their roles. The status of Paris as an open city was made public only on 13 June. That morning posters appeared on the walls of the town halls and the commissariats carrying the following text:

Paris having been declared an open city, the military government asks the population to abstain from all hostile acts and hopes that the people will remain calm and dignified in a manner which appears appropriate in the circumstances.

By this time, however, the majority of the population had already fled and the declaration came too late to have anything more than a limited impact. If people had known that Paris was going to be declared an open city, many of those who left would probably have remained at home.[91] Even for those who fully grasped its significance, it remained unclear whether the Germans would respect this open city status. The press had cited examples of German bombings of other open cities. Furthermore, the decree itself looked suspicious. The Germanic-sounding signatures of Hering and Dentz were an unfortunate confusion for the apprehensive few who now remained in the city.[92]

One of these was Paul Léautard who explained his reasons for staying, thus:

I am staying. I was always sure that I would stay. Now I am even more certain of it . . . I would not know where to go. I am a bad-tempered person. I don't want to go and live just anywhere with who knows what people. I don't want to risk finding nothing in my home when I come back. The very idea of packing hastily and organizing my departure makes me want to stay. I say to myself that my destiny here depends on the kind of people I come across. If I come across a brute, I could also come across a civilized man. I am an old man.

6. On 23 June 1940, the day after the signing of the Armistice at which Hitler was present, the Führer came to visit Paris with Nazi architect Albert Speer, to celebrate his victory. His two-hour early morning visit took in all the main tourist sites. It is said that he wanted to go up the Eiffel Tower but the French had cut the lift cables and they could not be mended in time. Hitler preferred not to climb the 1,792 steps to the summit. Within hours of his departure, the lifts were again operational.

I have no arms at home, I am an inoffensive civilian. What could anyone possibly have against me? I am staying put. It is not a courageous position. It is sang-froid, reason, indolence, and a don't care attitude.[93]

Those who remained had managed to resist the contagious panic which inspired the mass departure of three-quarters of Parisians.

Hardly any cars are left on the roads of Paris or the suburbs of the city. Post vans, fire engines, rubbish trucks have all been used to take away entire families. Even undertakers had left, making burials impossible for several days.[94]

On 13 June Léautard noted the following:

Paris is completely deserted. The best word for it is empty. Shops are shut. Passers-by are rare . . . The Cour of the Carrousel is empty. Not a single sentry in the Louvre. You could set it alight without bothering any one . . . The intermittent noise of cannons can be heard.[95]

For the English reporter of *The Times*:

Could this really be Paris? There were no newspapers, except one composite sheet, and only guarded announcements on the wireless to dispel the fear that the city might already be encircled.[96]

Everyone now expected the inevitable any moment.

The remaining population was waiting without any fervour for the first detachments of the Wehrmacht to appear on the boulevards. Each motor noise (vehicles had become so rare) made us quiver as we wondered if this could not be a group of panzer tanks which would suddenly appear.[97]

Late on 14 June, one day earlier than Hitler had predicted some weeks before, the Germans triumphantly entered the French capital as victors. They had won the battle of France in less than a month. Meanwhile, those who had left the capital in the course of the previous week were little prepared to cope with what was to face them on the roads of the exodus.

2

On the Road

France was confused, tangled up like an immense skein of wool being manipulated by a superhuman, evil power. Soldiers and civilians—soldiers without their leaders and leaders without soldiers—mothers who had lost their children, children who were lost and who were crying alone on the roadsides four days' journey from their bombed homes. Other couples were fleeing on foot dragging cases which were tied up with string, young people on bicycles overloaded with packages of all kinds . . . all this formed a deeply moving and pitiful mixture of bravery and panic, calm courage, distress, and (what a marvellous thing!) good humour, the will to live and fear of death.

André Morize, *France: Été 1940*

Once people had left home, the pressure of the German advance created the momentum which kept the floods of refugees moving slowly south and west. The crowds from Paris joined columns of other advancing civilians who had left their homes during the first exodus. Peasants from rural areas with their heavily laden carts set a slow, tortuous pace. Food became more and more difficult to find, and comfortable provision for shelter was increasingly thin on the ground. Refugees were obliged to sleep rough as hotels in towns ran out of space, local residents had no more spare rooms to rent out, and local farms and their outbuildings were already packed with those who had preceded them. To add to their discomfort, this human mass was an easy target for the German planes who sought to kill indiscriminately as well as add to the confusion by machine-gunning them down.

Departure

Families left their homes within hours of taking the decision to do so. Luggage was thrown together rapidly and without much thought. Preparations were often cursory. Clement weather and the time of year suggested to many that they should plan for some kind of 'early holiday' as this was often the only precedent they had for preparing departure. At the same time, it was hard not to take too much. The Englishman Rupert Browning who left Paris by bike described the need for self-control: 'Steadfastly I refused to look too long at my possessions, lest the temptation to try and take some of them might prove too much for me.'[1] Indeed, those who left in catastrophic haste were often forced to abandon heavy and useless goods on the way. The roads of the exodus, as well as the railway stations, were littered with abandoned personal possessions of all kinds.

Concern about what might be necessary or useful was superseded by the need to protect valuables from pillaging. Choices about what to take and what to leave behind tended to be more linked to emotional attachments than thoughts of what might prove practical. Women recalled packing and unpacking in an agony of indecision. Lack of understanding of the nature of the disaster made it impossible for them to predict what they might need. Many failed to take even the most basic supplies of food and drink assuming that they would be able to shop along the way. Most people simply had no idea of what they were getting themselves in to.

From the outset departure was intensely class-based. Time was the all-important factor and when people left their homes had a vital impact on the nature of their journey and their capacity to stay ahead of the German armies. Those who were better off had often made plans long in advance to ensure that if the moment came they would have somewhere comfortable to run to. These individuals for whom money was no object had organized rented accommodation well before events had taken such a dramatic turn. Less dependent on their incomes, there was no reason for them to prevaricate when the situation appeared to become dangerous. They were among the first to leave, equipped with the assurance of a definite destination to head for. The middle classes were not far behind them.

When it came to means of transport, once again wealth put them at an advantage. Most middle-class families were likely to own cars or have access to them. Cars became such valuable currency that any that moved, however pitiful their state, were seen as desirable. They not only allowed for the transport of heavy luggage but they also seemed to offer the prospect of reaching relative safety reasonably fast. Quite how long petrol supplies would last was a question rarely considered by most Parisians who were prepared to chance their luck. Once again, most assumed that they would be able to fill up in the normal way on the journey. Car owners found themselves solicited by relatives and acquaintances on all sides seeking lifts if not for themselves, then for their children. Georges-Alexandres Pros recalled how at 10, on leaving his home in central Paris on 12 June, while he knew he should be grateful for the lift, departure was a terrible wrench.

> My mother disappeared out of sight. A dagger in my heart would not have been more wounding. I wanted to cry out 'Mummy' but I was relieved when this did not come out of my dry throat. I was too old and too proud to cry. It was already a miracle that I was in this overcrowded car at all when so many people who were trying to find a way to escape found themselves unable to do so. Very late the previous evening my mother had implored our neighbours, 'Take him with you. Take him with you.'[2]

Such requests were difficult to resist and cars left the capital overloaded with passengers as well as luggage. Children recalled feeling squashed and claustrophobic in the back of stuffy cars, an uncomfortable experience which they sometimes had to put up with for several days.[3] Mattresses were frequently tied to the car roofs in line with the widespread belief that this could somehow protect passengers from bombing or attack from the air. They also proved useful to sleep on at improvised stops and shelters.

Once the decision to leave had been made and the stress of packing and organizing departure was over, these Parisians could often feel more relaxed in the belief that they were doing their patriotic duty. Those who headed southwards believed that, on crossing the Loire, they were sure to find themselves on the French side of the battle lines where they imagined they would then remain throughout the hostilities. In this way, not only would they avoid finding themselves under German occupation, but they also hoped to make some contribution to the ongoing war effort. Many still thought that all was not lost and remained optimistic, comforted in the belief that they had made the right decision both for themselves and for their country.

This sense of optimism in the early part of their journeys pervades many accounts of those who left Paris early in June. Testimonies often refer to an atmosphere of holiday adventure. The roads were not too congested, the weather was good, and they were able to sleep in the open air; these journeys took on the allure of a kind of forced camping holiday when people stopped for picnics and breaks in a ritualistic way.

> If I wanted to conform to common practice, I would describe the exodus in tragic terms. But I can only recount what I saw. Others doubtless witnessed

desperate escapes, the bombing of crowds who were crushed at the entrance
to bridges. They saw soldiers throwing their arms into ditches, roads littered
with human debris . . . I have to say, at risk of scandalizing some readers, that
the departure of Parisians appeared to me as a large countryside party. The
queue that our car joined, at the southern exits from Paris, included all kinds
of vehicles . . . In the factory lorries where there were complete families, they
were passing one another pieces of saucisson and litre bottles. Every time the
traffic queue stopped, and that was about every 100 m [328 feet], people
spread out over the plain, and went into houses from whence they brought
back the crusty end of a loaf of bread and a bottle of water. The sun was
beating down strongly on the joyous crowd.[4]

Marie-Madeleine Fourcade, who was later to become a distinguished leader
of the Resistance movement, also marvelled at the picnics people produced
from their cars. Some people even went as far as unfolding tables and chairs.[5]

The working classes, on the other hand, especially factory workers, were
trapped in the capital until the very last minute. Dependent on their wages,
workers had to wait until word came from their bosses that the factory was
leaving or being evacuated. Certain companies were more helpful than others
in arranging transportation for their employees in an effort to relocate to an
area further south that they imagined would be beyond enemy lines.
Thoughtful and far-sighted employers distributed delivery lorries and vans
to their workers to enable their escape. As many people as possible packed
themselves into these trades vehicles and numbers of passengers often increased as the journey wore on. In the state sector, the government prevaricated over what to do with the specially designated workers who found
themselves at the mercy of orders and counter-orders. Sadoul met a worker at
the aviation factory Gnome in the Paris suburbs on 13 June who complained:

'I don't know what to do. One day they say one thing to us, the next day they say
the opposite. The day before yesterday specially designated workers like me all
had to leave. Yesterday, we were told the opposite. We have to stay to show the
Germans that we are not afraid of them. But if we stay they are going to make us
work for them, and I don't want to do that. I'd rather leave. In any case we will
see what they say to us later.'

We later learnt that all those who appeared at the gates of the factory that
morning found it deserted with orders to reach Bordeaux by their own means.[6]

The Armaments Minister Raoul Dautry had wanted to keep industry
working until it was absolutely clear that the Germans were arriving. This
decision, which was doubtless motivated by the best intentions with a view
to promoting the war effort and to avoid appearing defeatist or create panic,

seriously backfired. Ultimately, it worked to the benefit of Germans who were able to recover much of the material which was left intact as a result of the rushed last-minute desperate departures of many of these workers. The Germans were sometimes able literally to walk in to the abandoned factories, take control, and immediately start up the factories again, sometimes employing exactly the same workforce as before. The dismay and bitterness of these workers was often compounded by the discovery that employers who had failed to arrange evacuation for workers had themselves managed to escape. Many workers were left stranded in this way and had to decide for themselves their best course of action.[7] In the absence of clear instructions, many took their chance in the rush once they had learnt of the government's defection and joined the numerous women, children, and elderly who were abandoning the capital.

Since few were able to run a car, their main option was the train. As crowds of Parisians flooded the mainline stations, the French railways

7. The crowds struggle to board the last trains leaving for Brittany at the Gare Montparnasse in Paris.

struggled to cope. Aren Arenstraum who was due to take a sleeper to Bordeaux on 10 June recounts the scene.

> The train leaves in four hours time. About 20,000 people are massed in front of the station, most of them seated on their belongings. It is impossible to move and the heat is unbearable. In its present state of nervous tension the crowd has lost all its charm, and has none of the friendly gaiety that normally characterises the French *en masse....*
>
> The human body can evidently stand much more that one suspects in normal times. I have now been standing wedged in this seething mass for over three hours ... A woman standing near us has fainted. Two policeman force their way through, and carry her off over the heads of the crowd. Children are crying all round, and the many babies in arms look like they are being crushed to death. The Police Officer in charge of the entrance gates orders all babies to be handed over to the Police inside. This human baggage is gradually passed over the heads of the crowd by outstretched arms, and the babies are assembled on a table within the station gates, until the mothers can get through to collect them.[8]

By 12 June the situation was even worse. Eugène Dépigny observes:

> The train stations are full to bursting. People that were left behind by the last trains of the evening are sleeping out in the open in courtyards and adjacent roads. Passengers include women, children, the elderly and with them they have their cases, their dolls, and their toys.[9]

These people eventually realized that their uncertain and difficult wait was likely to prove futile. Some sought a different means of transport. Bicycles proved ideal. Not only did they surge ahead of the frustrating and paralysing queues, they could also serve to transport luggage. Anything and everything that moved was mobilized: prams, pushchairs, and any other contraption on wheels. In the absence of any other solution, people set off on foot. As Rupert Downing put it:

> the sight for a couple of fledgling refugees was amazing ... There were lorries, cars, bicycles, horses, perambulators, and wheelbarrows all mixed up with pedestrains of every age, type, size, and description. Some of the cars were straight from the showroom; others looked as if they had been rescued from refuse dumps. And every vehicle was laden to its capacity with anything you can think of, from an empty parrot cage to a grandfather clock. The desire to save as much as possible from the invader was later to spell tragedy for many, and from the next day onwards we were to see hundreds and hundreds of cars with smashed axles lying by the roadside—while their owners either trudged on with what they could carry or helplessly waited for assistance that never came.[10]

8. People left Paris with whatever means of transport they had at their disposal. If all
else failed they walked.

There were many pedestrians among the floods of people leaving the
capital after 10 June. Yet despite the dramatic circumstances, the early stages
of their journeys do not seem to have been marked by undue panic.
Commentators once again likened this mass departure to that of a holiday.
Roland Dorgelès, the novelist, commented that the crowds he met between
Paris and Tours did not appear fearful. They looked more like they were on
holiday than being hunted down by the enemy. They had less the appearance of being in flight than of trying to escape the heat. 'This fuss really
reminded one of a holiday rush more than anything else.'[11] Georges Sadoul,
whose journey took him round the capital, noticed the contrast between
those who had been caught up in the exodus for several days and those who
had just joined it. He described the Parisians he came across on 13 June near
Longjumeau in the suburbs of the capital:

The mass of people, more dense than a crowd returning home after the 14 July fireworks, is still fresh, even well turned-out. The elderly and disabled who are pushed in wheelbarrows appear courageous. An elderly lady . . . who looks as if she would normally be fearful of taking too long a walk in the Luxembourg gardens, cheerfully goes on her way with two heavy cases and a yappy little dog on a lead. To those who ask her, she simply answers that she is going to Orléans on foot to catch a train there.

The young women are powdered, well made up with lipstick. The women's magazine *Marie-Claire* must have had advice to give those who were leaving as among Parisian salesgirls there seems to be a desire to start a new fashion, that of the refugee chic. They wear relatively short grey or light-blue trousers, with a navy blue jacket or cardigan. On their hair a handkerchief is no longer knotted in the peasant style according to last year's trends but now in 'madras' style . . .

The happiest of them all are these 18-year-olds who dash by in gangs on bikes, boys and girls travelling light who appear almost cheerful in their (newly gained) freedom heading towards the unknown.[12]

Indeed, for many younger refugees caught up in the hiatus of the exodus who were perhaps less conscious of the more serious side of the situation, the atmosphere could certainly be said to have resembled that of a holiday. Young people were perhaps better equipped to take advantage of these experiences as they were more adaptable and prepared to take life at face value and were not haunted by the spectre of what might be the true consequences of losing the war. Children also tended to travel with adults, normally their own parents, and this gave them a strong sense of security which affected their perception of events.

As Parisians left the city they encountered other rural populations from the Seine department as well as those travelling south and west from the first exodus. Bottlenecks were created by the heavily loaded peasant farm carts drawn by horses and oxen. These enormous vehicles set the pace for everyone travelling along behind them. Georges Adrey described their painfully slow progress:

We advanced down the road with difficulty, taking a step at a time in the middle of a formidable traffic jam of cars and vehicles drawn by animals or humans taking up the full width of the road and overtaking one another in spite of the clamours of pedestrians who persisted in trying to make a passage through it for themselves. Broken-down cars, rearing horses, fallen cyclists, and people who were feeling unwell or who needed a break from their vehicle, all this added to the disorder, made circulation more difficult, and obliged us to stop frequently.[13]

9. This family on a road near Chartres is using their bike to carry luggage. The children appear quite heavily dressed for a warm day. Dad has a helmet at his waist suggesting that he might be part of a civilian defence structure. The older girl has brought her gas mask and her dog unlike many Parisians who abandoned their pets. Countless dogs were left to run wild in the streets of the capital.

Those who were not used to covering long distances on foot soon found themselves forced to return home. Few had dressed appropriately for an extended period of walking. Many soon regretted decisions taken in haste to dress in several layers of clothing in spite of the unseasonably warm weather or to wear heavy coats to avoid carrying them.

The presence of others was reassuring for those who were less sure about their decision to leave.[14] Most enjoyed the friendliness of recognition of those they had met along the way. Rupert Downing expressed it thus:

> We met and remet quite a number of people during that fortnight—motorists, cyclists, all sorts. Car-owners we had met and talked with hours and days back on the road we would meet again farther on, they having been held up for lack of petrol. Pedestrians we passed in the morning would be seen in the evening

waving to us out of the back of a lorry in which they had secured a lift. And they all seemed as pleased about these chance encounters as we were. At such a time in a stricken country the sight of a face you know (however slightly) can bring a curious glow to the heart.[15]

People soon realized that, despite the delays, they could move faster in motorized vehicles than travelling on foot. Military convoys had priority on the roads and could make headway more easily. Although these trucks were not supposed to take on civilians, this stipulation was widely ignored (along with many others at a time when rules and regulations had little or no meaning). Georges Sadoul recounted how his work colleague 'is so happy to get a lift, he abandons his wife and even forgets to take his stick with him. However, as the lorry is only going as far as Étampes, they promise us that they will wait for us there and that we will head on together.'[16] Convoys would take civilians some distance and then leave them elsewhere, at which point they had no means of contacting or rejoining their party. People invited opportunities to separate if it looked as though this would advance the elderly or the young who were less equipped to cope. Agreements were made to meet further down the journey. Sadoul recorded an incident on the road near Longchamp where his group came across a family picnicking. The party consisted of several women, three men, and five children—two were infants.

> A convoy appeared on the road and the soldiers offered to take the women and children. Within a minute they were all installed . . . and the men raced along behind them, crying
>   'Where are you going?'
>   'We don't know but you are sure to catch us up', the women shouted back as the lorry accelerated and disappeared.
>   The three men remained stupidly at the crossroads next to a pile of prams, luggage, and bikes.
>   The grandfather was the first one to react. He broke out in a rage, swore at his son and his grandson, and started to hurry off in the direction of the lorry. The others tried to hold him back . . . The grandfather continued his cursing and then all three men continued down the road in a complete panic, abandoning all their prams, luggage, and even their bikes on the side of the road.[17]

Such well-intentioned spontaneous initiatives often left families in agonies of worry about lost family members with whom there could be little hope of being reunited. In cases where the separation was not planned, or the difficulty of meeting up again had been underestimated, this could be extremely traumatic and difficult for all concerned. Children were particularly vulnerable. More astute families would make sure that the children carried some kind of identification on them, sometimes details were slipped into their socks in case they were separated from their shoes.[18] Mothers, exhausted by carrying children or struggling to keep up, welcomed the offer of a lift for the children from an unknown quarter and subsequently could not track them down.

It may now seem extraordinary that mothers were prepared to take these kinds of risks, but the very fact that women were prepared to do so suggests that losing a child was less of a worry than attempting to ensure its safety. Most people had no idea of the scale of the disaster and imagined that they would easily catch up with those sent ahead later in the journey. Towns along the roads leading south were covered with chalked messages and notes left at official buildings in a effort to inform relatives of the whereabouts of other family members.[19] The numerous messages later published in the papers to this effect are testimony to volumes of personal dramas and tragedies of this kind.[20] Had they been given clearer instructions, it is possible that much distress could have been avoided. Reuniting these families was to prove one of the most lasting and acute problems of the exodus. However, these dramas only came to light later on. In the early days, on the contrary, people were preoccupied with forging travel companions, enjoying picnics in the open air, and there certainly seems to have been little evidence of revolt and dissatisfaction. Most people tried to make the best of difficult circumstances and passively accepted their fate.[21] Dorgelès noted that 'these families in full flight did not seem particularly worried. At that time, we were only concerned about what was most pressing; eating and finding petrol.'[22]

On leaving the capital most refugees, whatever their transport, naturally tended to stick to the main well-established routes towards the south and west. Most left Paris and made for Chartres, Étampes, or Fontainebleau. From there they either branched towards Le Mans, and on west to Brittany and the Atlantic coast, or they headed for the south or south-west, on the N20 or the N7 towards the river Loire (see Map 3). For those working their way southwards, crossing the Loire seemed to promise safety. Léon Werth described a peasant woman who invoked the Loire as the place she needed to reach in order to be safe from all peril. 'Once we have crossed the Loire, we will be safe . . .' was a common refrain among all the refugees.[23] This natural frontier seemed to be the obvious place for the front to reconvene and once again historical precedent reassured refugees. In 1870 Gambetta had rallied the

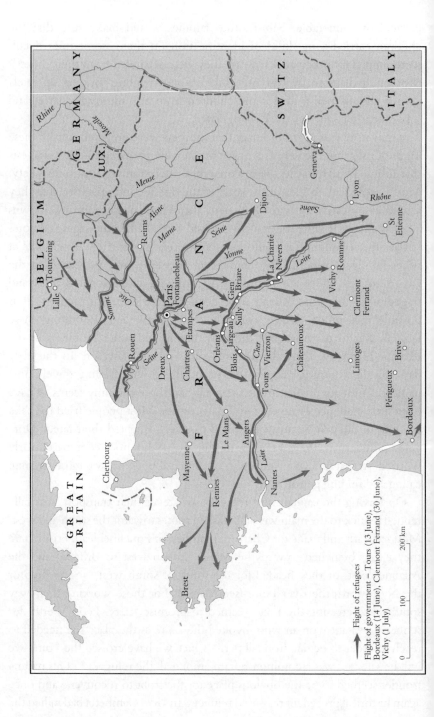

Flight of refugees

Flight of government – Tours (13 June),
Bordeaux (14 June), Clermont Ferrand (30 June),
Vichy (1 July)

GREAT
BRITAIN

GERMANY

BELGIUM

LUX.

SWITZ.

ITALY

FRANCE

Rhine

Moselle

Meuse

Marne

Aisne

Reims

Seine

Yonne

Saône

Rhône

Lyon

St Etienne

Geneva

Dijon

La Charité

Nevers

Loire

Roanne

Vichy

Clermont
Ferrand

Limoges

Brive

Périgueux

Bordeaux

Châteauroux

Vierzon

Cher

Tours

Angers

Loire

Nantes

Le Mans

Mayenne

Rennes

Brest

Cherbourg

Rouen

Seine

Dreux

Chartres

Etampes

Orleans

Blois

Jargeau

Sully

Gien

Briare

Paris

Fontainebleau

Oise

Somme

Lille

Tourcoing

0   100   200 km

French armies against the Prussians along the Loire front and it seemed logical that the river would once again offer the military the opportunity to prove that after all it could defend itself. Werth describes how

A group in the road, massed together in front of a half-open window, are listening to the radio. I approach them. I would be unable to remember the news in the periphrases that the radio news was communicating. The advance of the Germans was barely mentioned. I seem to remember that that morning I heard an extraordinary 'behind Paris' which reminded me of the battles west of Brussels, when it had not even been announced that Brussels had been taken. However, for the nomads that we had become, it was still only the German advance in the headlines of the papers. They advance, they pass the Somme, the Oise. Even if they pass the Seine nothing is lost. We will fight them on the Loire. We will have no shortage of rivers and strategy is the science of rivers.[24]

Soldiers gave momentum to people's desire to cross the Loire. They too sought to reach places where rumours suggested that they would be regrouping. Official communiqués continued to cultivate this belief until very late in the day.[25] Dorgelès later accused himself of naivety:

as absurd as it may appear, I could not believe that all was lost. In 1914 we had the Marne, this time we would have the Loire. I was convinced of it. (This in spite of being better informed than most.) In spite of that, I still hoped for a miracle.[26]

I imagined that the invaders would stop on the Loire to discuss terms, which would give the US time to intervene, perhaps even allow the Soviets to change sides, and in these circumstances there would be no point in continuing the journey.[27]

In the face of appearances, and sometimes only after they had encountered German troops, or when their trip had become impossible, people still clung on to the belief that some kind of front was going to be fought along the banks of the Loire.

Unless they had made plans in advance, the majority of refugees did not have a clear idea of their final destination. In 1936 French workers had benefited from laws allowing them paid holidays for the first time. Recent holidays by the sea were often their only experience of travel and reaching these resorts became a possible objective for them. Others decided to head to friends or family where they were likely to receive some measure of welcome. Parisians who had taken note of their publicized evacuation destinations attempted to make for their allocated departments. Few could conceptualize the distances involved, nor the nature of the terrain, nor indeed the climate.

Class was once again a determinant when it came to reaching destinations. Car-owners normally possessed maps and could plan their journeys to avoid the more congested routes. Those who left the main national and departmental roads were likely to make faster progress even if routes were sometimes longer or less direct. Of those on foot, few had planned their journeys in advance and most had little knowledge of the geography of the country. Those from rural areas were rarely even familiar with areas within their home departments. Women and the elderly who formed the majority of the crowds assumed that they would reach safety by following those ahead of them. 'People followed along in a line as if we were all going to the same place.'[28] It was rare for them to own a map though some used departmental maps situated on the back of calendars distributed to homes by the post office. Those who did have access to decent maps or who had any knowledge of the local countryside could more easily escape the jams and they were much more likely to have been able to reach the Loire in good time.[29]

The true nature of the disaster was slow to dawn even on those who found themselves in the most difficult of circumstances. Signs that all was not well could be explained away at this stage, often in the face of all evidence and indications to the contrary. News was sparse and even if what they did hear did not bode well, people were reluctant to believe the worst. The appearance of soldiers in groups and regiments reassured refugees who assumed they were heading for the new front on the Loire. The presence of stray, dishevelled soldiers was more confusing. Marie-Madeleine Fourcade explained how one exhausted man interrupted a picnic and burst into tears, explaining that he had been walking for four days and four nights and could not find his unit. The picnickers reacted to this with disapproval. This man, in uniform, mobilized to defend the nation, had allowed himself to turn up like some kind of refugee. 'It is not to be believed, not to be believed,' they all murmured.[30] Other civilians found it reassuring to have soldiers amongst them and turned to them for advice. One French soldier in retreat later told how he passed 'through towns and villages where a frantic population is trying to join the already overcrowded columns, asking me when we are forced to stop what to do. My answer is invariably the same, "stay where you are, you are safer in your own home than on the road". How many listened I do not know.'[31] In their endless and often futile search for figures of authority, refugees on the road perceived uniformed soldiers as having some official status. On Sunday 16 June Sadoul reported of his arrival in the town of Sully,

I get down from the lorry. A woman calls me over. I answer her. There are soon thirty refugees calling me, asking for advice, because I am a man, in uniform, and for hours they have found no one to ask, no official policemen, no agents, not even a local councillor... Firefighters left with their equipment, agents with their authority and their coshes, but nowhere on the roads of our withdrawal has there been anyone to put out fires or organize circulation at crossroads.[32]

Most soldiers, like Sadoul, when they found themselves amidst civilians, did their best to help out and share with them whatever resources they had left at their disposal. When it came to finding somewhere to sleep, hotels were often the first port of call for the fleeing refugees. Most attempted to accommodate as many people as possible, often allowing their large salons and lounges to be used by people passing through, but were soon overwhelmed by the volume of the arrivals. In Chartres, situated 100 km (62 miles) south-west of Paris on one of the main arteries leaving the capital, refugees gravitated to one of the two hotels in the town centre. Jean Moulin (at the time prefect of the Eure-et-Loire), who later became de Gaulle's emissary, described the scene in one of these establishments:

There are people everywhere, in the rooms, in the lounges, and on the steps of the staircase. People eat on tables which are full of the leftovers of previous guests. The silverware is dispersed across the furniture. In the corners of the room entire exhausted families have installed themselves on mattresses. Those who could not get inside the building have installed themselves outside on chairs and armchairs from the hotel next to their luggage. All classes, all ages, both sexes are mixed up in this tragic overcrowding.[33]

His efforts to persuade people that they should not take to the road again and his reassurances that he would do what he could to help them were often in vain. His repeated appeals that they must 'resign themselves to staying here' were largely ignored and, as they moved on, more arrived to replace those who had just left.[34] As they went on their way, people slept where they could find shelter, in cafés on overturned tables, in station halls, in the entrance halls of buildings, and in cinemas. Dorgelès described the situation in Vendôme, just north of the Loire, where he hoped to find accommodation for the night.

The little town was packed with refugees. The early arrivals had found somewhere to sleep in hotels or with locals, those who followed them had managed to find space to lie down in school playgrounds or in cafés but now all of these are full. Many people were sleeping in their cars, others in the open air on deckchairs or mattresses untied from their car roofs.[35]

As towns became saturated, locals tended to be readily prepared to help those with young children or infants: farmers often made barns and outbuildings available if people approached them directly. But sleeping in a bed was a rare luxury and most refugees did not see a bed with sheets until their return home. Lack of information about what was going on meant that people left one shelter in the morning with no idea at all as to where they might find themselves that evening. Their only preoccupation was to move, to escape danger, and to avoid the possibility of finding themselves caught in bombing attacks. If all else failed, people would just sleep rough and this was the common experience of the majority. Cars offered some degree of shelter, otherwise the generally good weather made sleeping outside less uncomfortable than it might otherwise have been. In Moulins, just south of the Loire,

Many, overwhelmed with fatigue, fell asleep in cars, on benches, and on the ground. Others stepped over them. I can still see four children lying next to one another on a mattress between two carts. They washed themselves and their washing at the fountain . . . Sometimes, a fire was lit on four stones and a few onions started to sizzle. And on the cobblestones of the road, more went by and then still more, the inexhaustible caravan of France which was moving on, while those around them had a break as if in an oasis . . . for one hour, there was a 'camping' atmosphere almost like that of a picnic.[36]

As the momentum of the exodus continued, its dynamic drew in others along the way. Emmanuel d'Astier, who created the Resistance movement Libération, recounted:

They were all on the roads and there was nothing in the sky. In the fields there was no activity or it seemed to be in a strange abeyance. The wheat was maturing. Only in the small villages, the towns, those fleeing gathered around hotels, cafés, or petrol pumps. They brought contagion with them, and people who had never considered departure were suddenly seized with a fever on seeing them.[37]

Such newcomers joined the throngs of people already on the roads. Peasants who initially wrote off the hordes of Parisians, believing they had over-reacted, rapidly revised their positions when they saw the carts led by peasants identical to themselves. The sight of them so shocked and affected them that they too felt drawn to join their flight. 'They watch all this, they are astonished by it, they make fun of it and then as a result of watching it continuously, they themselves become overwhelmed by the panic and take their places in the columns of queuing refugees.'[38]

10. Peasants with their carts attempt to distance themselves from the battle zone.

Those who thought that they had finally reached safety along the way soon found that the wave of panic caught up with them. Some days into his exodus, Léon Werth found a comfortable place to rest with a kindly peasant family. He and his wife enjoyed the luxury of a real bed with sheets, comforted in the belief that they had managed to distance themselves some way from the battle front.

> I woke up suddenly, someone was knocking at the door. I recognized Abel's voice. I got up and opened the door... Abel told us 'The mayor has had the order to evacuate the village of men between 16 and 45. The women can stay.' It is two hours after midnight. It is dark outside. We deliberate in a confused way. Wisdom suggests that it would perhaps be best to stay or to leave the women to look after the farm. But it seems impossible for the men to leave their women. We know nothing of the Germans except for the behaviour that that was attributed to them in Poland by the papers...
>
> We prepare to leave. Madame Deaveau puts the mattresses on the floor and takes sheets out of a cupboard. She has tears in her eyes... 'What should we take?' she asks my wife as if she holds the great secret of evacuation.

And so they departed once again.[39] Evacuation orders like these added more refugees to the throngs of people already on the roads. Sadoul and his colleagues found their efforts to persuade people to return to their homes could have little impact when the authorities had given them opposing advice.

> These people were not involved in a spontaneous evacuation. The evacuation order had indeed been given by the prefect of the Loiret department. This was madness and sabotage because these farmers ran no risk of danger in their own homes spread out across the rural areas of the Gâtinais [due south of Paris]. Whereas on the roads, mixed in with the military convoys...[40]

Mounting Fear and Panic

In order to confuse and disable the Allied armies, and to prevent the possibility of organizing defence south of the Maginot line, the Germans set about an extensive bombing campaign and gunned down the columns of refugees who were attempting to escape from the embattled areas. These attacks were extremely frightening. They appeared to come out of nowhere. Unlike the noise of the Stukas which could be heard immediately before and during the bombing raid, the machine-gun attacks came without warning. Once an attack was underway, refugees would take whatever action they could to try and protect themselves. 'People lie in the ditches, hide in the woods, and glue themselves to the trees in the courtyard. Children hang on to their mother's skirts. Women go round the trees and hide their faces in their arms, like a child who fends off a slap.'[41] One witness recalls, as a child, avoiding the guns on the road to Avallon, in Burgundy, 100 km (62 miles) west of Dijon. 'We dived into a ditch when we heard someone shout "They are machine-gunning us!" We felt like we were playing at Robin Hood or Cowboys and Indians. We were playing, yes, we were playing. We didn't realize how serious it was. No one was hurt. We got up and carried on.'[42]

In the event of attack, parents would throw themselves over their children in the hope of protecting them. Cars would stop and their incumbents would pour out and head for any form of shelter. The ever-present mattresses offered little protection against the raids, and the split-second it took to get out of the cars and dash for shelter meant that car drivers and passengers were more likely to be caught in the blast or struck down by a bullet. Those on foot had valuable extra moments which allowed them to get to shelter. André Morize described the aftermath of these attacks:

I saw and touched the lacerated cars. I saw blood on the cushions of the seats. I saw the car from the Ardennes and among the bundles and the cases, rolled up in blankets was the body of a little girl whose father was looking for a cemetery. I saw a 10-year-old boy whose shoulder was fractured by a bullet. I saw a woman who hardly knew how to drive at the wheel of an old Renault taking her three children away with her because her husband was killed on the road in the Pas-de-Calais.[43]

Those who travelled by rail were not spared these attacks. From mid-May railway stations became prime targets in German efforts to disable transport services. After each attack, destroyed wagons and carriages were abandoned and the convoy continued with whatever elements that could be saved. On occasion, the railways were so damaged that the passengers were obliged to continue on foot. Or, after a very slow period of advance, they were then able to re-embark. It was soon decided that trains should travel at night with all lights extinguished in an effort to avoid the bombings and escape enemy detection.[44] Similarly, many preferred to travel on the roads, at night, believing that it would be less crowded and that they would be less visible and therefore less likely to suffer attacks. Using headlights was discouraged so people were obliged to try and manage without or turn them on and off for short spells.[45]

In the absence of news of what was happening, Werth interpreted the condition of the soldiers he saw as one of the few ways of marking the progress of the war or lack thereof.

Some were lying down, asleep. The others, standing, contemplated the caravan splitting up in the village. I approach them. They had been in the Somme. I expect them to clarify the situation, give me some hope. But I find myself confronted with mysterious, resigned soldiers. I try to find their souls... They reveal no secrets. They are weary. I only get from them a few expressions like 'You must not worry'... [46]

The disorder and disarray of the French army was shocking to those who saw them. The absence of officers was particularly peculiar. As Browning asserts, 'what puzzled me was the number of French officers—in uniform—driving cars with civilian passengers. *The cars were moving south*. It seemed a curious way of defending la Patrie. Something was very wrong somewhere.'[47] The sight of the fleeing soldiers was for many the most convincing sign of the seriousness of the situation. As attacks became more frequent, refugees realized that the uniformed soldiers among them were attracting the attention of the German pilots and putting them in danger. Where their presence had initially been read as a reassuring sign, it had become apparent that these soldiers were not engaging in some organized withdrawal with a move to creating another front, but were themselves in much the same position as the civilians, fleeing in confusion with virtually no idea of where they were going, short of heading away from the Germans.

For their part, individual soldiers who found themselves among the civilians had often become separated from their regiments. Cut off from their superiors, without access to any orders or command from their hierarchy, they were forced to fall back on their own capacity to survive. Aware of the turmoil around them, news that the Germans had taken Paris could only add to their sense that everything had collapsed. Sadoul mused, 'Why carry on now that Paris has been taken?'[48] Many considered themselves relieved of their duties and sought refuge in civilian life. These men had little regard for the demoralizing impact their presence created both among those civilians they met en route and among their loved ones if they reached their homes.[49]

The slow pace of movement of the queue of cars and the endless stopping and starting (cars had to be cranked up) meant that many broke down. Desperate car owners offered money to military convoys and peasants in exchange for a tow. 'As the cohorts fled further south, cars became increasingly rare. Drivers carried on using bikes they had loaded onto their cars, or

11. The true impact of the defeat can be read in the eyes of these despondent soldiers in their dishevelled uniforms on the roadside. They look on helplessly as civilian refugees pass by.

did a deal with peasants to have horses which then pulled them along. The progress of civilization moves backwards.'[50] If all else failed, they attempted to keep up for a while, pushing their cars, but once all possibilities had been exhausted most were forced to abandoned their vehicles, rescue whatever possessions they could carry, and join the ranks of those who were fleeing on foot. Cars which had run out of petrol were unceremoniously pushed off the road by other furious refugees. In this way, affluent members of the population who may have set off by car, found themselves on the road with other hungry refugees. Those on foot all ended up taking on the same appearance and they all looked equally miserable in their flight. Sartre represented this in his fictional account of the exodus.

> The crowd terrified her. The people in it walked slowly, painfully and misery imparted to all a family likeness. Anyone who joined them would soon look just the same. I don't want to become like that. They did not look at her, but avoided the car without turning their eyes in her direction. They seemed no longer to have any eyes.[51]

To this extent the experience of exodus and being a refugee proved a social leveller. Money was of no influence in a situation where resources could not be found at any cost. Where at first the obviously rich had been distinct from the obviously poor, all social classes eventually found themselves confused into the same crowd. Certain commentators have pointed to this to suggest that there was a certain equality of experience on the roads and railways of France. In the introduction to Georges Adrey's account, Jean Dupaquier suggested that 'Their common suffering brought them together in misfortune, the barriers which separated them fell away, class disappeared for while and then, suddenly, this human solidarity faded away, egotism and individualism soon reappeared.'[52] While there is evidence of solidarity and good relations, especially in the early days of the exodus, such behaviour was also accompanied by lawlessness of all kinds. Pillaging was widespread as was petty thievery.

Collapse of Social Structures

By this point, physical conditions had become increasingly acute. Most Parisians had made little, if any, provision for food supplies. After a day or two, what people had brought with them had run out and supplies in the shops had become virtually non-existent. Parisians often left without so much as water and immediate provisions for the journey, believing that they would find everything that they needed on the way. They quickly panicked when they realized that this was not so. Only the peasants had thought to load their carts with adequate stocks as Sadoul noticed.

> I admire the phlegm of the peasants of Picnigny who managed to be more rested, more at ease after four weeks of travelling than a family who left the parc Monceau in Paris in their large car covered in a mattress forty-eight hours ago. The Parisians left without bread, without petrol, counting on buying everything on the way, as if going to the Côte d'Azur on holiday. When those who are normally accustomed to aquiring their potatoes not from the fields, but from bags filled at Les Halles market arrived in the country where the shops were empty, they became scared and frightened as soon as a plane flew over or a motor stopped working properly. These nervous outbursts of the Parisians contrast with the placidity of the peasants in the face of defeat and misfortune.[53]

Official arrangements tended to be patchy and inadequate and consequently refugees had a variety of experiences in relation to attaining food.

Canteens which managed to keep stocked in the early days of the exodus soon found themselves swamped and unable to cater for the volume of demand. Reception centres at train stations struggled to maintain a semblance of a service for arriving refugees. In the absence of proper information about arrivals, it was often impossible to anticipate their needs. Much depended on the organization of the various departmental administrations. When it came to food, therefore, luck was a huge factor. On the outskirts of some towns, local authorities established road blocks where food and drink were provided. In certain areas peasants took food to people on stranded trains. Some shopkeepers left the doors to their shops open when they departed, encouraging people to help themselves to what they needed. The military was certainly not equipped to offer help on the scale that the situation required. Those who lived in the countryside took a dim view of people tramping across their fields searching for food and water.[54] In some infamous cases farmers would demand money in exchange for a jug of water at a time when running water was still a rarity. This has been an enduring aspect of the collective memory of the exodus. Those who had restaurants or other outlets also took advantage of refugees by charging ridiculous prices. In this regard, where food was available, it was only at a price. In these cases, social difference once again came into play and wealth was an advantage. Most refugees struggled to find enough food and sustenance along the way.

While certain communities were organized to help passing refugees, others had nothing they could offer.

> The people from the areas of Limoges or Poitiers saw those from Lorraine pass through in September and the Belgians in May; they no longer have any pity for the first floods of Parisians. They shut out the arrivals with closed faces. These starving populations who always ask for the same thing, always wanting what they do not have—bread, petrol—this ends up exasperating them. They answer without even opening their mouths, making discouraging signs instead... The same scene repeats itself twenty times. A convoy of refugees appears, with cars being towed... In a voice exasperated by tiredness, the leader of the column asks for beds. At the war memorial where the local council is congregated, the mayor replies that there are none. They soon get into a quarrel. The refugees wish upon the villagers famine, bombing, and all the calamities they now feel they endure... Eventually the column moves on, with a noise of motors, while the villagers stay in place with their eyes on the north awaiting the arrival of those who will cause the next skirmish.[55]

Towns unable to cater for refugees had no hesitation in moving them on. In Poitiers they were directed along a promontory which prevented them from gaining access to the centre. People started to go hungry and feared that they might even be at risk of starvation.

As it became clear that the normal channels had broken down, inevitably, in the absence of any law and order, hungry refugees soon started to help themselves to whatever they wanted or needed. Pillaging was the common reaction to the absence of proper organization as Georges Adrey explained:

> Above all the problem of food supplies started to become an issue if we did not come across the odd shop abandoned by its owners. Without such providential windfalls we really faced the prospect of dying of starvation, the communes we crossed were evacuated, the shops shut, and the authorities absent.[56]

Rare were those refugees who did not witness pillaging to some degree during their exodus. French soldiers who helped themselves to what they fancied during their withdrawal often set a precedent in this regard. For soldiers to take food when their own supplies became exhausted was probably a normal reaction on the part of the enemy in a time of war, but it was resented by local communities when carried out by their own armies. Sadoul was horrified at the extent of the systematic pillaging he witnessed. 'At every moment people carrying empty bags go into houses, people carrying full bags come out... Not a single officer, not a soul tries to stop this shameful behaviour.'[57] He did not know how to respond to the vociferous complaints of those concerned, reflecting, 'How can we expect people who have just lost everything to respect the belongings of others?'[58] If pillaging by the army was a normal consequence of war, so was that of hungry refugees who felt free to wander into other people's homes. Abandoned properties provided shelter and their gardens sometimes contained fruit and vegetables which passing civilians happily consumed. Some sought to make this behaviour appear more acceptable by claiming that at least their gain would mean less provisions for the Germans. Others took advantage of the extraordinary circumstances to pillage in a more systematic way. Nicole Ollier recounted how certain individuals approached a village and started to rush around it crying, 'The Germans are coming.' They then hid nearby until the inhabitants left. After a period in hiding they wandered into the now empty village and calmly took whatever they wanted.[59]

Stories of widespread petty thievery were also common. Jean Moulin cited the case of a woman who arrived in Chartres having been stripped of all her belongings by travel companions made on the road: 'One woman came from Paris on foot with a lady who had shared her tribulations and whom she came to trust. This lady had just left her, brusquely stealing her 6,000 francs, all her fortune. I give her something. She cries and asks me if she can kiss me.'[60] Georgette Guillot met friends along her journey who also experienced misfortune. They left Paris with their aged aunt who died on the way. Finding nowhere to leave the body, they put it on top of the car out of sight of the children who were rather frightened of it. They finally decided to stop for a rest in a barn. The following morning, the car had disappeared, aunt and all. Their regret at leaving Paris, now declared an open city, was intense but the most frustrating aspect of their journey was the fact that without the body they could not get a death certificate. The absence of this documentation would prevent them from claiming their inheritance.[61]

Pillaging and thievery were the result of the general collapse of familiar social structures. It seems likely that there was a corresponding relaxation in moral norms which sometimes even led to a transgression of what was considered to be appropriate behaviour between men and women. Certain accounts suggest that women who attached themselves to groups of French soldiers in retreat found that they were expected to offer sexual favours in exchange for this protection. If they demonstrated any reluctance to do so, these soldiers did not hesitate to take it by force.[62] Gilles Perrault, the author, who experienced the exodus as a young boy, claims that while sleeping in the open he was kept awake by the noise of the repeated screams of women being raped.[63] While evidence of this kind remains rare and anecdotal, and it is difficult to establish the extent or likelihood of such behaviour, it must certainly have been the case that women travelling alone or with young children—as many were—were especially vulnerable at this time.

The widespread sense of the collapse of social structures was reinforced by the lack of reliable information about what was going on. Hunger, combined with general exhaustion after several days of sleeping rough and coping with intense anxiety brought about by the unpredictable nature of events, left many refugees extremely susceptible to the influence of rumour. In this atmosphere of growing desperation and panic, they had no way of identifying where they were, no idea of their destination, and had lost all their normal and familiar points of reference. Figures of authority were absent. Instead of government officials, teachers, clergy, police, firefighters, and so on—all their normal official interlocutors—they had to depend on often casual acquaintances met on the journey. To offset this feeling of abandonment and disorientation, people were often all too willing to ignore their normal judgement and adopt the opinions of others who appeared in the know.

After all, the sheer force of numbers of people in the crowd seemed to lend a certain logic to the action of going along with them. In the midst of these throngs of people, refugees often lost a sense of their own identity and found themselves acting and behaving like those around them, picking up and repeating to others the ideas and rumours that were circulating.

Rumours assume a particular importance in times of crisis and trauma. Reliable information about what was happening was absent. To appear to have knowledge, even if it was invented or came from unreliable sources, gave refugees respect at a time when people were desperate for some sense of order and organization, even authority, in the chaos. 'The first person to know a rumour felt filled with self-importance,' Anti-Nazi writer Lion Feuchtwanger wrote while in an internment camp near Aix-en-Provence, and there was no shortage of rumours on the journeys of the exodus which covered every aspect of people's lived experience.[64] People discussed the whereabouts of the Germans, the government, even aspects of everyday survival, where to find food, shelter, and particularly petrol. 'But the news about petrol is now the same as that concerning the war. These are myths which circulate and come from heaven knows where.'[65] Rumours spread about the nature of the invading armies and the course of the war: 'Hitler's soldiers are in shirtsleeves! They are fighting bare chested! They are all wearing a scapular decorated with a picture of their Führer! No planes are covering the strategic withdrawal of our armies! The English are re-embarking! The Belgiums have abandoned us!'[66]

Rumours also concerned the incompetence of the French leaders and this chimed well with the personal experiences of the refugees who felt horribly let down by them.[67] The road became a 'floating forum of open debate' which in some cases exposed people to interpretations of their situation that they had no way of challenging but also which implanted ideas and lent credence to hypotheses that they might not have considered or taken on board before in a very serious way.[68] The crowds drew on this information in an effort to make sense of their situation. Their incomplete understanding was fraught with contradiction and ambiguity. Bitterness prevailed as refugees realized that they were completely at sea and had been left to their own resources and many expressed resentment at what they saw as the desertion of the government and officialdom. Léon Werth was struck by the number of people he came across who needed to find someone to blame. 'They shouted and cried expressions along the lines of "We have been sold out! We have been betrayed!" This popular accusation, that I have heard several times since on the road, seemed to suffice in itself. I was never able to get a reply to the question "By whom?" '[69] Those passing by in their expensive cars were assumed to be Jews. 'The Jews sold us out!' people cried.[70] As refugees struggled, their anti-Semitism grew. Such feelings laid the way for people to be sympathetic to Vichy's later anti-Jewish statutes. The notion of fifth columnists was also widespread and those on the move surrounded by strangers of all kinds felt especially vulnerable. It seemed logical to many of them that spies may have been planted amidst them. The atmosphere of suspicion was particularly menacing for young men and led to many mistakes about the identity of those who were not immediately recognized as 'ordinary' French soldiers.[71] From the point of view, therefore, of trying to make sense of what was going on, it was much easier to blame things on the enemy than attempt to face the extent to which the French themselves had helped create such a mess. As Rupert Downing observed, 'In some ways it was far easier to believe in German cunning than in French treachery.'[72]

The Fifth Column

The psychological impact of the fifth column is apparent from its frequent mention in nearly all accounts. Belief in its existence was clearly present in the minds of many French people. Both Weygand and Reynaud made declarations which pointed to fifth column responsibility for events. Weygand for example, when accounting for the defeat of Corap's Ninth Army, warned that, 'Above all, the action of the fifth column must not be underestimated.'[73] Similarly Reynaud, in his speech to the Senate on 25 May when he admonished those military commanders he posited as responsible for the defeat, added, in speaking of the general situation, an accusation that the fifth column had also played an important part.[74]

Propaganda during the phoney war had so effectively prepared people for the idea of a weakened army eaten into from within that, at the time of the defeat, the responsibility of the fifth column for the collapse seemed self-evident. So successfully had the idea penetrated the collective unconscious that André Morize who had previously worked at the Ministry of Information and escaped to the US after being caught in the exodus, wrote in an American newspaper just six months afterwards that the fifth column had been 'not a legend but a deadly reality'.[75] Edward Spears, writing in 1955, was also convinced that 'the Germans had evolved a brilliantly organised system of deception, whose instruments were believed to be specially-trained and highly-trained Swiss and Belgians who could pass as Frenchmen'.[76] The notion was widespread that the Germans sent agents into France beyond the battle lines whose role it was to spread rumours of their imminent arrival and work local populations up into a panic so that they would leave their homes.

The departure of populations and the congestion of the traffic was studied by German High Command in the minutest of detail in order to stop or make more difficult the movements of the French army. The Germans commenced the bombing of the frontier towns of the Nord department. Some individuals had been given instructions by telephone in the name of French High Command to order the evacuation of the civilian population; the towns and villages soon emptied.[77]

In the atmosphere of fear and panic of May and June 1940 when many officials were looking for an excuse to leave, mayors and others in elected offices seized the opportunity to communicate orders for the evacuation of towns and villages on the basis of telephone calls (the authenticity of which were not always verified at the time or later). Many certainly came to believe that these orders could well have emanated from German sources. Vidalenc reports that in several communes people unknown to the locals announced the arrival of the Germans and this had the immediate effect of emptying the entire area of its inhabitants.[78] Morize attributed 'collective panic and departed villages' to 'the brutal work of false orders or telephone orders from the Fifth column'.[79] Spears was to conclude that

> The German organisation was so thorough, the experts engaged so superlatively good, the plans on which they worked so meticulously thought out that the confusion they engendered led to stupefied bewilderment over wide areas. From prefects to village mayors, no one knew whether to believe or disbelieve, obey or disregard an order.[80]

Radio Stuttgart fed these fifth column fears in an extremely effective manner by emphasizing the success of the invasion and urging people to leave their homes. The notion of the fifth column cultivated by German propaganda evidently contributed to weakening the morale of the French people.

It is impossible to fully evaluate the extent to which the German armies infiltrated France, hidden amidst the fleeing refugees. In a sense this is to miss the point. What is important is not the enemy agents who may or may not have actually existed but the widespread belief in their ubiquitous presence. How much of the belief in a fifth column was a reaction to sleep deprivation brought on by fear of bombing or a phenomenon symptomatic of a widespread mass panic born of the sense of loss of control of the situation, it is impossible to gauge. It seems highly probable, however, that the actual role of the fifth column belongs more to the realm of myth and the power of rumour and other associated irrational fears than the actual activities of enemy agents on the ground.

The Exodus as a First Form of Resistance

The high numbers of people who left their homes when they could in reality have stayed put, did so because they were determined to avoid German occupation. In so doing, the historian Jean Vidalenc argues, they were not just attempting to escape the rumoured terrors occupation might bring, but they were also demonstrating their faith in the French army's capacity to stop the enemy, ensuring that extensive manpower was prevented from falling into the hands of the Germans. He therefore interprets their flight as an early referendum against collaboration and any form of coexistence with the enemy and, as such, suggests that it was an early form of resistance.[81]

It is difficult to apply this kind of interpretation to the majority of the women, children, and elderly people who took flight from Paris in May–June 1940. It does, however, have more resonance when considering the motives of the men who left their homes. Evacuation arrangements for those designated to work in industries linked to the war effort were certainly mishandled in terms of timing, as we have seen. Orders, if they existed, came so late that many workers were forced to join the surge of people leaving the capital at the eleventh hour. Most believed that departure was nonetheless their best course of action to avoid finding themselves constrained to work for the Reich.

> We were escaping famine, but also occupation... Until 17 June 1940, and even still at that point, there were men who continued to deny the evidence, to believe that even if they crossed the Loire, we would establish a front on the Dordogne or Charente rivers. Until the seventeenth, official communiqués led everyone to believe that a military recovery would still be possible. Escaping the enemy became a duty... this black syrup of the exodus was also its 'human supplies', factory workers and future soldiers.[82]

This colossal population displacement would also have a considerable influence on the later emergence of resistance activity, much of which originated in the south. Many individuals who fled Hitler's armies did so with a determination to safeguard their freedom. Flight for them was the only credible alternative to submission to the Nazis. Marie-Madeleine Fourcade wrote of leaving Paris: 'We left on 11 June in the middle of the exodus without knowing how we would do it, but with the firm conviction that we should not abdicate in the face of this power, with the incredible presumption that we had to represent something in this midst of this defeat.'[83] This departure distanced them from their normal activities and habits. When he reached the south, Roland Dorgèles stopped first in Marseilles, 'the capital of the exodus', then carried on to nearby Cassis, before moving once again to Saliès-du-Salat, near Toulouse: 'for four years I wandered from town to town, camping here, renting elsewhere, moving further away, always seeking a safer place to take shelter'.[84] This imposed leisure or 'forced holidays' as Dorgèles put it, brought him into contact with others in the same position. Individuals like Marie-Madeleine Fourcade and Roland Dorgèles, as well as many others including André Chamson, Henri Frenay, and Emmanuel d'Astier, all experienced a similar odyssey. Their shared experience of escape and exile brought them together and fostered a common desire to react. Thus, if Vidalenc's analysis does not appear to coincide with the reality of the experience of the majority of those who left their homes during the exodus, escape was, for many, a precondition for later resistance.

The sense that they were exiles was also common to many of those involved in later resistance.[85] For those caught up in the exodus, consciousness that they had become refugees was at first difficult to grasp. Rupert Downing expressed this sentiment thus when, soon after his departure from Paris, 'the realization came to me with a bit of a shock that I had now joined the ranks of those who had fled from Poland, Belgium, Holland, and now France. We were refugees.'[86] Unlike Downing the Englishman, however, the vast mass of French people who had abandoned their homes had become refugees *in their own country*. The enormity of this cannot be over-emphasized. Their capacity to survive at a time when all their normal points of reference, all the normal structures of their daily lives evaporated, served as a key learning experience which would influence their later reactions to events. Whatever their class or social background, as refugees marched down the roads of the exodus, fought for standing room in the trains that were taking them to hoped-for safety, or struggled with overloaded cars along crowded streets, they were nursing a growing bitterness which taught them not to trust what they were told and to dismiss the authorities who had massively let them down. Their sense that everything had collapsed around them was reinforced by their experiences on these journeys. The majority coped as best they could in the absence of any controlled or organized help. They realized that their survival depended on their capacity to focus on their own concerns. There was little room to show compassion or interest for others as the business of their own survival and that of a close family or friend or companion was a full-time occupation and left no energy to think about the repeated and anguishing dramas that were engulfing those around them. The very fact of their own survival was what was important. They had survived German attack at close hand and had discovered that they could fend for themselves. This pattern of behaviour was one that many would adopt later. There was little place for altruism on the road and this was a lesson many later applied during the Occupation. It was this which would prove to be the lasting importance of the exodus for the majority of those who survived it.

To return to the sad populations who were struggling along the roads of France. 'Where are we going?' Georges Adrey complained. 'When will our exodus come to an end?'[87]

If only we had a target, if only we knew where we were going, that would give us courage and would release the energy we need to carry on. But nothing is more discouraging than walking into uncertainty, nothing is worse than walking straight ahead, on the off-chance, without being able to stop somewhere and say 'On such and such a day, at such and such a time, our ordeal will come to an end.'[88]

There was nothing but chaos and confusion.

In this mass of people, nobody could find anybody else. Nobody knew where they were going. People just moved on, that was it. Towards the south, far from the 'others'. They fled. They fled from real or expected horrors. People who took to the roads crossed others who were going in totally the opposite direction.[89]

As they moved to the south and west they brought with them a message of collapse which carried the reality of the defeat to the communities they reached. Saturated towns could offer them no shelter as all arrangements that had been put into place for them had been exhausted and refugees were forced to move ever further on. Their minds full of fears of possible attack, they looked around with suspicion lest there be an enemy in their midst. The prospect of supplies of food and drink running out was terrifying.

Refugees understood that they would probably have been better off and certainly safer if they had stayed in their own homes and this added to their feelings of bitterness and betrayal. Léon Werth recounted: 'I am the prisoner of a road I have not chosen. I have become a refugee. And I have no refuge. I am tired. Why carry on?... Have we done the right thing by going? Would we have been safer if we had stayed at home?'[90]

Reaching the Loire did not provide the hoped-for safety nor did it bring their journeys to an end. The Germans, not unaware that the Loire was believed to be the site of a possible battle line, targeted these areas heavily, rendering the situation acutely dangerous for those seeking shelter there. French High Command decided that it would try and hold up the enemy by blowing up the bridges to allow the retreating army time to keep ahead of the invaders.[91] Many found themselves caught in this battle zone. The Loire valley between Orléans and Nevers underwent fierce bombing raids in which many civilians found themselves the unfortunate participants. Gien, Jargeau, Tours, Blois, La Charité, Sully, and Roanne were especially heavily targeted by the Germans as they offered key crossing points for retreating

12. Refugees were anxious to cross the river Loire by whatever means they could to reach safety and distance themselves from the Germans. These lucky few have managed to get across the river on a ferry. A queue of waiting cars can be seen on the opposite bank.

soldiers and their armaments as well as for civilians in a last desperate bid for escape. Nicole Ollier described the scene:

> In fact, there were not thousands, but hundreds of thousands, of refugees who stagnated on the right-hand bank, while a few dozen others who could not swim in desperation took the risk of crossing on flat barges. But the overloaded boats sank. Only a few rare swimmers made it over to the left bank.[92]

For those who did make it across the river, their hopes of escape soon evaporated. Demoralization and dejectedness set in very quickly. The news that the Germans had had no particular difficulty crossing the Loire further aggravated their feelings of anguish. On the one hand, it seemed that if the Germans had not been prevented from getting across the Loire, they would also invade the Midi so there was no sense in carrying on their journey. But on the other, as they had been lucky enough to get across the Loire, unlike many who must already have found themselves under occupation, it seemed to make sense to carry on southwards while some hope of escape still remained. Many had reached the end of their tether. Disappointment made their journeys harder to bear. Soldiers had even started to hope for capture as a way of bringing their seemingly hopeless journeys to a close.[93] Military and civilians alike were losing faith and called for the battle to end:

> I hear only one thing repeated all around me. All my friends say:
> 'Why carry on, why massacre poor sad souls when all is lost? What are they waiting for to make peace? . . . '
> 'Peace, peace, peace, what are they waiting for?' is all I hear around me. They also say:
> 'We can't continue to let women, children, and civilians generally be massacred on the roads like this, we have to end it immediately'.[94]

PART II

Reactions to Defeat

3

Death of the Third Republic

It is not the first time in our history that the military have lost a war because of their incompetence and lack of imagination. But it is doubtless the first time that in sanctioning a disaster they took power. The Republic often feared a dictatorship of victorious generals. It did not think to be wary of them in defeat.

Jean Zay, a radical-socialist deputy in 1940

Initially, as the French government took to the road, the immediate turn of events, though dramatic and serious, seemed to fit with previous history and many of its members were comforted by the thought that their departure from the capital was not unprecedented. However, in the absence of any defence, Hitler's Wehrmacht remained unopposed and was able to forge its way ever southward. After a couple of days, Touraine no longer seemed a safe enough distance from the threat of direct German attack, so the administration moved on, making its way to the city of Bordeaux which, like Tours, had historically acted as its wartime host. Here, amidst chaos and confusion, the ministers were forced to choose which path to pursue. The alternatives centred around whether to carry on the fighting or not, decisions which were to have an important bearing on France's future role in the war. Faced with these stark choices, disagreements in the cabinet led the government to tear itself apart in a process which was eventually to undermine and destroy the Third Republic in votes taken on 10 July 1940.

Touraine

During the night of 10–11 June, most members of the government managed to reach the area around Tours and in so doing, often gained first-hand experience of the conditions of the exodus. As Minister of the Interior, Georges Mandel had decided on the evacuation of all ministerial and administrative staff as well as those with political responsibilities. Georgette Guillot's departure with her fellow employees from the Ministry was described earlier. Her party took several hours to reach Tours where they finally arrived the following afternoon after a difficult journey:

> the town was crowded with cars, refugees were arriving in their thousands, they were camping in the avenues, in the gardens. There were cyclists, pedestrians, Belgians, people from northern France, and many Parisians ... A terrible spectacle of anxious faces, nervously apprehensive about what future calamities they may face.

They moved on to their allocated chateau which seemed totally ill-equipped and unprepared to receive them.

> Since September 1939 various evacuation plans had been drawn up, a woman was even sent there to organize it all. According to the reports she returned to us, everything was in place for us to arrive night or day. But we soon realized that in fact nothing had been arranged ... directives had indeed been passed on to the mayor or his deputy and arrangements were put into place in September, but in June the war was already meant to be won and over with.[1]

This was a common experience and the arrangements facing most members of the government and their staff once they arrived in Touraine were confused and improvised. The prefecture of the department of Indre-et-Loire had been told to prepare for evacuation and find chateaux to lodge everyone and this was largely achieved; however, the practical arrangements as to how the government would function had been completely overlooked, as Paul Baudouin, Under-Secretary of State in the War Cabinet, described:

> We are quartered in the Château de Chamilly in the little village of La Roche, and the offices of the Ministry of Foreign Affairs are packed into the Château de la Chataignerie, near Langeais. A single telephone connects us with the post office at Langeais. All the ministries are scattered throughout the vast extent of Touraine. Direct telephonic communication has been promised, but in the interval messengers have to be used, and that wastes a great deal of time as the roads are blocked with traffic. This rural disorganisation is paralysing the Government at the very moment when circumstances call for rapid decisions.[2]

The British ambassador, Sir Ronald Campbell, was apparently alone among all those in the entourage of the French government in having thought to bring along a field radio. Reports in telegrams to the Foreign Office in

London related how on arrival in Touraine the British diplomats had found all the ministries of the French government variously spread across the local countryside, sometimes miles apart, with little or no means of communicating with one another. Viscount Halifax wrote:

the only way to get in touch with anyone was to get into a motorcar and go to what was supposed to be a headquarters but frequently was not, over roads thronged with refugee traffic of every description . . . our activities during the whole of this period were considerably hampered by the conditions in which we were living and working. The government had persistently refused to face up to the possibility of having to remove from the capital, with the result that, when it had to do so at short notice or risk falling into the enemy's hands, it was obliged in the absence of other arrangements to fall back on the scheme prepared before the outbreak of the war to meet the event which then seemed probable, of Paris being subject to constant aerial bombardment. The essence of this plan was to spread executive and administrative services over a wide area in Touraine rather than to concentrate them in one spot such as the town of Tours itself, where they would have offered a single and tempting target. During the three days of our stay in Touraine, it was thus extremely difficult to maintain close contact with Ministers or their departments.[3]

It was in this context that the French government was forced to try and take stock of the situation and decide what was the best course of action and by this time a series of different alternatives had opened up.

One of the options under discussion was to carry on the combat even if this meant that the government would have to retreat to Brittany and thence go abroad. The attraction of withdrawal to Brittany was that the remaining French armies could be mobilized to hold off the Germans, thereby winning time for the government who would have the option to escape by sea when it became necessary. This alternative, known as the 'Breton redoubt', had the advantage that it left an opening for a move to London from whence continued resistance to the Germans could be coordinated. This was an option strongly favoured by the British who would attempt to force it upon the French with a later offer of Franco-British union. Others saw Brittany as a step on the way to French colonial territories in North Africa which could provide the military with a base and allow continued battle with the Germans and still maintain some degree of independence from the British. A final option was that of admitting defeat and ceding to the Germans. This would mean either military capitulation or negotiating armistice terms with the enemy.

Exploring the Alternatives

In early June both General Weygand and Marshal Pétain had already started to indicate that, in their view, opening negotiations with the enemy was soon likely to be necessary. On 9 June, when the news first came through that the Aisne front had collapsed, Pétain had read a memorandum to Paul Reynaud and the cabinet insisting on the necessity of asking for an armistice.[4] His unshakeable belief that such a request should be made without delay was painfully apparent in his contributions to the discussions of the Supreme War Council on 11 June. Churchill had flown into Touraine to meet with Reynaud, Weygand, and other members of the French government at Briare, on the Loire, 80 miles (129 km) from Paris, the site of the new Army Headquarters which had retreated there from Vincennes in the suburbs of Paris. At this meeting, to the horror of the English, Weygand soon made it clear that he held out no hope whatsoever of halting the German advance on Paris. 'I am helpless, I cannot intervene as I have no reserves,' Edward Spears, Churchill's envoy recorded him as saying.[5] Once he overcame his shock at this news, Churchill attempted to encourage the French to continue the battle, drawing on their common experiences of the First World War and urging them that the tide could still turn as it had in the Marne in 1914 and again in March 1918. The French should still fight on, even in Paris itself, he pressed. To which Pétain retorted, 'To make Paris a city of ruins will not affect the issue.'[6] Again Churchill tried to galvanize the government, encouraging those present to act to deter the Germans and slow their invasion by conducting a guerrilla war. It seemed extraordinary to onlookers that the Germans were able to progress across the country, facing so little resistance from either the military or civilians.[7] Finally, Churchill pressed for the idea of withdrawing all the available remaining forces to the north-west of the country, thereby creating a bridgehead for the implementation of the Breton redoubt plan.

Reynaud was sympathetic to this idea as he was determined to hold back the Germans for as long as possible by whatever feasible means. Despite pressure from Weygand and Pétain, he steadfastly refused to contemplate making overtures to Hitler, convinced that no honourable terms could be expected from him, and insisted that the armies should fight on. If France was now crushed, the struggle had to be carried on from elsewhere; if necessary the government should leave the country.[8] The Breton redoubt had first been mooted as a possible strategy in late May, and despite

Weygand's ferocious opposition to it and his repeated warnings that he did not have enough men to make such a plan viable, Reynaud kept returning to this project as a potential way forward. Withdrawing to Brittany had the strategic advantage of allowing the government to keep its options open by assuring access to the coast in the event that the decision was taken to leave the country. The North African colonies were the preferred destination, as relocating there would allow the government to remain symbolically within the French empire, thence strictly speaking still in France. Fired by Churchill's enthusiasm, Reynaud was now spurred to instruct General de Gaulle, a strong advocate of the plan, to actively start to implement the necessary arrangements. By the close of the Briare meeting of the Supreme War Council, it seemed that this option was one that the government might seriously pursue.

Soon after Churchill's departure from Briare, however, Weygand again began to forcefully express his view that French territory could no longer be defended and that armistice should be requested as soon as possible.

He was convinced that before all else it was necessary to avoid the total disintegration of the French army, a stampede, and the scenes of disorder in which soldiers and refugees would be mixed up; he said it was his duty to ask the Government to address an immediate request to the German Government for an armistice. All the Army Commanders agreed with him that this request should be made without further delay.[9]

Pétain, too, declared that the government should ask for armistice urgently in order to save what was left of France, and to allow the reconstruction of the country. Any delay would be criminal: 'Let us think of those who were fighting, and of the millions of civilian refugees who were on the roads.'[10] Both men now also linked this need for armistice with the idea that the government should remain on French territory come what may. Scaremongering about the potential danger to public disorder, Weygand repeatedly articulated his fears that the current absence of law and order might leave an opening for a communist coup.

Weygand wanted to take France out of the war, but only once he was satisfied that the army had been seen to have fought with honour. By waiting for the outcome of the Somme and Aisne front (the so-called Weygand front) before publicly coming out in favour of an armistice, he believed that he had offset the possible criticism that the army had not made every effort to defend the country against the Germans. He, like Pétain, was now anxious to bring the fighting to a rapid conclusion in order to preserve some vestige of the army through which he planned a rebirth of the country. These wider ambitions were behind his preference for an armistice and his refusal to contemplate military capitulation. An armistice would allow the military to emerge from the disaster relatively blameless and unscathed, as it would only implicate politicians. So determined was Weygand to pursue this strategy that he would actually refuse to follow Reynaud's orders to arrange for a capitulation, declaring that 'It was for the government who had declared war to face up to its obligations.'[11]

Furthermore, those government ministers like Ybarnegaray and Bouthillier who were swayed by Pétain and Weygand in favour of the armistice also had a very ambivalent, even hostile, view of the British. They blamed the British for committing France to a war for which neither country was adequately prepared, and then for failing to invest equal military effort during hostilities. Pétain retorted to Reynaud when told that they needed to respect the needs of their allies: 'The interests of France should pass before those of England: they put us in this situation, let's now try and get ourselves out of it.'[12] They projected Dunkirk as evidence of egotistical behaviour on the part of the British. Weygand, for example, blamed the British for the failure of his front which he claimed would have had more chance of success, 'if the English had not been continually looking over their shoulders at the sea'.[13] Despite Churchill's efforts to ensure that a significant number of French soldiers were evacuated, more members of the British Expeditionary Forces had certainly been saved there: 123,095 French soldiers were evacuated, 102,570 in British ships, compared to 338,226 British soldiers.[14] Churchill also persistently refused to accede to French requests for more air support and would not transfer RAF fighters to France. At Briare, Churchill adamantly held this position, explaining that air fighters were the 'only weapon with which they could hope—and he was confident that they would succeed—to break the might of Germany, when the time came'.[15] The efforts of Britain to safeguard resources for reasons of her own defence in the event of a French defeat leaving her alone to face the Germans single-handed were not viewed sympathetically by the French. On the contrary, this behaviour was interpreted as betrayal and refusal to help an ally when they most needed it. The attitude was posited as grounds for France to break the agreement made in March 1940 which forbade each of the signatories to make any separate peace or to engage in armistice negotiations without the agreement of the other. The possibility of breaching the terms of this agreement were raised during Churchill's visit to Tours on 13 June for what was to be the last meeting of the Supreme War Council.

Soon after the meeting began, it became clear to the British that those in favour of an armistice had gained ground. Reynaud immediately began to press Churchill to explain the British position, 'should the worst come'.[16] He claimed that it was now too late to pursue the option of the redoubt in Brittany and the government could not escape captivity if it remained on French soil. It now looked as if France was going to be obliged to negotiate a separate peace. This apparent change of position stunned the British and Churchill urged that France should turn to Roosevelt for help rather than contemplate such a step. But despite his firm refusal to release France from the March commitment, his efforts to communicate in French left the way open for Baudouin later deliberately to misrepresent his position to suggest that the British were in fact sympathetic to the French desire to ask for armistice.[17] Although Weygand was not present at the meeting, it was clear that he had brought considerable influence to bear on the morale of the French government and Spears was later to explain that 'It must be realised how very difficult was the task of civilians assailed by doubts as to their confidence in the face of strong violent opinion of the soldiers in favour of peace.'[18]

The meeting finished inconclusively and the British left despondent, unaware that the French cabinet were expecting to meet Churchill immediately afterwards.[19] Reynaud had evidently promised this, but his failure to carry it through only compounded the situation and was interpreted by many government members as a sign of Britain's lack of interest in France's plight. Spears expressed deep regret at this missed opportunity in that it 'undoubtedly played its part in swaying the majority of the Cabinet towards surrender'.[20]

Later the same day, at the subsequent cabinet meeting, Reynaud admitted that the only decision arrived at during Churchill's visit was to send an urgent message to Roosevelt pressing for active intervention of the United States. Reynaud broadcast this appeal to the US for the benefit of the population. 'He asked America to give France, even from afar, the hope of victory, necessary for every fighting man.'[21] Only after this reply was known would the government decide whether or not to pursue a request for an armistice. This provoked Pétain to read a further note which placed a fundamental choice before the government. He claimed that the military situation was so serious that if the government failed to ask for an armistice immediately there might be panic such that they would not then be able to undertake any manoeuvres at all. He did not believe in the Breton redoubt and the idea of carrying the battle from there and thought that such a departure would 'kill the army and thence make France's rebirth impossible'. For Pétain, the issue was not whether or not the government should ask for armistice, but whether or not it stayed on French soil. 'But I personally refuse to leave French soil: I will stay among the French people to share its pains and its miseries.'[22]

The choice facing the government was a dramatic one either way: to abandon the struggle and break the alliance with the British in order to deal with the Germans, or to transfer the government, the navy, the air force, and as much of the army as could be saved to be regrouped in the south-west to Brittany or to North Africa.[23] The main difficulty facing the supporters of those who wished to carry on the fight against the Germans was to persuade members of the government that departure would not be tantamount to abandoning the French population to an invading army, as Pétain was repeatedly at pains to point out. Moving to North Africa also seemed difficult to accept at a time when most associated the colonies with a place for the relocation of people 'who had committed some kind of indiscretion' when they were young.[24] Reynaud remained persuaded that the country should carry on fighting despite evidence that the armistice option was gaining support around him and that many of his entourage appeared to moving towards Pétain's position. He believed that if the American President could be persuaded to provide military aid, his position would be strengthened and such a step would firm the resolve of the government to stay in the war. But reports of the continuing approach of the Germans, and the fact that tanks had broken through at Evreux and were heading south, potentially reaching Tours during the day, led the government to interrupt discussions. In the light of this news, the idea of the Breton redoubt was abandoned and it was agreed that the government should withdraw instead to Bordeaux to await news from Roosevelt before taking any further action. At this last meeting in Tours, still only six ministers out of twenty-seven had supported Pétain's position. Ministers left for Bordeaux on the evening of 14 June.

The further move to Bordeaux posed extra problems for the government which was no longer sure how it should manage its staff. Should they be brought along or allowed to make their own arrangements? Eventually it was decided to give all government employees who were part of the ministerial party the option to choose.[25] Guillot, who as we know was travelling with the Minister of the Interior, considered this to be most unsatisfactory, complaining that it was far too late for such a proposal to be made and that they should have been asked to make such a decision before their departure from Paris. The government could not now expect to abandon people, having brought them so far. Accordingly, the entire party opted to carry on to Bordeaux in spite of the increasingly tenuous nature of the arrangements for their accommodation and transportation.[26] As the government left Tours, it gave orders to prefects south of the Loire that people should no longer be allowed to leave their homes.[27] However, such orders could have little impact on a population already on the move, conscious of the rapid enemy advance, and who had learnt that the government itself was now on the way to Bordeaux.

Armistice or Capitulation?

The situation facing ministers on their arrival in Bordeaux was little better than it had been in Tours. Despite finding themselves somewhat less dispersed as the various ministries occupied most of the larger buildings in the centre of the city, once again they were not able to contact one another by phone.[28]

> In the hotels there were no more rooms, no baths, not even a mattress. By virtue of an accommodation coupon, Parisian state officials were invited into patios frequented by Bordeaux's high society . . . Last minute refugees without lodgings were reduced to wandering around the streets. In the wide avenues, on the quays, and in the public gardens . . . an immense human torrent moved around ceaselessly. The parliament was reduced to a hundred members and met on the benches of a room as empty as a schoolroom.[29]

For Pierre Mendès France:

> The confusion had reached maximum levels. Everywhere people were in a state of panic and fear. In Paris, until the end, people had remained calm, peaceful, and magnificent... The opposite was true of Bordeaux where the pressure of the crowd was increasing hourly. The refugees filled up every corner of hotels, cafés, roads, squares, and people's homes. State officials, military officials, ministers, journalists... all of them were seized by this free-for-all, crushed into the crowd in the general confusion.[30]

In Bordeaux, in the apparent chaos which reigned there, parliamentarians found that they were the target of public anger and dissatisfaction as Paul Boncour, a socialist deputy, noted:

> The population, which was swelled by all those who had joined it along the roads of the exodus, wondered how this disaster could have happened and naturally pointed to those in authority, who could be considered to be those who should have exercised it, as being responsible. All defeats require scapegoats. The attacks directed at the parliament grew in ferociousness in line with the scale of events.

Thus the disasters of 1940 had a corresponding impact on people's faith in the parliament. And this was what the public made clear to us on all the streets and the public spaces of the city.[31]

These kinds of criticisms and frustrations with the apparent failure of Republican government would have serious consequences as events continued to unfold.

At the first cabinet meeting held in Bordeaux on 15 June, debates focused around the alternatives between armistice and capitulation. A purely military capitulation would lead to the cessation of hostilities and while it would admittedly require abandoning the population to the victor who would probably occupy the whole country, it would have the advantage of leaving the government free to carry on the battle from elsewhere (this was the position that had been taken by Norway and Holland subsequent to their defeat, for example). Armistice, on the other hand, offered a very different prospect. It was a political rather than a military agreement which would forbid any continuation of the war and would mark an end to the involvement of the two parties in hostilities. In theory, the defeated populations would therefore be protected from any further danger as the war would be at an end. The 'peace' which would be the result of such an armistice, Pétain's supporters believed, would provide them with the opportunity to introduce and implement their essential plans to rebuild the country.

By now, although most were agreed that it was no longer possible to continue the battle on the mainland, the cabinet was divided exactly in half between those who felt that armistice was the best way forward, and those who wanted to carry on the war from abroad. Reynaud, along with Mandel and de Gaulle, remained confident that the 'Anglo-Saxons' would eventually win the war even if the first leg of it was lost in France and this influenced their belief that they should continue to honour their alliance with Britain and attempt to carry on the conflict even in exile. 'The future of France depends on England and the US,' said Reynaud on 12 June; 'the Anglo-Saxon world will save France and it alone will be able to rebuild it.'[32] Others, like Weygand, had no confidence in the ability of the British to stand up to the Germans and was sure that Britain would soon have 'her neck wrung like a chicken', as he had retorted to Reynaud at Briare.[33] This conviction that Britain could not possibly hold out alone against the Nazis was to prove the crucial stumbling block which undermined the notion of departure. If Britain collapsed, the French would find themselves in an even worse position. This belief made the armistice appear the best way of securing France's position in the longer term in a Nazi-dominated Europe. Would it not be in France's best interests to negotiate terms with Hitler while she still had the chance to do so and before the defeated British came on to the scene and muddled the picture? Pétain was able to further force his point by playing on the chaos brought by the exodus both for civilians and the sad remainder of the army. How could the government contemplate abandoning the French population at a time when it was undergoing such trauma and distress?

Amidst violent bickering as supporters of each of the possible options sought to win over opinion to their side, and as no one wanted to publicly expose the lack of unity in their discussions, a compromise solution was reached. This was promoted by the former Prime Minister, Camille Chautemps, in the interests of maintaining a unified front. It was agreed that the government would approach the Germans in order to establish the possible form that an armistice might take in the event that the French government decided to pursue it. Chautemps's argument was that once the expectedly draconian terms of a potential armistice were made public, the French people would immediately understand why departure of the government to North Africa was the only possible way forward in the circumstances.

> He said that the whole resistance of the French people against the invader, especially the moral resistance, would reach its maximum effort once our fellow-countrymen realized there was nothing to be hoped from Hitler. It was thus necessary to prove this, and a request for the conditions on which hostilities could end would best serve the purpose.[34]

The government would then establish itself abroad and British support as well as the eventual backing of the Americans would allow the battle for the reconquest of the mainland to commence. Before the Germans could be approached, however, the French still had to persuade the British to release them from their March agreement.

While this seemed a feasible plan, the following day, Sunday 16 June, brought the disappointing news that Roosevelt would offer no military help. This now forced Reynaud's hand to negotiate with Britain in order to establish the basis upon which Britain would relieve France of her promise not to conclude a separate peace. But, before these negotiations could be completed, the British took the dramatic and imaginative step of offering Reynaud the possibility of presiding over a union of France and Britain. The text of the terms of this proposed marriage went thus: 'The two Governments declare that France and Great Britain shall no longer be two nations but one Franco-British union . . . Every citizen of France will enjoy immediate citizenship of Great Britain, every British subject will become a citizen of France . . . And thus we shall conquer.'[35] The dynamic behind this extraordinary suggestion was the British desire to keep the French in the war for as long as possible. The idea for union had originated with Jean Monnet who, as president of the Franco-British committee of cooperation, was based in London. De Gaulle, who was also in London to organize the transport of the government and troops to Algeria, immediately warmed to the idea and put it to Churchill who, although initially reticent, agreed to the plan believing that it could provide a new stimulus to help Reynaud carry his cabinet to North Africa and continue the war from there.[36]

So it was that with de Gaulle at his side, Churchill called Reynaud and offered him the chance to join in issuing a declaration announcing the immediate constitution of closest Anglo-French union in all spheres in order to carry on the war. Reynaud took to the plan immediately, convinced that this declaration would tip the balance in favour of continuing the war. But his obvious enthusiasm for the project was not enough to carry his fractured government, many of whom treated the British offer with suspicion. Those pressing for armistice, led by Pétain, refused to even consider the proposal seriously, fearing that it would relegate France to the status of a dominion. Pétain even claimed that 'it would be a marriage with a corpse!'[37] For Ybarnegaray, 'It was better to be a Nazi province. At least we know what that means,' to which Reynaud retorted, 'I prefer collaboration with my allies rather than my enemies'.[38] Churchill was to report in his memoirs, 'Rarely has so generous a proposal encountered so hostile a reception.'[39] The offer was put to the vote and defeated 14 to 10; it subsequently collapsed of itself amid comments that it bore no relation to the immediate problems that required settlement.[40] Discussions soon moved back to that of armistice.

Reynaud did not counter this nor did he fight back. Although most of the government still seem to have been in favour of carrying on the war, on the evening of 16 June, overwhelmed with anger and frustration at his failure to gain support for the project of union and convinced of his lack of support in the cabinet, Reynaud resigned in a fit of pique and failure of nerve. In fact it appears that only nine ministers were active supporters of armistice, and that twelve, possibly even fourteen, still supported him.[41] Perhaps Reynaud had confused those who supported the armistice proper with those who supported the idea that asking for terms would facilitate and justify a government departure. After Reynaud's resignation, President Albert Lebrun followed his advice that Pétain should be asked to take over as Prime Minister, and when approached with this proposal, Pétain calmly produced from his pocket a prepared list of the names of those he intended to choose to form his government.[42] Reynaud evidently believed that the terms of the armistice that the Germans would impose would be deemed as unacceptable and that even Pétain would feel obliged to reject them. In this way, after a short period of time, Reynaud anticipated that he would soon be called upon to return to power.[43]

In the confusion around the discussions relating to possible Franco-British union, Churchill had also responded sympathetically to Chautemps's request that the French be released from the March agreement with the proviso that the French fleet should immediately sail to British ports pending negotiations. The future of the French fleet and the fear that it might fall into German hands and be used against Britain haunted Churchill. At Briare, just before leaving, he had expressed these worries to Admiral Darlan, Minister of the Marine, who assured him that the fleet would never be surrendered to the Germans—such a move would be 'contrary to our naval tradition and our honour'.[44] Reynaud had never divulged the contents of Churchill's reply to the cabinet since these telegrams had been withdrawn and replaced by the offer of union. Reynaud also doubtless preferred to keep it quiet, fearing that knowledge of British acquiescence to Chautemps's request would further undermine the project for Franco-British union which so excited him. In any event, it soon became obvious that the new French government had little concern for the British as they undertook to make contact with the Nazis whether the British liked it or not. That very evening, the Spanish ambassador in France, Felix Lequerica, sent a telegram to his government requesting it to act as intermediary between Pétain's government and the Germans with a view to ceasing hostilities and to find out their proposed peace conditions.[45]

Pétain's New Government asks for Armistice

The next morning, 17 June, at 11.30, without waiting for a reply from the Germans, Pétain broadcast the substance of this decision to the French nation. First, he declared how he had taken over direction of the country. Rather than dwelling on the routed and defeated army, he focused instead on the plight of the refugees, women, children, and the elderly, implying that his approach to the enemy was predominantly motivated by a desire to bring their suffering to an end. In this way, Pétain constructed an argument which privileged compassion for the innocent civilians caught up in the war, and suggested that it was first and foremost for this reason that hostilities had to stop, rather than because of any shortcomings on the part of the military who had performed 'heroically', providing 'magnificent resistance'. In offering himself as a gift to France in its time of need, he assured people that if they followed his orders he would ensure that the chaos of exodus came to an end. This assurance formed the basis of his legitimacy.

The terms of his request were not at all clear to those who heard it. Was he calling for those who were still fighting bravely to put down their arms? Was this then essentially an appeal to desertion? Or should the soldiers hold out until such time as the terms of the ceasefire could be worked out? This kind of ambiguity could only exacerbate the confusion and chaos that already existed on the retreating front and across the country. Moreover, Pétain had carefully sidestepped the use of the term 'armistice' in this first broadcast although he had not shrunk from its use in recent governmental discussions. He simply made euphemistic reference to 'the means to bring the hostilities to an end' which for some, of course, could mean military capitulation rather than a politically agreed armistice.

Despite this confusion, it was now clear to everyone, especially the British, that the battle of France was over and the government intended to bring the war to an end. Chautemps's suggestion that discovering the potential terms of the armistice could form the basis for a departure of the government now looked increasingly far-fetched. When the cabinet decided unanimously against handing over a single warship to Germany or Italy whatever the consequences, Pétain exclaimed, 'In that case, I shall remain on French soil and the enemy shall take me prisoner.'[46] It was clear that Pétain had no intention of leaving the country: staying with the suffering population appeared to be crucial to him.

> The Council was very divided on the subject of leaving France. The Marshal and a certain number of ministers . . . have made up our minds not to quit the country whatever happens. It is in France that its future will be decided, and not in an overseas empire which has been drained of troops and which possesses neither munitions nor factories. Those who can assist in the moral and material revival of France must remain in the country.[47]

The Drama of the *Massilia*

The Germans did not reply immediately, and continued their advance south. It became apparent that the Germans might soon take Bordeaux and certain members of the government felt that this would undermine their capacity to give free consideration to the terms of the armistice. The presence of invading armies in the city would inevitably put them in a position of extreme weakness. Chautemps and Lebrun both favoured the idea that the government should be divided into two with some members remaining in France and others departing for North Africa. Once again, Pétain refused to leave the country but agreed to delegate powers to Chautemps and to order their departure so that it would not appear that they were taking flight.[48] In this context, it seemed sensible for certain key government members to make their way to relative safety in North Africa where they would be able to carry on the work of government and in the worst case scenario the other institutions of government would follow. So on the afternoon of 18 June, it was agreed that the President of the Republic, members of parliament, its presidents, and several ministers would embark on the ship *Massilia*, which was put at their disposal by Admiral Darlan.

At some stage the following day, however, Pétain changed his mind. This may have been because the British government had decided to formally recognize his government, but it was most likely to have been because he had heard from the Germans that they were prepared to negotiate. These two factors seemed to confirm his position and gave him a good measure of legitimacy. For Pétain, therefore, there was no longer any need for half of his government to depart. One of his trusted new ministers, Raphäel Alibert, developed a ploy designed to persuade certain key members of the government that they should stay in France, especially those who were considered absolutely necessary. He first spread the false rumour that the Germans had not yet crossed the Loire, hoping that this news would undermine the sense of urgency of the need for departure. When this failed, he sent explicit orders on Pétain's behalf that they should not board the ship.[49] Consequently, until the very last minute there was confusion over whether the ship should depart. When it finally left on 20 June a number of deputies were on board, including seven ex-ministers. Among them were Daladier, Mandel, Zay, and Mendès France. Many were Jewish. Both Lebrun and Chautemps remained in Bordeaux.

Hitler's rapid response to Pétain, indicating that an agreement with the government could be reached, was precisely calculated to avoid the prospect that the government might depart to North Africa en masse and continue hostilities from there. Those who left on the *Massilia* essentially did so under false pretences without Pétain's agreement. Their position now appeared rebellious. Mendès France claims in his memoirs that he and his colleagues knew nothing of Pétain's decision to rescind orders for their departure to North Africa. Stranded in the estuary of the Gironde, those on board were told nothing of this counter-order.[50] It would seem that a trick had been played on them, designed to distance the forty patriotic deputies from Bordeaux. Some of them were very influential and opposed capitulation and were likely to have refused the terms of the armistice which Pétain later accepted. That they were victims of a plot became even clearer when the press was instructed to begin a campaign against them which projected them as cowardly runaways. On learning by telegram that the armistice had been signed, the majority of the deputies on the Massilia wanted to return to Bordeaux to openly oppose this decision.[51] This proved impossible. The ship continued on to Casablanca where it arrived on 24 June. Several of those aboard were arrested for desertion.

De Gaulle's Extraordinary Gamble

In the meantime, de Gaulle, sensing that he was *persona non grata* in Pétainist circles and fearing arrest, had decided to leave Bordeaux with Spears. Both men left the country on 17 June 1940. De Gaulle pretended that he was simply accompanying Spears to his plane until the very last second before departure when he jumped aboard with his aide-de-camp Geoffroy de Courcel.[52] Once in London, de Gaulle was determined to put out a call to the French forces and urge them to continue to fight. He immediately visited Churchill who authorized him to speak to the French nation on the BBC.

Those who for many years have led the armies of France have formed a government.
This government claiming the defeat of our armies has contacted the German army in order to cease combat.
It is true that we were, we are submerged by the enemy's mechanical force both on land and in the air . . . but it was the tanks, the planes and the tactics

which surprised those that lead our armies and which brought them to the point at which they are today.

But has the last word been spoken? Should all hope now disappear? Is defeat definitive? No!

Believe me, I know what I am talking about when I say that nothing is yet lost for France. The same methods that were used to conquer us can be used to bring us victory one day.

Because France is not alone! She is not alone! She is not alone! She has a vast Empire behind her. She can join with the British Empire which rules the sea and which is carrying on the battle. She can, like England, draw on the infinite resources offered by the immense industries of the U.S.

The war is not limited to the sad territory of our country . . . This war is a world war.

He appealed to the soldiers, officers, engineers, and armament workers, exhorting them to join him in England, and specifically London, to continue the fight to ensure that 'the flame of French resistance should not be extinguished'. This first appeal (18 June) was written down and then read out on the BBC several times within a twenty-four-hour period. The text was published in the British press the next day. A few days later, on 22 June, on the announcement of the conditions of the armistice, General de Gaulle launched a new radio appeal to rally people to take position against it.

De Gaulle's rebellion against Pétain's government, his refusal to accept the armistice from the outset, and his decision to leave France and embrace exile was an extraordinary and daring gamble, particularly since it flew in the face of the French military tradition of subservience to a civilian government which held supreme authority.[53] However, in the early days, de Gaulle had relatively little success in rallying support. His future role as a leader of the French Resistance and ultimately the French state was by no means a foregone conclusion. He himself did not anticipate that he would be able to motivate and rally crowds of people. His main concern was to show that there was an alternative path to that taken by Pétain.[54] De Gaulle had already won the admiration of Churchill. Spears wrote that on a visit to London on 8 June, he 'had made an excellent impression on all who met him: cool, collected, completely "unrattled" '.[55] Nonetheless he was viewed with some uncertainty by the British cabinet who saw him as a rather unknown quantity and who would have preferred to deal with more established politicians like Mandel, Reynaud, or Daladier. However, their attempts to contact Mandel and Daladier on their arrival in North Africa were frustrated.[56] On arriving in Casablanca on 24 June, the status of those on board the *Massilia* was unclear. The Vichy government ordered that the ship should remain at sea until the situation could be clarified. The British envoys Duff Cooper and Lord Gort who arrived expecting to find a government in exile were discouraged by the local authorities from meeting with Mandel and were finally obliged to leave without seeing him. Only after the departure of the British diplomats were Mendès France and Mandel allowed to disembark, at which point Mandel was immediately placed under arrest.[57]

Unlike the majority of French people, de Gaulle was exceptionally well placed to refuse the French defeat, reject the armistice, and take the decision to leave. His insight into military affairs informed his conviction that the Germans would lose a lengthy war and his recent political involvement reinforced his belief that both the Americans and the Russians would eventually join the battle. His refusal to be taken in by the cult status accorded to Pétain also contributed to his decision. His training and allegiance to the military seems to have left him untarnished by the traditional republican view that exile was an unacceptable taboo.[58] However, for others, going to join de Gaulle in London did not have such evident logic. Doing so would force them to adopt the status of dissident or force them to take a position against the Marshal who, to all intents and purposes at this stage, appeared to most people to have unquestionable legitimacy.

Members of the armed forces, who were the initial target of the 18 June appeal, viewed Pétain with the greatest of respect. They were also profoundly anglophobic. Most officers were convinced that the Germans had now won the war and that there was little sense in leaving their homeland to benefit a country which had failed to adequately support them.[59] These sentiments were seriously aggravated by events on 3 July 1940. British fears that the Germans would commandeer the French fleet in the interests of their own war effort came to a head. To prevent such an eventuality the British sunk the French navy ships at Mers-El-Kébir and 1,200 French soliders lost their lives. This tragedy considerably amplified feelings of hostility towards the British and thereby further undermined de Gaulle's position. The attitude of French officers towards de Gaulle was later summarized by General Eisenhower:

> It is possible to understand why de Gaulle was disliked in the ranks of the French army. At the time of the French surrender in 1940, the officers who remained in the Army had accepted the position and orders of their government and had given up the fight. In their view, if the course chosen by de

Gaulle was correct, then every French officer who obeyed the orders of his government was a poltroon. If de Gaulle was a loyal Frenchman, they had to regard themselves as cowards. Naturally the officers did not choose to think of themselves in this light, rather they considered themselves as loyal Frenchmen carrying out the orders of constituted civilian authority.[60] De Gaulle faced an uphill task to try and win over their support.

The Acceptance of the Armistice

Meanwhile, everyone in the political and military hierarchy waited anxiously in Bordeaux for news of the German terms for the armistice. The possibility still remained that these terms might prove impossible for the French to accept and Hitler was aware of this. He told Mussolini on 18 June 1940 that his main concern was to keep the government on French soil and prevent any possibility that it might make for London. He therefore went out of his way to ensure that the armistice would appear acceptable to Pétain's government. He did not seek to annex large areas of territory and did not touch the colonies. His ambitions regarding the territories of Alsace and Lorraine were not mentioned. He did not require the fleet to be handed over, he simply demanded that it be disarmed in order to prevent it from falling into British hands. Pétain's cabinet, convinced that Germany would soon emerge victorious, was predisposed to find the armistice acceptable and believed that agreeing to such terms would prevent France from experiencing a similar fate to that of Poland which had undergone repressive direct military rule. Hitler's readiness to tolerate the presence of their government on French territory seemed to augur well and suggested that they would be able to preserve a good measure of sovereignty and be able to introduce their planned policies for renewal of the country. The government, however, had to wait until 22 June to hear details of the German terms—in effect the enemy probably wanted to string out negotiations for as long as possible so as to pursue their advance to ensure their advantage.

General Huntziger was chosen to play the role of key negotiator for the French contingent. He reported to Weygand that the terms were very harsh, but they contained nothing dishonourable.[61] The clause which concerned him most was that of article 14 which required the French to hand over all the anti-Nazi refugees. Huntziger objected and asked for it to be deleted as it was 'contrary to French honour and the nation's practice of asylum'.[62] Despite meeting three times to discuss the German propositions, and despite the fact that eight members of the government had severe reservations about it, Pétain and Weygand agreed to the terms. They were much relieved that Hitler had not demanded the fleet which would have put them in a compromising position towards the English and might have forced their hand in a different way.

Although evidently acceptable to Pétain's government, the terms of the proposed armistice agreement were harsh. The country was to be sliced up and separated into zones. The two most important of these were divided by a demarcation line which cut through the centre of the mainland south of Dijon to the east, passing just south of Moulins, Bourges, and Tours, then due south parallel to the coast, east of Angoulême and Bordeaux as far as the Spanish frontier (see Map 4). Its position more or less represented the extent of the advance of the German armies in June 1940. Those territories north of the line would remain under German occupation in the area designated as the 'Occupied Zone' whereas the so-called 'Free Zone', south of the line, would be unoccupied and contain the centre of the new government situated at Vichy. Pétain believed that he would be able to unite the country under his national government and had a feasible area in which to enact his planned changes. He could also claim sufficient autonomy to silence those who had pressed for government in exile. For Hitler, the continued existence of a French government was bound to reduce the potential for resistance to the armistice while the Occupied Zone still gave the Germans the chance to exploit what was most economically useful to them. It also ensured that the German army was present in force in places where it could potentially be under threat from the Allies and established a Forbidden Zone along the entire length of the French Atlantic coast. According to further clauses of the treaty, the French would bear all the costs of the Occupation and would allow the Nazis to hold the 1,600,000 French prisoners of war who would be transferred to German territory pending the conclusion of peace. These men would effectively be held hostage as a means for the Germans to ensure that the French were accommodating towards them. The public mistakenly believed for some time that the conclusion of armistice would bring demobilization of the French military and that the men would soon return to their homes. In apparent agreement to all the terms of the treaty, the Marshal gave orders on 22 June that the armistice should be signed by the French representatives. The Germans insisted that this signing should take place in a ceremony steeped with symbolism, using the very same coach at Rethondes which had been the site of the German humiliation of November 1918. The armistice treaty would take effect from 25 June 1940, a day which Pétain declared should be a day of mourning.

Once the armistice had been dealt with, Pétain turned his attention to the business of government. In his plans for French regeneration he had little thought for the institutions of the Republic, referring only to the need for a new order in the vaguest of terms in his broadcasts. Other members of his entourage, however, had long held them in contempt. Most notable of these was Pierre Laval whose name was among those on the prepared list of ministers which Pétain produced when Lebrun had called upon him to form a government after Reynaud's resignation. Laval, however, did not take office immediately and only became Deputy Prime Minister on 27 June. Having first entered the Chamber of Deputies in 1914 and the Senate in 1927, he had held government office several times during the 1930s and served as Prime Minister on a couple of occasions. Opposed to Germany at this time, his skills as a canny negotiator were demonstrated by his success in crafting the Stresa Front between France, Britain, and Mussolini's Italy in 1935. He also hoped to persuade Stalin's USSR into alliance against Hitler. In early 1936, however, Laval was forced to resign as Prime Minister when his efforts to find a solution to the Abyssinian crisis with the British Foreign Secretary, Samuel Hoare, were denounced as appeasement to Mussolini. Laval also had a reputation for being a rather dubious character, not just because he had made a fortune in ways that were suspected to border on the illegal, but also because his track record in politics suggested that he was an opportunist. Since starting his political career as a left-winger, he had moved over to become an independent supporting the right. His allegiance to Pétain was now evident. Like many of Pétain's other ministers, his career in government had been cut short by the triumph of the left-wing coalition in 1936 when the Popular Front came to power. His subsequent exclusion from government had led him to despise the Republic ever after. Pétain now brought him into government as an ally in his plans for national renewal. This position provided Laval the opening he needed to help bring about the downfall of the Republic he so hated. While many others were also keen to bury it, Laval had the idea that it should vote itself out of existence. As Baudouin reported in his diary, Laval's argument was that 'It was impossible to govern with Parliament, especially with the Front Populaire Chamber of 1936. "This Chamber has made me sick," he said: "Now it is I who am going to make it sick." '63 Laval's personal role should not, however, be overplayed. If he successfully engineered its demise, he was helped by the Republic's lack of popularity and the widespread belief that the time had come for a major change in the institutions of government in the light of the defeat and the exodus.

Meanwhile, it had become clear that the government had to move. It could not stay in Bordeaux which fell into the Occupied Zone under the armistice agreement. It had to find a home until permission was granted for it to return to Paris. On 29 June it moved first to Clermont Ferrand which was dismissed as it was Laval's power base and was seen as too working class. The government then settled at the spa town of Vichy, chosen on the basis of its numerous hotels which could receive the various ministries.⁶⁴ This was to be the setting for the dramatic events which led to the demise of the Republic. The members of both assemblies variously made their way there and finally convened in the casino at Vichy on 9 July. Their numbers were considerably depleted by the absence of those who were under arrest, communists, and those who were elsewhere—aboard the *Massilia* for example—or those who were simply unable to reach Vichy because of the ongoing confusion and transport difficulties which made it difficult to get across the country. Ex-Prime Minister Reynaud was injured in a serious car accident and was not present. Of 849 senators and deputies, 649 made it to the meeting where both chambers voted first in favour of revision of the Constitution of 1875, and the next day, by 569 votes to 80, to give all executive and constitutional powers to Pétain. By virtue of these new powers, Pétain promptly declared himself head of state and adjourned the Chamber and the Senate indefinitely. 'That is how you overthrow a Republic!' remarked Laval allegedly.⁶⁵ In the event, the defeat had served the enemies of the Republic. As the Fascist sympathizer Lucien Rebatet was to remark in his memoirs: 'The operation we had dreamed of and called for so many years had taken five hours . . . Defeat paid better dividends than victory! It did away with vile parliamentarianism. A military triumph would never have given us this happy outcome.'⁶⁶

The ruling elites had chosen to put the nation into the hands of the Vichy regime which now had carte blanche. In the days that followed, it immediately set about introducing new legislation and soon embarked on a growing involvement and collaboration with the Germans. The French people, for their part, still traumatized and displaced, were slow to grasp the intricacies of what was going on. Let us now return to a consideration of the alternatives they faced at the time of Pétain's speech on 17 June 1940 with the exodus still in full swing. How were these events received and understood by the people stranded on the roads trying to make sense of their experiences, attempting to fathom how they could possibly take control of their lives again?

4
The People's Decisions

During these painful hours, I have in mind the unhappy refugees who are
crossing the country in a state of utter destitution. I offer them my
compassion and my concern. With a heavy heart I tell you today the
fighting must stop. I contacted the adversary during the night to ask him
if he is prepared to work towards finding the means to bring hostilities to
an end in an honourable agreement between soldiers.

Marshal Philippe Pétain, Speech, 17 June 1940

By placing refugees at the centre of his concerns, Pétain gave them hope
that their suffering might soon come to an end. In underlining their
plight, he also sent a clear message to communities swamped by these
arrivals: their priority should be to reinforce their efforts to provide shelter
and tend to their needs. As host communities attempted to rise to the
challenge, stranded refugees halted their journeys and started to consider
their next steps. Gradually, a series of alternative strategies opened up. Some
followed the advice of the authorities and stayed where they were. Others
chose to carry on, seeking less crowded areas with better food supplies. For
those that believed that German occupation might put them at personal risk,
and that this was a likely outcome of Pétain's decision to negotiate, it
became imperative for them to maintain their distance from the Nazis.
Many now had to contemplate the option of leaving the country.

Civilian Reactions to Pétain's Speech

Refugees recalled hearing the speech through open windows or in the homes
of others, a memory which reflects the displaced existence of those who had

left their own homes and were sleeping rough and living out of doors. Germaine Tillion and her mother heard the radio through an open window as they were passing through a crowded village. When Pétain's speech was announced they rushed into the first house they reached and listened to the news of the Marshal's armistice request in the family's kitchen. Tillion's reaction upon hearing it was to dash into the street to be sick.[1] But this was not the reaction of the majority. Most were simply relieved and felt that such a move was long overdue. 'We were at the farm when we heard Pétain. The farmer was listening to the radio and he called us over. We didn't understand much, but we cried. We thought the war was over. There will be no more killing, no more deaths. We were all so relieved.'[2] Alfred Fabre-Luce, a notoriously right-wing commentator, explained people's reactions perfectly:

The exodus . . . favoured amongst this mass of men, women, and children axed from and deprived of their normal infrastructures, victim of uncertainty and deprivation, suffering physically and emotionally, a feeling of abandonment which predisposed them to accept the armistice almost with relief. Had they been in their own homes, these same people would only have been ashamed to do so.[3]

Drawing once again on their understandings from the last conflict, most expected that armistice would be followed by lasting peace as in November 1918. France, they believed, was now out of the war. Rumour and word of mouth reduced the content of Pétain's words to 'The war is finished!'[4] Like Madame Perrot and Simone de Beauvoir who was conscious of her own lover, Sartre, on the front line, most women were relieved to think that no more soldiers would be killed, that their husbands, fathers, and sons no longer faced the possibility of death. The true meaning of Pétain's words, however, remained unclear. De Beauvoir was among those who at first understood him to mean that the French military had capitulated. 'It took me several days to understand the real meaning of the armistice.'[5] Indeed, in the week between 17 and 25 June, the French people who were on the roads did not know whether or not the war was over until they learnt that the twenty-fifth was to be a national day of mourning to mark the fact that the armistice was coming into force.

For those trying to reach places further south, the meanings behind the speech were of less concern than the fact that the speech in and of itself seemed to render any continuation of their journeys futile. The majority of the refugees therefore collapsed wherever they found themselves and rested until they could assess the likely turn of events. Others simply turned round

and headed towards home, often travelling along the same road they had
been following. For some this mistaken belief that the war had come to an
end would have tragic consequences. One witness reported that on the
morning of 18 June, at Thouars, 100 km (62 miles) south of the Loire, some
Parisians and other refugees from the north and east of the country took the
news that armistice was being requested to mean that it had been signed.
Finding no food supplies, they tried to return to the regions north of the
Loire, thinking that conditions might be better there. Here they came up
against refugees who were still flooding south. This mass of refugees was
victim to German machine-gun attack which, in the light of Pétain's
speech, they had believed would cease.[6] To the confusion of those who
now thought themselves out of danger, such attacks and bombings continued until the armistice officially came into operation on 25 June. Adrey
recorded the following on 19 June:

> We've been told that hostilities have ceased. It is not quite true and we have to
> believe that this pernicious war refuses to end as this afternoon we were aware
> of the noise of machine guns and some explosions, the last ones perhaps, could
> still be heard. A bomb fell on the road and killed two civilians. What is going
> on? We don't understand anything anymore![7]

And then on 20 June,

> No, the war is not quite over. There is less fighting, but the fighting is still
> going on.[8]

The area around the Loire valley where there was a tremendous concentration of refugees continued to be the location of ongoing battles in the days
immediately before the armistice came into force and many perished there.

In those areas where refugees were now overtaken by the Germans, they
too soon realized that there was little point in carrying on, and, like others,
simply turned round in an attempt to return straight home. Inhabitants of the
capital who had waited until 13 June to leave had often been unable to make
much progress, slowed by the crowds of people on the road. Those who were
less than 100 km (62 miles) from Paris were soon caught up by the enemy's
advance parties and overtaken by them between the Seine and the Loire even
before Pétain's speech. They had little choice other than to follow German
directives to retrace their steps. Other refugees, believing that they were
ahead of the Germans, arrived in towns only to find them already under
occupation. In the days immediately before and after Pétain's first broadcast,
the centre of France was marked by confusion of this kind. Reaching the

Loire had provided no certainty of escape. Many had arrived too late to cross bridges which had already been detonated by the French army. The relatively short distances involved meant that the return of those who had not managed to get far was relatively easily to organize. The sight of people returning home reassured others who concluded that all must be over.

Paul Léautard, who had stayed in the capital, noted people returning home as early as Sunday 15 June, just a day or two after their departure. He saw 'groups of two wheelbarrows, miserable-looking men, women, and children with three dogs. As they stopped to get their breath for a minute, I talked to them. A woman says to me, "The Germans told us 'Go home'. They gave us soup, and well, you know! . . . "'9 Thus, just four or five days after the fall of the capital 'thousands of Parisians had returned to their homes'. Roger Langeron, the prefect of police, who made this remark also noted 'a reflux of refugees' on 19 June: 'These people could not go on any further and have realized that the battles are over.'10 The German military commander in Paris, General Von Brieson, expressed concern about the returning refugees fearing they might create disorder, but Langeron felt that 'it seemed to be in everyone's interests and even that of his troops, that these unhappy people come home, that they don't overcrowd the roads, and that they reinvigorate the economic activity of their region'.11 Many were pleasantly surprised by the attitude of the Germans and commented on the fact that the Germans did not seem hostile; some claimed to have been given petrol to help them return home.12 If several tens of thousands of Parisians had returned to their homes in the second half of June, by the end of the month the city's population was still far from reaching its normal levels and there were many thousands who had not yet been able to reach their homes.

Unless refugees from Paris were reasonably close to the capital, the Germans encouraged them to stop and await orders to return. Adrey reported having overheard a German soldier tell some refugees 'that all the roads to Paris were blocked with traffic and that "Parisians", by which he meant us, would do well to wait three or four days before returning home'.13 Displaced civilians from the north and east of the country, as well as Parisians and others who had joined the flight along the path of the exodus, were told to stay put. On 19 June, appalled by the levels reached by the exodus, Charles Pomaret, newly appointed Minister of the Interior, broadcast the following:

> In the name of the government, I give the order to all French civilians, men and women, young and old, to stay where they are for the time being. The

immense and tragic exodus which has transported millions of men and women from the north to the south of the country is an enormous mistake. We must put an end to it.[14]

He explained how the government had taken the step of ordering the military generals in the regions and the prefects in the departments to forbid any further population movements. Appeals were widely reproduced in the press. These measures marked the first time that the government had taken a coherent line on the exodus and finally gave civilians a clear indication of what they were expected to do. In some areas of the country the advice had a dramatic and immediate impact in slowing down the progress of refugees. On Wednesday 19 June Sadoul reported that civilians had all but disappeared from the roads.[15] In other areas, however, these official directives had less influence on populations who were determined to pursue their flight and reach a satisfactory place to stop. Until the armistice actually came into force on 25 June, people continued to seek better conditions further south and, particularly, better food supplies. In the absence of proper information, many of those who were on the roads and who were not sure of the whereabouts of the Germans continued their journeys. In Brittany, the roads remained crowded with refugees marching west to Brest until 8 July, long after the region had been occupied.[16] The momentum of the exodus also continued for some days in the southern unoccupied areas. Morize describes the situation in Cahors: 'From 17 to 30 June, I can tell you that people continued to arrive, day and night non-stop.'[17] Having reached the end of their physical and emotional resources, the vast majority of refugees soon understood that with the German advance still underway, they would do best to follow directions from local authorities. Most heeded Pomaret's requests to stay put and wait.

Military Reactions to Pétain's Speech

Like civilians, soldiers almost universally viewed Pétain's broadcast on 17 June with relief. As Raymond Aron confirmed, in military circles, 'it was seen as a decision which was the natural result of the situation'.[18] However, for those soldiers who were having some success and who were still in the throes of battle on the Italian front, the apparent military capitulation was not viewed favourably. On all fronts, officers as well as individual soldiers had to consider how best to proceed as news of Pétain's speech filtered through to them. At first, some refused to take these reports seriously, assuming that such a move attributed to Pétain was a device to further undermine the French war effort. Rebatet recounted: 'The rumour was gaining credibility that Pétain's speech was a fake, a trap created by the fifth column.'[19] As soldiers came into contact with more reliable sources of information, they understood that these reports had validity, but how they should act was by no means clear. Should they continue fighting until they had formal orders to the contrary? Or should they give themselves up to the enemy? Should they participate in an orderly withdrawal? Or should they endeavour to escape on an individual basis and make for safety in the south?

To confuse matters, bombing continued apace in the days after the request for armistice. Raids took place in Le Mans, Rennes, Nantes, Tours, and especially Bordeaux where the government was present, and all this despite the fact that towns of more than twenty thousand inhabitants had been declared open cities. Divisions closer to the German front sometimes chose to keep up the battle until they had explicit orders to surrender. Soldiers who decided to carry on fighting and continue their efforts to halt the German advance found that they had to deal with the growing opposition of civilians who wanted an end to the hostilities and feared German reprisals. General Pagézy noted the following:

> As a general rule, each time defence of a village was organized . . . the leader was subject to complaints, grievances, and sometimes threats from the mayor. It was clear that from the time that the request for armistice was announced, the only thought that preoccupied the local population was how they could avoid possible bombings or reprisals.[20]

Mayors whose communes were caught up in the fighting sought to avoid military confrontation that could inflict damage on the civilian population and tried to persuade military commanders to leave or surrender rather than continue to fight. Local authorities contacted the government in Bordeaux in an effort to establish whether their towns qualified as open cities. Civilians, that is the local population as well as passing refugees, were even prepared to disarm French soldiers in order to avoid further conflict.[21]

In the absence of orders and often in the unshakeable belief that the war was now virtually at an end, many soldiers immediately threw down their weapons.[22] Countless demoralized and confused soldiers were easy prey for the Germans. Seizing the opportunity to benefit from the ambiguous nature of Pétain's speech, the Germans insisted that the war was now over and were often easily able to persuade these overwhelmed and devastated men to surrender without a fight, sometimes promising that they would soon be able to return home. 'War over, home soon,' the young German soldiers were heard to chant to their captives.[23] In some areas, *feldgendarmes* were overwhelmed by the mass of prisoners to such a degree that they did not know what to do with them. Columns of French soldiers were marched by their own officers towards Germany without so much as a German guard, in the belief that this would make a good impression.[24] Examples abound of cases where soldiers handed themselves over, sometimes even before the bulk of the enemy troops had reached the area. In one case, French soldiers allowed themselves to be guarded by volunteers from the local French village until adequate German reinforcements arrived to take over.[25] Many of those who allowed themselves to be disarmed in this way were regarded with undisguised disdain by the Germans who were surprised, even shocked, by the extent of their surrender.

> Then I saw our own men who had fought so well right up to the last moment, throw down their weapons, cast away their equipment, and join together dancing in the road and in the clearings. Forgotten were the disaster, the surrender, self-respect, the dignity which the defeated should maintain in the presence of the victor. No, I wasn't wrong: in the looks of the young German soldiers who passed I read astonishment and contempt.[26]

The most surprising aspect of all this was, as the historian Crémieux-Brilhac has pointed out, that neither Pétain nor the Military Command saw fit to remind their soldiers that once all possible means of fighting had been exhausted, it was their duty to do everything in their power to avoid falling into the hands of the enemy.[27] Doubtless many soldiers believed that this military duty had been overridden by Pétain's assertion that the fighting had to stop.

The Germans actively cultivated the belief that the liberation of the prisoners of war was imminent, perhaps only days away. Once the English had met defeat, everyone would soon be demobilized and they could return safely to their homes. French soldiers were urged not to write letters home to their loved ones as they would be home themselves before their letters could get there.[28] Thus, the French prisoners rarely attempted—despite the lack of guards—to escape from the makeshift temporary arrangements put into place in their early days of captivity before being transferred to Germany. E. M. Guibert relates how he was marched off in German custody and put to work by the Germans in areas where there were no guards. At one point, he arrived in Avallon with some other prisoners and they were given the freedom of the town. It was only some days later that he was rounded up and sent to a camp outside the town where he was grouped with eight to nine thousand other men.[29] It seems probable that prisoners decided to go along with the Germans because they thought that there was not much point in taking risks. They feared the possibility of reprisals against their fellow men or their families. Most importantly, they hoped that by complying with German wishes they could speed up the bureaucratic formalities that were necessary for demobilization and that this would make it possible for them to return to their civilian lives as soon as possible.[30] 'We could have escaped to civilian life a hundred times and changed our clothes. It simply did not occur to us. We were docile prisoners . . . And in any case they were going to free us immediately. This was the unanimous opinion.'[31]

In places where soldiers were distant from any direct threat of German advance, in an effort to protect themselves from being taken as prisoners of war or treated as deserters, they acquired civilian clothes. In some cases, they did so because they were told to by their superiors.[32] Others believed themselves relieved of their duties in the absence of any coherent orders or directives from the military High Command. Soldiers tended to drift away. Those who were less informed, believing that the war was now over, headed back to their homes and, if north of the river Loire, straight into the hands of the Germans and towards a prisoner-of-war camp.[33]

Many regiments had become separated from their officers, and soldiers from their fellow soldiers and officers. They decided that all they could do was to make their way south. Anxious to be demobilized, they listened to the radio for news from the government as to where they should go and whom they should report to. These stragglers made their way to Toulouse and Montauban where vast numbers of soldiers regrouped.[34] The fate of these soldiers who made it into the southern zone was also uncertain. Many of them, like civilians, were lost.

Those regiments who were able to keep together, eventually reached the places where their orders had directed them, often some time after the armistice had been requested. When Sadoul's battalion finally regrouped, it found at the roll-call that only 15 per cent of the regiment was present. Other regiments had more success, but all complained that withdrawal had been especially difficult in the region of the Loire. This was the case of the Seventh Army whose commander reported having taken a path from the Somme, via the Seine, and the Loire to the Cher. It had managed to sustain a 500-km (311-mile) retreat and avoided capitulation in the open field.

This, as Edward Spears pointed out in his memoirs, was the worst possible scenario for a soldier in the army. 'In the French language, there is no expression which conveys to the soldier and the civilian alike an expression of more dire disgrace than this one: "Surrender in the open field". To be starved out of a fortress, to be ridden down and decimated, are great misfortunes but surrender in the open field is utterly shameful.'[35]

As civilians and soldiers alike waited to hear the terms of the armistice, the assumption was widespread that France would escape with the loss of some provinces and then peace would ensue. Pétain and Weygand also fostered this belief. Weygand had repeatedly pronounced on the inevitable and certain defeat which the British would soon experience at the hands of the Germans. Pétain also seemed extremely confident of Nazi victory. He had recommended to Churchill at Briare that he too should seriously consider making peace with the Germans as in his view the British were unlikely to hold out for more than a month.[36] Soldiers who had participated in the exodus, along with the civilians, had witnessed first-hand the scale of the disaster and the extent of the collapse of all civil and military structures of authority. It was clear to them that any effort to resist was bound to fail. Their only plausible reaction was to accept Pétain's words, passively acknowledge defeat, and hope that they would soon be able to get home and be reunited with their loved ones. The exodus experience impacted on soldiers and civilians alike and the traumatic events became the crucial experiential basis which they brought to their understanding of the defeat and would help shape their responses to the later German occupation.

Armistice Terms

In the days following Pétain's speech, the population waited anxiously for news of the details of the armistice while the Germans relentlessly carried on southwards, ignoring orders from their generals that they should halt their advance.[37] It was not until Pétain's third broadcast on 25 June that most French people realized what the armistice would mean in practice. The population was finally told by Pétain on that date that France was to be divided into different areas, some of which would be occupied and others not.

A large part of our territory is going to be occupied on a temporary basis. In all of the north, and the west of our country, from the lake of Geneva to Tours, and along the coast from Tours to the Pyrenees, Germany will have garrisons.

These details were not always well received. One of Sadoul's colleagues retorted:

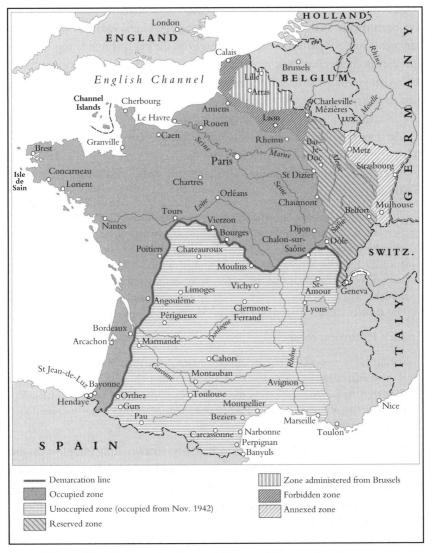

Map 4. The Demarcation line and Zones of Occupation, June 1940

That Weygand, he could not be bothered to organize any kind of defence on the Oise river, nor prevent the evacuation of Paris which made the defence of the Loire impossible. And now he has accepted these peace terms! ... I just cannot believe the victor of Verdun [Pétain] is under German orders.[38]

Displaced populations waited anxiously to hear whether the areas they found themselves in were likely to come under direct German occupation. As Downing put it, 'Obviously, the news was of vital importance to us. Just where were we? On enemy soil or what?'[39] The demarcation line had not yet been mentioned publicly and its exact geographical location was slow to emerge. Most people learnt of its position from the papers but first reports were not very accurate. For some days, those who realized that they were situated in areas that were earmarked for German occupation took action to leave. Their perception of the extent to which they might be in danger of persecution by the occupying forces was the main influence behind this decision.

On hearing the details of the terms of the armistice, many people, whether they had been involved in the exodus or not, sought to reach the Unoccupied Zone in the south. Dorgèles still harboured some illusions on reaching Bordeaux.

The Germans, I imagined, would not advance any further than the line where their troops had stopped. Sure of this absurd conviction, I committed my last error by renting a villa in Arcachon [a seaside resort 50 km [31 miles] from Bordeaux], for the whole season, paid for in advance ... This dream only lasted two nights. On learning that the victors were going to occupy the entire coast, I quickly had to pack my bags in the car again in order to reach the Free Zone. The same evening, delayed by German convoys, we arrived in Cahors.[40]

Stanley Hoffmann recalled

buying the papers on the twenty-third or twenty-fourth to find the positioning of the demarcation line. Bordeaux was going to fall within the Occupied Zone. We therefore had to leave before the Germans arrived. But where could we go? The first small town in the Free Zone was Marmande. So we headed there ... by taxi.[41]

At the other end of the country, in Brittany, many young people who did not want to find themselves trapped in occupied areas left by sea. The ports became scenes of frenetic activity.[42] Between 19 and 24 June, ships took hundreds of refugees to Bayonne from the French ports of Caen, Cherbourg, Granville, Brest, Concarneau, and Lorient among others. This evacuation came to about 2,245 people of which 150 were soldiers.[43] But many of those who were able to reach the ports of the Atlantic coast found that they had been beaten to it by the Germans who had already arrived in both Bayonne and Saint-Jean-de-Luz. Travel by sea carried its own particular dangers. One boat carrying 150 civilian passengers hit a mine and just fifteen people survived.[44] Further inland, Dorgelès asserted:

> I will never forget the sight of those soldiers, heads bowed, evacuating from the Occupied Zone in packed lorries, mixed in with the enemy convoys... I also came across fleeing groups of older kids who had packed their bags... to escape the control of the victor and who cried out, holding themselves proudly above their handlebars, 'They won't get me!'[45]

Even once the Germans had started to put the demarcation line into place, it was some time before it acted as the frontier it was later to become. Marie-Madeleine Fourcade recounted how 'the demarcation line was still weakly guarded by courteous members of the SS who were not yet searching the cars. We crossed it at Orthez without incident.'[46] It took the Germans some weeks to get established, and until September the line itself was far from definitive.[47]

Jews and the Exodus

A large proportion of the French and foreign refugees caught up in the exodus were Jews. Foreign Jews escaping Nazism had flocked to France from Russian, Poland, Austria, Germany, and Czechoslovakia throughout the inter-war period. This wave had accelerated in the late 1930s as war became more likely. Many were interned by the pre-war French governments. The Daladier government in a fit of fifth column anxiety that Jews might be enemies in disguise, extended the existing policy of internment of foreign Jews in the months before the outbreak of war. Camps had appeared across the country, originally constructed for the internment of refugees who had flooded over the border during the Spanish Civil War. They were mobilized by the authorities as a convenient, cheap way of housing to keep Jews and foreigners under surveillance.[48] After the German invasion, those interned in the north of the country were transferred by train to other camps in the south.[49] Severe overcrowding resulted from the need to absorb the growing numbers of refugees evacuated from the north. As the Germans advanced southwards and their victory seemed imminent, the chances of survival for the interned refugees deteriorated and panic overcame those in camps who risked being turned over wholesale to the Nazis.[50]

In May 1940 Jews were numerous among the early refugees who fled from Belgium, Luxembourg, and Holland. Among these refugees were Jews from Alsace and Lorraine who suspected Hitler's annexation intentions for the region and left immediately. Foreign Jews who had managed to escape internment had mainly gravitated towards Paris. They knew that capture by the Germans was likely to mean persecution. When the first waves of French refugees reached the capital, these foreign Jews took this as their cue to leave. They had little alternative but to follow the crowds and hope for the best.

The Jewish community in Paris was a thriving one. It is estimated that 90 per cent of French Jews lived there in 1940.[51] Most left during the exodus. Parisian Jews had been among the first residents of the capital to depart. Only those who could not afford it or who were too old or too ill to manage the journey remained in the city. Some had lived there for several generations; others had only come to the country in the previous twenty years and had recently adopted French nationality. Refusing to recognize their Jewish identity as a particular reason for their departure, French Jews, for the most part, were unaware of the risks that they would face from the German occupation. Sceptical about the stories of persecution brought by foreign Jews, they looked down on these foreigners, considering themselves to be in a very different position. Those who had taken French nationality, or who had been present in the country long enough to have fought as Frenchmen during the First World War, had a strong sense of national identity which reinforced their conviction that they had nothing to fear.[52]

When the defeat was confirmed and Jews were faced with the prospect that the Germans would soon be taking control of much of the territory, some of their former confidence started to evaporate. Pomaret, Vichy's new Interior Minister, strongly encouraged the Jews he saw in Bordeaux to emigrate.[53] Many started to think in terms of leaving the country. But exile abroad was a significant step, and if they felt that they had much to lose, some still preferred to wait until the true nature of the situation became apparent. They were also conscious of the stigma associated with running away and did not want to appear unpatriotic. While fleeing the Germans in order to escape the risk of occupation was generally perceived of as acceptable, leaving the country was quite another story. The reaction to the departure of those on the *Massilia* had made clear that exile was not an approved option. Publicity surrounding these departures was steeped in propaganda with a strong anti-Semitic slant. The

Pétainist press was at pains to portray the Jewish politicians who escaped on the *Massilia* as unpatriotic by comparison with Pétain and Weygand who were determined to stay on French territory and share the sufferings of the population. Large numbers of French Jews however recognized that it might be prudent to make sure that they were situated in the Unoccupied Zone. Pétain's readiness to deal with the Germans was more immediately alarming for foreign Jews. When the terms of the armistice were finally announced, news of article 19, which allowed the Nazis to extradite all those they wished to forcibly repatriate from both the Occupied and Unoccupied Zones, was received with despair by those interned. A wave of suicides, including that of Walter Benjamin, the author, swept the camps among Jewish refugees who feared that they would be handed over to the Germans.[54] The government had made no provision for those interned in camps in the event of a German victory and camp commanders were largely left to their own devices. Some complied with refugee demands for release and urged them to escape in order to avoid being taken by the Germans.[55] Others continued to detain them, believing that to do otherwise would be disobeying orders.

For those who were released from the camps, the logical step after locating other members of their family was to try and get out of France. This soon became the preferred option for French and foreign Jews alike. However, those in modest circumstances were soon forced to abandon this plan. Refugees wanting to leave the country needed to be persistent, have good contacts, and most importantly be extremely wealthy. Many hoped to board a ship or boat for Britain or North Africa from the French Atlantic coast. Casablanca was a sought-after destination. Locals with boats in the south Atlantic ports seized the opportunity to make vast amounts of money on the back of these desperate refugees. Many of those who were exploited by racketeers did in fact manage to reach safety. More than ten thousand people, mostly civilians, left France via Saint-Jean-de-Luz. More than half of them were Jews.[56] Spain offered another possible escape route. After crossing the country to Portugal, refugees hoped to take a ship from Lisbon.

It was time-consuming and costly to acquire the necessary documentation and visas which allowed access to a departing ship or permission to cross the frontier into Spain. Affluent French Jews who had planned emigration as soon as it became clear in May that France was likely to be invaded were among those who attempted to escape in this way. Some had followed the government to Bordeaux with the intention of accompanying it to London or North Africa. When it became apparent that the government would not

be leaving France, they were forced to organize their own departure.[57] Thus
in the period after 17 July, long queues of luxury cars waited at the border to
Spain at Hendaye around 200 km (124 miles) to the south of Bordeaux. These
refugees were subject to extremely long waits with no guarantee of making
it across the frontier into Spain. The barrier was rarely raised throughout the
day, allowing very few people through, as Downing recounted:

> All about us there were people in various conditions of relief or anxiety,
> because while a lot of us were British or American and feeling happy at last in
> the care of our governments, there were many other nationalities whose
> chances of getting out of France were slight. Many of the French were already
> turning back, grim faced and haggard.[58]

Until 15 June it had been relatively easy to get to Lisbon, but just days before
the request for armistice, the Portuguese authorities decided that their country was saturated and would only admit those with visas. By this time, Spain
was also becoming increasingly hostile to these floods of arrivals. After the
closure of the Spanish border, with the only large port in the Unoccupied
Zone, Marseilles offered refugees the best opportunity for all of those wishing
to escape from France. From June 1940 it became a place of congregation for
all those who feared persecution from both the Germans and Vichy

Choosing Exile Abroad

French citizens were unlikely to contemplate foreign exile unless they were
Jews. Even those fortunate enough to have gained passage on one of the last
boats agonized about their departure until the very last minute.

> Shortly before we sailed, some strange things happened on board among the
> French. Some of them were seized with a crise de conscience. They decided
> that they could not and would not leave their France. One man complained,
> 'It's a great drama! My wife does not want to leave France and I don't want to
> either.' He was in great anguish. Soon afterwards a launch brought a few more
> passengers on board, and took the Cains [this couple] back to France. And not
> only them, but several other people. When it came to the point, they decided,
> for better or for worse, to stay in their own country. There had been several
> crises de conscience like that among the French. The first night we were on
> board there was a French woman who insisted on being taken ashore; she
> came back to the ship the next morning; but that afternoon, she went back to
> France again—this time for good.[59]

Arguments against leaving the country could be compelling. There were practical issues relating to employment and income. Could the whole family leave? What would become of those left behind? Who would look after their property in their absence?[60] Those who did try to leave only tended to do so if they had serious reason to fear for their lives. Even gaining passage provided no certainty of safe arrival: harbours were often heavily mined, and ships were subject to German bombing.

In the face of such difficulties, for the majority of refugees trapped in southern and central France, exile abroad could not realistically be envisaged. In this context, it is perhaps remarkable that any French people joined de Gaulle. His speeches were little heard despite having been broadcast by the BBC repeatedly from 18 June onwards and being reproduced in certain local newspapers. A few individuals had no hesitation whatsoever in seizing the opportunity to leave the country. They refused to remain in France under German occupation and were determined to withdraw their support for a government that could make a deal with the Germans. Raymond Aron was among those who immediately decided to join de Gaulle in London—the fact that he was Jewish was evidently a key factor in his decision. His withdrawal south with his regiment had brought him to his home in Toulouse:

My friends ... who had not been called up for one reason or another, had already taken position against the Marshal in favour of the General whose appeal they had heard ...

I discussed the decision we should take with my wife. Should I remain in France or leave for England which we thought would carry on the fight ... Neither Marshal Pétain nor Pierre Laval would convert to National Socialism, but a defeated France, reconciled with the Third Reich, or subjugated by it, would have no room for Jews.

We envisaged two possible steps. Either I could stay at my post with my regiment and wait for demobilization which would probably follow the armistice ... or I could immediately head for England and enlist in General de Gaulle's troops.[61]

On 23 June he took a train to Bayonne and then on to Saint-Jean-de-Luz where he embarked on a Polish boat. René Cassin, the lawyer and statesman, was also on board. Both men later played a crucial role in the France Libre movement.

Most rank and file soldiers on the roads were unlikely to have heard de Gaulle's appeal. Few had any way of joining him in London even if they had wanted to. The exhaustion of the war made some unreceptive to de Gaulle's calls to carry on the fight.

'Go ahead and fight you bastard! You are sitting on your backside in comfort and you want others to go on getting killed . . . '

These were soldiers talking but the locals and the refugees agreed. The troops and the civilians had had enough. They wanted peace at any price.[62]

In the north of the country, a number of mothers, after hearing of de Gaulle's broadcast, persuaded their sons to leave from Brest on the last boats heading for England in spite of discouragement from certain officers.[63] On the Isle de Sein, off the coast of Brittany, all the male inhabitants left en masse to join de Gaulle but their exceptional situation—a predominantly fishing community equipped with appropriate transport—was a major enabling factor. Those on the other side of the country were less disposed to make such a move. Marie-Madeleine Fourcade recalled the atmosphere near the French Basque regions in the foothills of the Pyrenees:

> For the first time since the fourteenth century, Béarn felt the boots of the invader, but the youth of the area hesitated to cross the mountains to answer General de Gaulle's call. Painful discussions divided families. Relieved that their sons had escaped the rounding up of prisoners, parents forbade the slightest gesture of revolt. In all good faith, people believed that they could survive under the boots of the Germans. And anyway, 'the Germans will go home as soon as they have beaten the English, it's only a question of months . . . '[64]

Unlike de Gaulle, most French people did not have the information, knowledge, and foresight required to make a decision to leave at this stage, nor did they have the means to do so. No propaganda had prepared people for the possible continuation of the battle outside France. To join de Gaulle they were obliged to leave their social or family milieu. The first volunteers were relatively limited in number and fitted into Kensington Olympia, an exhibition hall in central London.[65] Those who presented themselves there were predominantly young men, with few family commitments. Others tended to be those who already had some experience of foreign travel, and had perhaps even visited Britain on a previous occasion.[66] But even those French servicemen who had been evacuated to England at Dunkirk were not keen to stay. They did everything they could to get home as soon as possible in order to be reunited with their loved ones in the face of the unknown dangers of German occupation.[67] Michel Junot noted this when he met some soldiers who had been caught up in the events at Dunkirk.

> All were very judgemental about the English and none wanted to stay in England after trying to be evacuated from Dunkirk some ten days earlier. Many among them were Jews, however, who a year later would give anything

to be able to find themselves outside the country, but such were the illusions we were under in the middle of June 1940 as much with regard to the outcome of the war as with regard to the fate awaiting French Jews.[68] A number of French personalities passed through London to reach destinations outside Europe. Few were tempted to abandon their plans to go to the US in favour of staying on with de Gaulle. As Elizabeth de Miribel put it, 'In June 1940, London was not a town where you arrived, but one from which you left.'[69] Even French citizens who had long been resident in London chose to return to France rather than join de Gaulle. De Miribel again: 'Some believed they could continue the battle in North Africa. Others were convinced that England would be rapidly invaded and defeated. The consciences of certain people were torn, should they return home and protect their family or stay to join a rearguard battle?'[70] In the three months after de Gaulle's appeal from London, he had still only managed to attract three generals (all from the colonies), one admiral, three colonels, and a few junior officers.[71]

Reaching the Unoccupied Zone

Thousands of refugees who were displaced in the south learnt with relief that the places they had reached were located in the Unoccupied Zone. Believing that the war was over, many imagined that they would soon be able to return to their homes and were anxious to do so as soon as the opportunity presented itself. The nature of their reception in the host areas had an important bearing on their later reactions to events and was very varied. While some felt they received a rather ambivalent, sometimes close to hostile welcome, others found that they were well looked after. Departments and towns were initially completely overwhelmed by the unexpected scale of arrivals. Some communes saw their population triple, even quadruple—an increase which would have strained existing facilities even in peacetime.

The efficiency of the structures that were put into place to accommodate refugees largely depended on the extent of advance planning undertaken by host departments. Local authorities worried that they would not have the necessary resources to cope. Prefects had instructed mayors that evacuees should be seen as a reserve army of labour for use in the positions that had been left vacant by mobilized soldiers.[72] In return for their labour, officials could promise evacuees free lodging in requisitioned apartments, hotel rooms, and rooms in private homes. Refugees would qualify for the state benefits available to anyone who was displaced from their normal place of residence. While French refugees would be given cash, foreign refugees would only receive help 'in kind' of food and accommodation.[73] Food was to be provided from local sources. The potential influx of large numbers of refugees also led to concerns that disease might easily spread among both refugees and local populations. In response to this, the authorities arranged for the provision of medical help to tend to the arrivals as a high priority.[74] Doctors were recruited to inspect refugee centres to ensure standards of hygiene were maintained at an appropriate level.[75]

Officials were also worried about the impact of the evacuated populations on the morale of local communities.[76] It was thought that their presence might create panic amongst those more distant from the battleground and less aware of what was going on. The possibility that political activists or spies could be among the refugees compounded fears that the arrivals might have the potential to stir up politically inspired disturbances. It was decided therefore that for reasons of security, as they arrived, the refugees should be continuously moved on to prevent their numbers from becoming too concentrated in certain areas. To avoid overcrowding, certain authorities made arrangements for the close supervision of refugee arrivals. On reaching railway stations or road blocks, it was anticipated that they would be immediately sent on to reception centres to be divided into small groups. They would then be allocated to communes widely dispersed across the department. In this way, they could more easily be controlled and kept under close surveillance.

On 17 May the prefect of the Tarn-et-Garonne warned the mayors in his department that the arrival of large numbers of refugees was imminent.

> For several weeks you have been preparing to receive these people and I know, both from what I have heard from my collaborators and from what I have seen for myself, that with the help of your local populations, you have managed to prepare sufficient accommodation.
>
> I am counting on you ... from today to make arrangements in whatever ways are available to you to feed our refugees as they arrive and ensure that they continue to have enough to eat subsequently.[77]

It soon became apparent that officials had grossly underestimated the numbers involved and plans that had been laid to deal with a reasonably organized evacuation were not equipped to cope with the waves of refugees arriving as a result of the German offensive. Authorities struggled to cope and appealed to local populations for additional help. On 23 May the regional paper *La Depêche de Toulouse* printed a report on the plight of the refugees which was designed to incite volunteers to come forward.

The convoys of refugees follow on and on without stopping ... In the face of their immense misfortune, the administrative authorities with the collaboration of the local authorities are trying to meet their needs. Everyone must help them in this demanding task. We once again appeal to our fellow citizens to relieve, in so far as is possible, the miseries of those who knock at our door. Letters that we have already received suggest that there is a high degree of solidarity across the region. Everywhere people are getting organized to provide shelter, medical care, and food for these unfortunate people ... Let everyone consider what they could be going through if they were in the same situation as these refugees! Let all our charitable feelings of generosity unite in this fraternal gesture. We are confident that this call, like preceding ones, will be heard.

Refugees who arrived by train were the easiest to organize. Prefects telegraphed ahead to advise of train departures and the numbers involved. They could not always accurately predict the arrival times of the trains, these were often disrupted, but such information did make it possible for the destination prefect to anticipate the numbers involved. Where possible, refugees would be dealt with on the day of their arrival, but if trains were late they would be put in temporary shelters overnight, before being allocated more permanent accommodation the following day. Those who were travelling independently, on the road, were more difficult to manage. They tended to stop according to their own inclination, and slipped through the controls, short-cutting official arrangements, finding accommodation as and when they were able to. Arrivals such as these were much more difficult for the authorities to monitor. Without a paper trail, many remained invisible to them. Such individuals were only identified if they appeared at one of the reception centres for a meal or chose to sleep in one of the shelters that were made available to them. The detailed registration procedures imposed on refugees slowed their progress and created long tailbacks on the roads and queues at all the reception centres.

By June 1940, large towns, swamped with refugees, were struggling to maintain services. Dorgelès's description of the situation in Cahors gives a sense of the scale of the problem:

The old town, ordinarily such a peaceful place, was choked with the volume of people within its walls. Refugees were stuffed all over the place: in large houses, public buildings, requisitioned homes and factories. At night they were everywhere, sleeping in doorways, curled up on pavements. The more privileged were sleeping in their cars. They stretched out on bales of straw and cooked out in the open. You would have thought that we had returned to the era of the invasions when entire peoples fled. Cars now replaced the peasant carts which in olden times would have formed a rampart around the encampment.[78]

André Morize, who also spent time in Cahors, estimated that the population of the city grew from its normal population of thirteen thousand to reach a total of between sixty and seventy thousand.[79] In the light of this kind of overcrowding, as refugees continued to arrive, towns attempted to limit new arrivals. In Béziers, road blocks and check posts were set up on the outskirts of the towns and refugees were permitted access only if they already had accommodation arranged. Similar arrangements were established in most of the large towns in the south, including Narbonne, Carcassonne, and Toulouse where refugees had to give proof of accommodation arrangements before being allowed into the city.[80] In Montauban,

> Those arriving by road were assembled together by the police and then sent to a reception post where they were given petrol tickets and then sent to neighbouring departments of Ariège, Hérault, or Haute-Garonne. Montauban had become so crowded that officials were placed along the external boulevards of the town and only those who had exceptional reasons for being allowed to do so were authorized entry into the city centre. Thousands of cars, lorries, bicyclists among others were checked by police. The cars belonging to civilians were put in parking areas and their occupants were taken to reception centres where they were fed and put up for the night before being sent on their way the next day. Those who arrived by train were taken to the town hall and fed and then also taken to the centres. Other arrangements were made for the large numbers of soldiers who turned up.[81]

Some officials proved particularly competent at managing this unexpected influx and improvised arrangements with considerable effect. Dorgelès was impressed with the way in which the deputy mayor of Cahors, 'the former minister, Anatole de Monzie', rose to the occasion.

> In his career he had held many posts; here he was holding the least expected one: Mayor of the refugees. He excelled at it as he had previously at the Ministry of Education or Public Works. For days he has not left this room. He gives orders, he imagines solutions, and he improvises. His only arm in this battle is his telephone, 'Hello! Hello!' He calls all the mayors in the canton, wakes up the local chatelaines, and scolds the hoteliers. He needs rooms, at all costs, that is to say for no cost at all. And he finds them . . . Then, pleased with himself, he throws his beret into the air in a familiar gesture.[82]

Accommodation on offer to the refugees varied from commune to commune. In some villages people came forward in response to the appeals and offered to take in two or three refugees. In these cases, refugees were asked to group together into families and friendship groups so that they could be allocated accordingly. In other communes, the refugees were all grouped together in one particular place, and chosen by their eventual hosts. Sometimes they were simply given a list of addresses and asked to find their own way. For some of the refugees this arrangement was only a temporary one, until such time as more permanent arrangements could be put into place. Understandably, some villagers were reticent to take complete strangers into their homes, at least at first. Refugees invariably found this process to be a difficult one. They felt themselves to be an awkward intrusion on the calm and peaceful life of their new hosts and often they sensed a certain hostility. Their embarrassment at their situation added to their sense of vulnerability. To quote the experiences of one Belgian family in Toulouse:

> When we arrived in the pink city, we were directed to the main square 'La Capitole'. Once we got there, I really felt like I was in a cattle market. We were spread out across the square and the people of Toulouse pointed out who they would take. 'I'll take that family there.' That's how we were taken on by the family who were actually very nice.[83]

Officially, for reasons of security, once refugees had been registered in a certain commune they were obliged to remain in the same place until they were informed otherwise. They were only allowed to move to another area if they had attained special permission to do so from the prefectoral authorities. Instructions to this effect were published in the papers and posters from the mayors appeared around the commune reiterating this advice.

Despite the difficult circumstances of the exodus and the problems relating to food supplies in several areas, the worst fears of the authorities were not realized. There was no outbreak of disease and there was little evidence of unrest in stopover towns and reception areas. Some reception centres evidently fell short of providing comfort as *La Depêche de Toulouse* reported on 19 June:

> I've seen these reception centres, simple covered enclosures where straw spread on the floor serves for people to sleep on. On improvised cookers, inadequate amounts of food are prepared. Admittedly, our soldiers may not expect any more than this level of comfort, but these refugees are generally women, children, the sick, and the elderly. They do not all have the same capacity to cope with this kind of situation.

Administrative reports, on the other hand, betray a clear satisfaction with the manner in which they had succeeded in stretching their facilities to cater to demand. When reflecting back on arrangements in Castelsarrasin, 30 km (19 miles) from Montauban, the sub-prefect's report of 30 August 1940 expresses a real sense of achievement and pride in his local community:

All refugees were provided with shelter. The first arrivals were allocated empty houses. The last arrivals were the least well served. Nonetheless, the local population demonstrated total devotion to them and everyone who had a room, or even a spare bed, took in refugees.

Most school premises which were not already occupied by the military were put at the disposal of refugees. Dormitories were organized in certain buildings which also served as reception centres for those refugees who were passing through. The warm season was a major bonus and facilitated the problem of accommodation. But the area was completely saturated.[84]

This attitude chimes in with Rod Kedward's assertion that managing to cater to the needs of the refugees became a matter of local pride, 'for a local victory won was more than a little compensation for the larger defeat'.[85] This dynamic was effectively mobilized by Pétain. By focusing on the human misery experienced by refugees in his speeches, Pétain not only won over the refugees themselves, but he also succeeded in equating the humanitarian activities of host communities with a demonstration of support for his cause. This meant that, whether they liked it or not, those involved in aiding displaced populations became associated with the patriotic appeal that Pétain represented.[86] When it came to repatriation, this would be played out even more explicitly.

Refugees, for their part, once they had found somewhere to settle, at least in the short term, found that feelings of relief were mixed with those of exhaustion. Many had become separated from families or travelling companions and experienced a sense of isolation. The friendliness of local communities could not always offset the fact that they were dealing with strangers and found themselves in unfamiliar surroundings. The trauma of their journey made it difficult for them to make much sense of what had happened to them. Soldiers awaited demobilization, anxious to get home to their families. In this way, most of those who were caught up in the exodus—host communities, refugees, and soliders—were prepared to accept the armistice without question.

Meanwhile, the immediate priority of the new Vichy government was to discourage any further movement around the country. Refugees were notified by the authorities that they should refrain from any attempt to commence their journey home until formal arrangements for their repatriation could be put into place. The demarcation line established by the Germans almost immediately began to function as a serious frontier between the two zones. The true nature of this division across the country soon became apparent both to the refugees and to the Vichy authorities. Returning people to their homes was likely to be much more difficult than anyone had originally anticipated.

PART III

Home or Exile

5

Summer–Autumn 1940

Lamalou ... with its numerous hotels and family pensions had become a
meeting point concentrating an army of refugees ... The most remarkable
thing was the harmony which reigned in this apparent mess. The people of
the exodus who arrived like wrecks, took on strength and courage, of
which they needed much because many of them had no news of their
mobilized husbands, brothers, sons, etc.—at best Germans prisoners of
war, at worst killed in combat. They talked amongst themselves, surmising
as to when they would return to their home towns and villages, most of
which were under German occupation ... Pre-written formulaic postcards
brought crumbs of news of their loved ones and their abandoned homes.
The demarcation line made Occupied France and Belgium seem as far off
as they were vague. Nonetheless, little by little, people went home. But it
was their own choice; the villagers never made them feel they wanted to be
rid of them ... On the contrary, everything took place in a sort of sad good
humour, a compassionate and decent dignity, in a climate of solidarity in
the face of an ordeal, that restrictions and passionate divisions had not yet
undermined.[1]

Stanley Hoffmann, Témoignage'

A witness, then a child living in the small village in the Pyrenees, wrote the
following account of the departure of the refugees from Trie-sur-Blaise:

In July those going to other areas of the non-Occupied Zone departed. The
proper process of repatriation took place in August. The people from Verdun
who were staying with me left on 6 August by train. The Belgians who were
with my grandmother went to Lourdes on 8 August and from there were taken
back to Belgium in coaches. Some wrote back that the return journey was
much harder than the exodus had been. Departures were spread out across the
whole of August. Some stayed much longer, notably the foreign Jews who lived
off American subsidies until they were rounded up and we never heard from
them again. People from Alsace and Lorraine were also around for most of the

war, leaving in 1945 and often returning soon after to settle in the village definitively. Others married or found work and stayed. Their accents and hair colours are now the only witnesses to this gigantic human emigration which for two months emptied entire provinces...My parents also talked of leaving; Heaven knows where we would have ended up if it were not for the Pyrenees.[2]

Once civilians had been able to satisfy their immediate physical need for rest, their thoughts turned to concern for separated loved ones. Impatience grew for news that the appropriate arrangements for their return had been put into place. By mid-July, repatriation was in full swing, and by the autumn, the majority of French people had reached their homes. A significant minority remained in exile until 1944–5. Some were destined never to return home, either because they emigrated permanently or because they perished as a result of German brutality during reprisals against the Resistance or subsequent to deportation.

The Anguish of Separation

The main preoccupation for the majority of people in the early summer of 1940, wherever they found themselves, was to be reunited with other family members. Women separated from mobilized sons, husbands, fathers, and brothers anxiously waited for news of their whereabouts, fearing the worst. The papers were full of notices from separated members of families seeking to find one another, along with those trying to recover possessions lost en route. Children who had been handed over to the French military convoys by well-meaning parents were often the most difficult to trace. Throughout the summer and autumn of 1940, local papers turned over their small ads columns to those seeking lost family members. Notices appeared about missing or lost children, separated couples, and lost elderly relatives. There were also numerous appeals on the radio. The *Courrier du centre*, for example, published the following on 4 July 1940:

An inhabitant of Perreux is looking for his 8½ -year-old son who went missing in Étampes.

A family from Le Mans is looking for 6-month-old Madeleine Dorée, 9-year-old Jean Dorée, and 10-year-old Francine Dorée who were picked up by a tanker between Poitiers and Limoges.

The mayor of Crèvecœur in Seine-et-Marne is looking for his 60-year-old wife, lost on 16 June on the bridge at Bonny-sur-Loire and seen that evening at the Place de Sully... [3]

Communication difficulties handicapped families who were trying to trace lost infants or other close relatives. Post office staff had often fled their posts during the exodus, leaving the telecommunications network unmanned.[4] Regions where the population had increased twofold, sometimes more, had seen a corresponding increase in telecommunications. Postal services were unreliable and telephoning was virtually impossible. Most post offices were open to the public by early August, but sending letters, parcels, or money orders across the demarcation line was strictly forbidden.[5] Families were forced to use pre-printed cards in order to communicate which provided limited scope to express any news short of information about serious illness or deaths. As the extent and scale of the disaster gradually became apparent, the authorities worked to try and bring together families who had become separated in the confusion. For some families, the laborious registration bureaucracy that had been forced onto refugees on their arrival proved an effective means of putting people in touch with one another as the authorities were able to cross-reference their refugee registers and reunite families.[6]

Parents refused to contemplate returning home until they had news. They wanted to remain close to the places where they had last caught a glimpse of their loved ones or stay in areas that had been discussed as possible destinations during the journey. Some unhappy families were obliged to wait for months before

13. Families check lists of names hoping to find mention of lost children or parents. Many families were reunited in this way, others had to wait long weeks before they had news of missing children and other relatives.

they had news of one another. From 1940 to 1942 the Red Cross tirelessly worked to reunite ninety thousand children with their parents. Parisian children are estimated to have been about 25 per cent of those who were lost.[7]

Other families took a different tack, deciding that returning home to their fixed address—the one which was known to all the family members—might be the only way they were likely to get news of missing relatives. It seemed reasonable to expect that those they were separated from would be equally anxious for news and that they might also be struggling to make their way home. Many women believed that demobilization was imminent and that if they had survived, wherever they were, their men would probably make for the family home. Simone de Beauvoir put it thus:

> When the clauses [of the armistice] were divulged on 21 June, I was mainly interested in the one concerning prisoners. It was not very clear, or at least I wanted to find it rather obscure. It stipulated that the soldiers interned in Germany would remain there until the hostilities came to an end. But surely the Germans were not going to take hundreds of thousands of prisoners that they had rounded up on the roads back with them. They would have to feed them all, and to what advantage? No, they would all be sent home. Many rumours were circulating. Soldiers hidden in basements and in the thickets had managed to avoid falling into the hands of the occupiers. They were reappearing in an improvised way, dressed in civilian clothes, in their villages, and at their farms. Perhaps Sartre had managed to find a way of reaching Paris?[8]

Soldiers, like those mentioned here, were appearing everywhere and they too set about contacting their families and trying to trace their fellow soldiers in order to acquire demobilization papers. One woman wrote in her diary on 25 June 1940: 'Unarmed soldiers are wandering around aimlessly. In our only local paper a long column publishes messages not just from families seeking one another, but even from officers who would like to find their companies or regiments! What have we come to?'[9] Many of those who had escaped being taken prisoner were directed to regrouping centres. Montauban was one of these.[10] In these camps they were forced to wait their turn for repatriation like everyone else. Some were able to join their families in their places of refuge. Monsieur Fee, a soldier who had been part of the retreat, found himself first in Montauban and then in Toulouse. There he was contacted by his wife who had found shelter in the Charente with their young daughter. Fee was able to use the document issued by the mayor of her commune which confirmed her status as a refugee, to persuade his officer in command to release him so he could join her there.[11]

Concern to be reunited with loved ones was understandably the over-riding preoccupation for the majority of those who were away from their homes and was to become a lasting legacy of the exodus. Many had to wait many long weeks or months before they found missing children or learnt that relatives had perished on the road. One hundred thousand civilians are estimated to have died during the exodus.[12] News of deaths, casualties, and those who had been taken prisoner was slow to arrive. Mistaken identities added to the torture of separated families who sometimes found they had followed up leads to missing family members only to find that they had been given the wrong information. Such dramas continued well into the post-war period. For those who had been able to travel together or who were successfully reunited, concerns then turned to other family members, those who had been called up or left behind. This preoccupation with finding young or vulnerable members of the family distracted them from the events of the war. Believing that peace was imminent, many took little active interest in what was going on politically and despite disappointment at defeat, the majority of civilians thought that they had done their patriotic duty and were now released to focus exclusively on their own immediate personal concerns which for the majority meant returning home.

While anxiety for loved ones was the most likely reason to drive refugees home, other factors also came into play. Many had little confidence in local authorities who appeared overwhelmed by the logistics of assuring a steady food supply for their extra visitors. These populations were particularly receptive to propaganda claiming that life was returning to normal in Paris and fostering the idea that food supplies might be better there. Although they were advised not to head home immediately, the Parisian and national press under the control of the Germans reproduced numerous articles designed to reassure the population and encourage them to go home. From late June, articles appeared demonstrating that life in Paris was getting back to normal. *Le Matin* carried the following front-page headline on 19 June: 'Paris remains Paris, and we can announce that shops have now reopened; water, gas, and electricity supplies have also been reconnected.' These reassurances were welcomed by those refugees who were struggling financially and were anxious to get home to their jobs and get on with their lives. Announcements which seemed to promise a return to normality had a compelling resonance among traumatized and displaced populations who longed for their nightmare to come to an end. Returning to a familiar environment offered the first step towards getting back to normal again.

Fear that their homes and possessions might have been damaged or pillaged by passing armies and refugees was a further worry which added to their sense of urgency. In areas where the Germans had invaded, and which were destined to remain a part of the Occupied Zone, there seemed little point in staying put. They might just as well be under occupation in their own homes as among strangers.

Early Returns

Logistical problems meant that the majority of refugees could not be officially repatriated immediately. At the end of June, the demarcation line was still far from being definitive and German authorities were absorbed with installing their armies of occupation along the line. It took some time before the demarcation line was properly established and had begun functioning as an active frontier.[13] This transitional period before the administrative structures of the Occupation had been completely put into place, provided an opening for some persistent refugees to get home. Indeed, at this point the Germans were evidently prepared to help ferry people around the country. Simone de Beauvoir was among those who refused to wait for news of official repatriation arrangements: 'For the last four days I have not been able to stay in the same place. I have persuaded myself that Sartre could make an impromptu return to Paris and in any case once there I might get news of him. And I wanted to see Paris under Occupation; I was bored.'[14]

The main handicap facing those who wanted to get home was that train services were not running and petrol had now become almost impossible to find. Car drivers therefore found themselves trapped, dependent on the goodwill of the French or German authorities to help them out, if they were to have any hope of making an early departure. As André Morize recounted, in Cahors, people were extremely resourceful in their efforts to acquire petrol.

> Petrol was all-important. After interminable waits in the prefecture, refugees able to produce all their papers, and state officials who could prove they were on official business, managed to acquire 5 litres...We all discussed the question of petrol between us as if we were connoisseurs talking about our wine cellars and our most precious wines in better days. There were incredible tricks, infinite machinations which were used to procure a small container of this most valuable of liquids. The army still possessed a little, and beautiful

women headed for the local barracks in the evening with the mission of acquiring 5 litres of contraband petrol that they carried home with them as if it were champagne. In an obscure corner of the town a sort of 'bootlegging' business appeared which the police soon put a stop to.[15]

Desperation even pushed some normally respectable citizens to steal fuel, as Madame Perrot recounts. Camping in a barn in a property close to the Châteauroux airfield, some boys in the party managed to pinch some petrol left there by the French soldiers in retreat, before the arrival of the Germans.[16]

De Beauvoir, having decided that she could wait no longer and needed to find a way to get home, managed to gain a lift with some Dutch friends on 28 June. The party did not get far, however. Although the Germans had been distributing 25 litres of petrol to those who were prepared to queue for it, the Dutchman, impatient to get going, had decided to leave with just 10 litres in his tank, convinced, wrongly as it proved, that he would easily be able to stock up with more on the way. They first came to a stop at Le Mans, where, after queuing among hundreds of refugees, he managed to acquire 5 litres, but this did not go far. They soon again found themselves stranded in a small village. At this point, de Beauvoir decided to abandon her friends and to attempt to make her own way home. Managing to hitch a ride on a German lorry full of other refugees, she eventually reached Mantes, just 40 km (25 miles) from Paris. For the final leg, she jumped aboard a Red Cross van.[17] An elderly woman also on the lorry to Mantes had commented thus on their German drivers: 'She said that for two days the lorry drivers had stuffed them with cigarettes, food, and champagne. They were really nice and did not appear to be following orders but seemed to want to help out in a spontaneous way.'[18]

This kind of friendly behaviour marked these early contacts between Germans and French civilians. The Germans were frequently helpful to lost and stranded refugees, picking them up on convoys and distributing petrol where they could. Their amiability was no accident. Hitler was well aware of the importance of these crucial first impressions and set out to win the trust of the French people with the full force of all his propaganda machine behind him. In areas which came under occupation the Germans took care not to frighten people more than was necessary. If the invasion in May 1940 had rekindled memories of German atrocities for the French population, these memories were no less present in the minds of the Germans. Hitler had learnt a bitter lesson from the disastrous impression created by the atrocities committed during the First World War. Acutely aware of the manner in which the Allies had propagandized German brutality so successfully to influence public opinion and undermine the German occupying forces attempting to keep these territories under control, the Nazi leadership was determined to avoid making the same mistakes.[19] Indeed a good deal was at stake. Anxious to minimize civilian resistance, the Germans wanted at all costs to prevent the type of guerrilla warfare that had marked their previous period of occupation (and which would again become increasingly widespread from 1942 once the French Resistance was organized). Hence, German military units were all given strict orders to behave impeccably and any soldier guilty of inappropriate behaviour was brought to trial. Hitler personally ordered the Wehrmacht in the clearest of terms on 7 July 1940 to 'exercise restraint in their dealings with the population of the occupied enemy territories as befits a German soldier'. He further warned that soldiers who committed 'punishable acts' against the population would face 'ruthless prosecution, in serious cases even the death penalty!'[20] This approach, incidentally, did not apply in Eastern Europe.

Propaganda was used in an attempt to humanize the Germans and reassure French populations in the Occupied Zone. Posters appeared depicting a smiling German soldier with a child in his arms with another two children curiously looking on (see Illustration 14). Press reports also sought to reassure the population that none of the rumours about the atrocities were true. The front page of Le Matin on 22 June denied some of the more alarmist rumours: 'No, the people of Paris have not been molested...Rumours have spread among evacuated populations, particularly those on the banks of the Loire affirming that the Germans were deporting young people, torturing women, and maltreating children...If only people would stop brainwashing us with these supposed barbaric acts.' The often total absence of French authorities played into their hands. Their apparent failure to assure basic supplies in certain areas offered the Germans an invaluable opening to bring succour and relief to distressed populations. The Germans did not hesitate to take advantage of this propaganda opportunity by distributing tracts along the following lines:

> Poor French people, see how your government and its prefects have abandoned you, how they have lied to you and presented us as barbarians, raping women and massacring men, when we are all ready to help you even if the armistice conventions stipulate that the French authorities should also stay in place. But since they are not doing anything for you, the German army will come to your aid.[21]

14. This propaganda poster urges: 'Abandoned populations, put your trust in German soldiers!'

In numerous communities the Germans were able to appear as generous victors offering food to abandoned French citizens. Much was made in Nazi propaganda of examples of German soldiers shepherding people back to their homes.

Organizing Repatriation

Officially, the Germans took a similar line in their attitude to repatriation. Claiming that the chaos of the exodus was the responsibility of the French, it was up to them to put the situation to rights. Article 16 of the armistice required the French government to organize the return of refugees to the Occupied territories with the agreement of the competent German services.[22] In reality, the Germans also saw repatriation as a high priority on a number of levels. They sought to help French civilians return home not just

15. These unarmed German soldiers on foot appear to have nothing better to do than help these heavily burdened refugees. This kind of contrived scene was a favourite of the German propaganda services.

to gain their confidence but also to reduce the likelihood of incidents of disorder and enable them to establish control with a minimum of manpower and maximum speed. It would also help them to achieve one of their primary objectives which was to harness the French economy to their own war effort as rapidly as the situation would allow. This required the return of civilians to their homes, both in the capital and in other areas of the Occupied Zone, so that the war factories could immediately be put back to work. Paradoxically, however, on occasion they also had no hesitation in slowing down the process in order to humiliate the French still further and show their superiority. In these early weeks, the Germans sometimes prevented people from returning to the Occupied Zone in order to keep numbers under control so as to facilitate the organizing of food supplies. This also enabled them to sustain their image as generous benefactors in contrast to the increasingly overwhelmed French authorities in the south. The newly installed Vichy regime therefore became anxious to organize repatriation as a matter of urgency. Aware of the importance of first impressions, it was keen to show its efficiency in getting the French back to their homes both to win public support and because it imagined that this would enable it to prove itself as an effective partner to the Germans. In this way, the desire to return home on the part of huge numbers of refugees was matched by an equally urgent and parallel desire on the part of the French authorities who had everything to gain from a quick and smooth repatriation of the displaced populations.

The authorities were determined that the return home would be a more organized and efficient process than leaving had been for the majority of those involved. The disastrous circumstances of departure were now used to discredit the regime which had been in power[23] and Vichy felt itself under considerable pressure from the Germans to show it could succeed in reverse where the previous regime had failed. Therefore, rather than dragging their feet and taking advantage of what might have proved an opportunity to resist the German invaders by making it more difficult for them to establish themselves, the French authorities immediately set out to repatriate as quickly as they could as an indication of their goodwill, a pattern which was to foreshadow more serious collaboration. The high concentration of refugees in certain areas was also seen as a possible threat to public order. Authorities were already stretched and if these populations were allowed to go hungry or remain in difficult circumstances for extended periods of time, officials feared the consequences. The most pressing priority for the Vichy authorities was to take stock of the situation and to ensure that food supplies reached areas where crisis might be looming[24] and where repatriation, therefore, seemed to be a more urgent problem than elsewhere. Officials were instructed by the Vichy ministries to calculate the numbers involved and also to indicate where the refugees came from; they set about attempting to collate these figures. On 28 July the prefect of the Tarn-et-Garonne sent a request to all the mayors in his department asking them to inform him of the numbers of refugees that were present in their communes.[25]

Despite the often genuine efforts to calculate the numbers of refugees, it is impossible to know with any certainty the number of people who found themselves displaced. Figures provided by the local authorities were frequently massaged upwards to allow them an extra margin when it came to handouts from central government for resources in food and heating.[26] Not all refugees had bothered to register and they often moved from place to place, searching for work or lost family members. However, the existing calculations give a sense of the scale of the problem. During a meeting held on 2 July 1940, the Ministry concerned with refugees put the number of refugees in the country at eight million, of which the vast majority—put at 6,200,000—were French. A further 1,800,000 were Belgian, and 150,000 were from Holland and Luxembourg. Of the French contingent almost a third—about two million—were believed to be Parisians; 800,000 were from the departments of Alsace and Lorraine, of which 550,000 had been evacuated under official evacuation procedures before 10 May 1940.[27] Three and a half million were thought to have taken refuge in each of the zones.[28] When the SNCF conducted its own count in August 1940 for the purposes of organizing appropriate transportation, their figures showed up strong concentrations of populations in certain areas.[29] The departments south of the demarcation line in the west and south-west of the country were unsurprisingly those most affected. According to these figures, the highest number of refugees was situated in the department of Creuse with more than three hundred thousand refugees; Dordogne and Corrèze were close behind with more than two hundred thousand each; Hérault, Tarn-et-Garonne, and the Haute Garonne had about one hundred thousand refugees each. The six Breton departments including Mayenne also each received nearly two hundred thousand refugees. These figures, though only approximate, provided adequate guidelines for the authorities to arrange transport to coincide with the apparent need.

Once the scale of the problem had been established, another crucial issue which had to be resolved before repatriation could seriously get underway was that of repairing war damage. The destruction of rail and road bridges by the French armies to prevent the Germans from catching up with them, and the numerous German bomb attacks, combined to bring chaos to the networks of communication across the country. Hundreds of bridges had been blown up, well over a thousand railway stations and hundreds of kilometres of railway had been destroyed. This was all in urgent need of repair, a process which now delayed the implementation of a repatriation plan. The disruption of the railways was compounded by the fact that many rail workers from Paris and surrounding regions had themselves been evacuated and had taken much of their material to the provinces with them. 'Of the thirty thousand rail workers in Paris and surrounding area, only five or six hundred have remained at my disposal,' explained Monsieur Barth, Head of Personnel for the SNCF on the front page of *Le Matin* on 22 June 1940. Pierre Girard, a regional head of the SNCF, was recalled to Paris from Clermont-Ferrand where he and his team had been evacuated. His experiences on this journey, which should have taken a matter of hours, indicate the scale of the problems faced by the railways. After leaving Clermont-Ferrand on 28 June, following numerous detours caused by damage to the line and persistent delays as well as administrative confusions created by the demands of the German military authorities, they finally arrived in Paris an incredible eight days later.[30]

Repatriation Begins

Eventually, from the end of June, a preliminary period of repatriation was put into place during which government officials and those employed in essential public services were to return home. The earliest trains were reserved for those who were considered to be vital to the reorganization of people's daily lives and the social fabric of the country. Some areas applied different priorities, but generally these included: those working in law and order (members of the police and gendarmerie, firefighters) or administration (government officials and public servants of all kinds), those essential to the economy (bankers and those employed in banking), those in sanitary work and responsible for the utilities (water, gas, and electricity), those in the medical sector (doctors, nurses, pharmacists, and health workers of all kinds), those in the food industry (agricultural workers, shopkeepers), those in industry (factory workers), and finally everyone else.[31] Prefects were urged to ensure that these orders be carried out to enable economic life in the Occupied territories to resume. The trains leaving Bordeaux on 18 July, for example, carried 1,700 railway workers, 728 workers at Peugeot, 450 aviation factory workers, 264 working in Air Liquide, 106 Electro-Mecanique.[32]

Despite clear instructions, many refugees who did not belong to the required categories refused to wait their turn and took their chances in trying to get home more quickly. But whereas earlier in the month many had managed to get home, as the German authorities took control of the transport system, it became more difficult to slip through. Once the Germans had secured their position on the demarcation line, it was virtually impossible for refugees to cross from the Unoccupied to the Occupied Zones without the appropriate documentation. Those refugees who ignored the advice of the authorities and set off to take their chances found themselves swelling the population of the already heaving and overcrowded towns and villages immediately to the south of the demarcation line.[33] As one relief worker observed: 'the Parisians have been authorized to return home but at Vierzon they are being turned back towards Châteauroux by the Germans. How can it be arranged to feed all these people and get around? There must be close to forty thousand refugees between Vierzon and Limoges.'[34] The possibility that the refugees might find themselves stuck en route in even worse circumstances with less access to food supplies and more uncomfortable conditions than they had experienced in their previous places of refuge led the authorities to counsel patience. The papers repeatedly urged refugees to stay where they were until it was their turn to leave.[35]

Lack of petrol meant that the main bulk of the return was arranged by train and eventually, from late July, displaced populations from across the country were invited to present themselves at train stations according to instructions published in the local press and notices posted at official buildings, town halls, and departmental prefectures. Although transport was free and refugees simply had to sign up or turn up on the day allocated to their home commune, they did have to ensure that they were carrying all the appropriate documentation. They needed their identity documents to prove that they lived in the departments concerned as well as a 'repatriation certificate' delivered by the mayor of their host commune.[36] A further visa issued by their local French military commandant made it possible for them to claim a transport voucher for rail travel or petrol if they were travelling by road. These certificates were non-transferable and applied only to those who were travelling. Luggage had to be kept to a minimum with an allocation of 30 kg (66 lb) per person. Bikes could be put in the luggage compartments on trains but many chose to leave them behind. The enormous volume of abandoned or lost possessions meant that most refugees returned with far less than they had brought with them.[37] Finally, they were also advised to take at least two days of food supplies, though this was not necessarily a guarantee that their journey would be completed in that time.

On 20 July the Director of Armistice Services announced that a certain number of daily trains would be departing from the Unoccupied Zone 'designated exclusively for refugees originating from the departments of Seine, Seine-et-Oise, and Seine-et-Marne',[38] thus the first priority was for the repatriation of refugees who lived in Paris and its surrounding departments.[39] In this way, during the three weeks between 26 July and 15 August, nearly a million Parisians, and those living in the suburbs or in the departments of the north, arrived at the three main train stations. *Paris Soir* reported that the number of people present in the department of the Seine had increased from 1,938,832 on 18 July to 2,350,000 on 1 August.[40] The local refugee offices in the Tarn-et-Garonne prioritized towns with the highest number of refugees for repatriation, and between 22 July and 22 August 4,000 Parisians returned home.[41] This focus on Paris soon led refugees from other areas to become impatient for news of when they too would have trains laid on for them. In Brittany, as soon as word got out that trains were working again, whether true or false, refugees descended on the stations without waiting for official confirmation from the town hall or the prefecture. The waves of refugees who came to Rennes in this way on 14 July were such that they had to be relocated to reception centres in the city and provided with food and accommodation until such time as their trains were arranged.[42] In most areas, the problem was not getting the refugees to turn up on their departure day, but persuading them to wait their turn.[43] Repatriation arrangements were progressively extended to the rest of the country and notably the Occupied Zone from 11 August. By the beginning of September, the line of demarcation was being crossed every day by thirty-five trains and four thousand cars, nearly all the major bridges which had been destroyed had been replaced with provisional ones, the roads had been cleared, and much of the railways repaired. Trains could circulate on about two-thirds of the normal peacetime network and the average speed of the express trains had climbed from 45 km (28 miles) an hour to 70 km (43 miles). In the same way, telecommunications were working almost normally.[44]

Refugees travelled along two main rail itineraries which were designed to ensure they passed through certain transit stations where they could stop regularly for food.[45] The obligatory two days' worth of food was supplemented by halts along the journey organized by the French railways and the local prefects. Hot milky coffee was distributed to children and the elderly.[46] But trains were crowded and uncomfortable. Georges Adrey described the rail trip which finally brought him home to Paris. He and his wife were able to catch a train from Étampes.

> At 15.00 travellers are allowed in to the station. We abandon our wheelbarrow on the road and passively follow the crowd. The organization is quite good. Those carrying bikes and prams go first. Priority is given to those accompanying children, the elderly, and the sick. But, when the most significant part of the crowd come in there is such a scuffle that the soldiers dealing with the organization are overwhelmed and don't know what to do next. People were screaming. People were shouting. Who should go first? All the savage instincts of the group are released; it is an example of egotism and brutality in all its ugliness. The Germans then lose patience and get angry. They hold up their bayonets and one of them even shoots into the air in an effort to intimidate the crowd and oblige it to back up though this has the opposite effect of increasing their nervousness.
>
> To prevent people storming the train, the Germans only let a few refugees on to the platform at a time. In the next moment, it is our turn to climb into the cattle wagons in which several families are already installed more or less comfortably. Then another storm of cries breaks out. There are vehement protests. The people who have already comfortably settled themselves in a nice seat are not pleased to see more people come aboard and are not keen to squeeze together to make room for them. 'There is no more room', they cry. 'Oh come on, of course there is', the others say; 'Just push over a bit, you are taking the space of four people!'

This painfully slow journey finally came to an end, arriving in Paris five or so hours later, just after curfew. Passengers had therefore to sleep rough in the station and were forbidden to leave the premises before 5 a.m.[47]

Conditions on trains were such that they failed to provide the most basic of necessities. On 5 September one refugee wrote to the prefect of Aveyron demanding that each goods wagon being used for the purposes of repatriation include a bucket or some appropriate installation for hygiene purposes.[48] Despite the fact that mayors in the communes had been asked to put together departure lists to aid efficiency, and that civilians were supposed to be informed two days before the departure of their train, in practice this arrangement rarely functioned properly.[49] Officials were obliged to let trains leave with empty carriages because they had no advance warning and were unable to organize refugees to catch the train. On other occasions, refugees lined the platforms expecting to embark on a train, only to find that when it arrived all their allocated places were already filled with refugees from earlier stops.[50] Controlling the traffic on the roads was seen as a high priority after the problems experienced some weeks before. Strict guidelines were implemented whereby vehicles were classified according to their average speed and allocated corresponding routes which were clearly signposted. Parking and stopping along these roads was prohibited with the threat of severe sanctions. As with those travelling by train, refugees returning home by car also had to ensure that their paperwork was in order, especially if they were intending to cross the demarcation line. The Repatriation Commission in Toulouse announced in the local press that departures would be spread over a two-week period. Petrol stations, each able to cater for 1,500 to 2,000 vehicles, where people could acquire food and petrol, were organized at regular intervals along their routes. Refugees had to present their certificates at each of these stops and these qualified them for an allocation of 5.5 litres of petrol.[51] Drivers were instructed to ensure that they had sufficient food supplies to enable them to reach their destination—that is, a day of supplies per 200 km (124 miles) by car—but they were to avoid taking any unnecessary stocks.[52] Refugees sometimes advertised for lifts in cars which had the space to accommodate them, and they were prepared to pay generously.[53] For many, however, the return trip was as uncomfortable as the outward journey had been.

> In August 1940 my father demobilized without so much as a scratch and joined us in Amélie-les-Bains . . . At the end of the month, he took his wife, son, and mother-in-law to Saint-Étienne and experienced a return journey exactly identical to that of departure: hellish heat, distant fires, hordes of unhappy people shuffling along bombed roads, dirt, sweat, dirty and sticky hands, hunger, thirst, endless stops, petrol shortages, those picked up to help them along the way, allowing them to rest for a few minutes, those who had to be left on the roadside with a pleading or resigned look to them.[54]

The Demarcation Line

As the repatriation process got underway, it soon became clear that control of the demarcation line was the key issue which would impact on the flow and efficiency of repatriation arrangements. French officials were frustrated by the fact that they were never told in advance of German intentions and refugees were frequently prevented from crossing it with no advance warning. 'One day the barrier was open at Moulins, to be closed in Vierzon; the next day it was opened in Vierzon to be closed in Moulins—constant vexations which were exasperating and paralysing.'[55] This procedure also led to the accumulation of horrendous jams. On 13 August repatriation was suspended and on 16 August the demarcation line was closed for an extended period.[56] Morize recalled the impact of these unpredictable closures:

> I remember how one morning at Saint-Pourcain, the last large market town before the frontier post at the bridge in Moulins, after several days of normal traffic flow, the commandant of Moulins suddenly ordered the closure of the barrier. Traffic continued to arrive on the roads from Vichy and Giannat and built up to such a degree that on the shaded square . . . there were between 1,200 and 1,500 cars, and these people had no idea where they were going to eat or sleep.[57]

These closures interrupted train services in a similar way, and this also considerably slowed the flow of repatriation.[58]

The Germans intended to use the demarcation line to introduce a harsh policy of border controls. Once they had established checkpoints on the roads and railways at particular crossing points, they were ruthless about preventing certain categories of people from gaining admittance to the Occupied Zone. In some cases such refusal was provisional; in others, refugees would find themselves prevented from returning to their homes for the entire duration of the war. The first group of refugees to be affected by these measures was those whose homes were located in the Forbidden Zone. This zone had not been mentioned in the armistice agreement. Its creation was announced at the end of July 1940. It comprised those departments along the north-east borders including the departments of Nord, Pas-de-Calais, part of the Somme, Aisne, and Ardennes (see Map 4). These areas had been seriously devastated by the hostilities and were to be treated differently from other occupied areas. Despite repeated requests to allow local people to return in the interests of rebuilding these communities, the Germans only permitted access to some key officials, bankers, and specialist factory workers. The majority of residents were obliged to wait until the area had undergone extensive repair and reconstruction.[59] More ominous was German policy in the two departments of Alsace and Moselle in Lorraine. While refugees were encouraged to return to these annexed areas, now renamed Gast Westmark (Moselle) and de Bade (Alsace), if they could not prove their family origins were from there, they too were prevented from going home. The Germans also refused the passage of Jews—both French and foreign—and other foreigners—ex-Austrians, Czechs, Poles, and stateless people. Those refugees the Germans intended to single out in this way were clarified in mid-September 1940, when lists of the categories forbidden from crossing the demarcation line were sent to the French authorities. They included members of the French military who had not been demobilized, people from Alsace and Lorraine who were not of German origin, North Africans, and those from the French colonies.[60] At certain points along the demarcation line, Jews who attempted to cross were threatened with extreme sanctions. Gritou and Annie Valloton related the experience of one of their co-workers at the demarcation line on 19 August 1940: 'At the line she was told that if a Jewish man or woman was found in the car, he or she would be immediately shot.'[61] From 27 September 1940, this was formalized when the Germans passed an ordinance forbidding those Jews who had left the Occupied Zone from returning there. In this way, the line became a surveillance point designed to prevent the passage of any 'undesirable' individuals who did not meet with Nazi approval and who they believed might have the potential for political opposition. If the Germans suspected that individuals belonging to any of these groups were nonetheless being issued passes by the French authorities, they closed the line without hesitation or warning sometimes for several weeks at a time.

The unpredictable nature of permission to cross the demarcation line meant that throughout the summer of 1940, those refugees travelling home both by train and in private cars were forced to take their chances at getting across. Arbitrary closure of the line was the subject of numerous complaints by the local authorities who were left paralysed and at a loss as to what to advise refugee populations. The sub-prefect of Castelsarrasin reported that repatriation had started in earnest at the end of July with five hundred refugees returning to Paris by rail daily. For a week this regularity of trains was maintained but the occupying authorities suddenly decided to close the demarcation line and sent one of the trains back. From that time and throughout August, all French refugee trains were suspended. Only one train of five hundred professionals was permitted to leave on 25 August. Most of those left waiting were from the Paris region: 'They appear at the prefectoral offices or the town halls of the municipalities close to their places of residence on a daily basis asking when the expected trains will leave. It is difficult to provide them with any answers.'[62]

A significant minority of those who were free to return home, and indeed were encouraged to do so by the authorities, were more reticent and held back when their turn came to be repatriated. Evidence of this was apparent in the department of Corrèze where many refugees refused to enrol on departure lists and ignored orders to contact refugee services. They may well have been discouraged by news that some of those from the north who had managed to cross the demarcation line were being held in camps.[63] It is also the case that some refugees voluntarily took the decision to stay in exile for as long as they could, believing themselves better off in their places of refuge than they would be in their own homes. Decisions taken by refugees about returning home mainly depended on their personal circumstances and whether they had been able to trace, even reunite with, family members. But their experiences of exile also had an important bearing on their feelings of urgency about getting home.

Experiencing Exile in France

Food supply and quality of accommodation were crucial factors in the decision as to whether to stay or to leave. In an exact reversal of their reasons for departure, the threat of food shortages in the unoccupied south increased the anxiety of many refugees to return home. Convinced by the German propaganda, they imagined that the situation must be better in the Occupied Zone. A local paper in the Aveyron reported thus on 27 July:

> Refugees are continuing to show their impatience to return home as soon as possible. They are besieging town halls and the subprefecture to try and learn of the exact intentions of the authorities behind the often contradictory news in the press and on the radio. There is no doubt that problems related to supplies are a primary concern for them. It will be much simpler when the refugees have been able to return home.[64]

The authorities evidently also awaited the departure of these added charges with some impatience. In the meantime, different strategies were implemented. In certain areas, officials opted to withhold refugee benefits and invest the money directly in canteens whose kitchens were often run by local restaurant owners.[65] This was found to be the most cost-effective way of providing nourishing meals for the extra population and meant menus could be adapted according to the availability of foodstuffs.[66] Other authorities chose to allocate refugee benefits directly to the individuals concerned, thereby making it possible for them to shop and cook for themselves. Shops were sometimes required to stay open for longer in order to cater for the increased demand in areas where there was a high concentration of refugees.[67] Families preferred this kind of arrangement which allowed them to be more independent and made it possible for them to sustain a more intimate family existence.[68] However, their dependence on the refugee allocations which did not go very far, made them more acutely aware of the fluctuations in food supply, especially when locals hiked up prices to take advantage of the increased demand. Furthermore, lack of electricity in some places meant cooking had to be done by hanging pots and pans directly over an open fire, or food had to be wrapped and placed in the embers. This process did not come easily to Parisian women who were used to more sophisticated arrangements for preparing food.

Similarly, while many Parisians relished the advantages of rural life which could offer better access to food, the more rudimentary nature of living arrangements came as a shock. One Parisian, a child in 1940, remembers her impressions of the village of Morlasse, near Pau, where her father took the family during the exodus.

> The village was really tiny. We were looked after by an old peasant woman. We were astonished to find that the house only had an earth floor. There was just one house in the village with parquet floors ... My mother, father, and brother slept in the attic where there were five sacks of maize under the mattress. We had never seen anything like it. What seemed strange to us was that we were in our own country and we had discovered another world. The difference from our lives was incredible.[69]

Refugees protested about the lack of running water, privacy, and comfort. The absence of toilet facilities in houses was often remarked upon. Many were moved to engage in major cleaning operations on their arrival, others complained about the overcrowding.[70] Sleeping arrangements and the comfort of the refugees depended very much on the goodwill of their hosts and the possibilities available. The ubiquitous mattresses which had provided little protection from air attack on the road could now at last be put to some real practical use. As Madame Perrot recalls:

> We had brought a mattress on top of the car which we now used to sleep on, and we stayed with the eighteen others we had travelled with in the barn ... Our mayor came to see us regularly and we went up to the main house to get food. We lived in a communal way. The farmer would let us heat foot in their kitchen, but one day we really had nothing to eat so we ended up eating

nettles. We were a bit uncomfortable, all mixed together on the straw. We were not used to living together in this way. We really wanted to get home. We stayed about three weeks; it was quite long enough.[71]

But, although they frequently complained, most refugees warmed to a friendly reception from their fellow citizens despite their unfamiliar ways of doing things. Different eating habits, cultural differences, warmer temperatures, and the absence of their normal working routines all combined for some refugees to create a holiday feeling, particularly if it was the first time that they had ventured beyond their immediate environment. Being far from one's home and habitual routines, having no control over one's destiny, though stressful for some, was strangely reassuring for others. Even under difficult conditions, some were able to use this forced exile to indulge in a bit of tourism and many experienced a first trip to the seaside.[72] As one historian put it:

> However unpleasant the initial experience, terrible conditions on roads, shock of exile, scattering of families and the realisation which would often come as a great shock that they were total strangers in their own country, the *exode* was for many a voyage of discovery of a wealth and freshness that no travel agent could achieve.[73]

Those French refugees who had not yet had the opportunity to benefit from the relatively new laws relating to paid holidays were able to get to know other regions of France through this experience of the exodus.[74] Some were so delighted with what they had found in their adoptive homes, they did all they could to prolong their time before having to return home to Paris to less comfortable surroundings.

> Notwithstanding the official granting of paid holidays in 1936, the factory workers and Parisian employees had perhaps never escaped from their immense collective blocks divided into miniscule apartments. The department of Charente paid the refugees a daily allocation of 10 francs. At the *auberge* they were paying just 12 francs a week for full board including drinks. They were definitely not going to make the mistake of bringing to an end these cheap holidays on the banks of a river well stocked with fish until formal orders required them to do so and to shut themselves back up in their caged homes.[75]

Good food supplies, comfortable accommodation, and a holiday atmosphere could be a combination which was hard to give up freely and in exchange for what? People had no idea what to expect on returning to their homes.

Others were not so happy to find themselves in a position of enforced idleness, and struggled to manage without a proper income. While government officials and rail workers still drew their salaries,[76] most refugees had to manage with the modest benefits of 10 francs per adult and 6 francs per child and were not as lucky as those in Charente who had found such reasonable accommodation. Many were determined to find paid employment to supplement their income. When evacuation had originally been envisaged, it was imagined that the refugees would provide a helpful labour force to replace workers who were at the front. It may even have been for this reason that the Germans attacked the columns of refugees so relentlessly.[77] Local authorities attempted to place those they could in useful employment so that they could contribute to the local economy and represent less of a drain on resources. In cases where refugees had an obvious expertise, as in the case of miners or railway workers, they were quickly directed towards work in these areas. Lists of professions were collated which could be of help to the economy, and those looking for work also advertised in the press. Lawyers and doctors, for example, attempted to attract a local clientele in the following way: 'M. X, doctor [dentist or lawyer], is pleased to offer his services to his fellow evacuated countrymen and -women as well as the local population.'[78] Others went round knocking on doors asking for employment. Those in towns stood a better chance of finding paid work, though by the time many of them reached their places of refuge the labour market was already saturated, and any jobs which had become available in the absence of soldiers were already filled by the early evacuees from September 1939. Refugees from Paris and the industrial north who were more used to factory work[79] and who found themselves in rural areas, were ill-equipped for employment in the agricultural sector.[80] They rarely found full employment, but they tried to be involved in general tasks such as chopping wood or helping with the harvest. The risk of losing their refugee benefits made them reluctant to take low paid jobs.[81] In more remote communes there was little work and for those who were used to being busy, this enforced idleness could lead to boredom and depression. This, coupled with their isolation from their normal friendship networks and channels of information, could reinforce the sense that everything had collapsed and made them more anxious to return to their homes.

Those who had managed to find satisfactory employment were less likely to want to return home. Even short-term employment such as working in the vineyards, could persuade them to postpone departure for a few weeks, even months, since the prospect of working for the Germans did not initially appear to be a very attractive one. Others were alert to the reassurances that everything was getting back to normal in Paris. Specially designated workers like Georges Adrey who had been unable to meet up with relocated factories or offices felt that now 'peace' had come they would be expected to try and re-establish contact with their employers, and a failure to do so might count against them.

Those playing host to these flocks of refugees were also torn as to whether they wanted them to stay or to leave. In the early days, for the most part, officials commiserated with them and were anxious to show hospitality. This remained the overriding sentiment in many areas where the authorities were generally able to adapt and cope with the demands made upon them.[82] As worries about food supply increased, so did resentment that these visitors were taking more than their fair share, even possibly eating their way through stocks put aside for the winter.[83] Those who were prepared to be charitable in a time of crisis became indifferent, even hostile, to populations which they now perceived as lazy and taking advantage of the situation.[84] Such feelings were aggravated by the fact that refugees themselves did not always act with appropriate tact, sometimes appearing judgemental and arrogant to the host populations. In some areas, relations continually deteriorated as the weeks passed with everyone becoming equally impatient for repatriation. One refugee who found himself in Brittany recalled: 'They did not like us much, they called us refugees. When we passed by they said, "Here come the refugees!" We didn't like that because we were still French after all.'[85]

For their part, local authorities became frustrated by these populations who posed numerous administrative difficulties and were seen as a tremendous drain on their resources. Not only did refugees need to be managed in terms of food and accommodation but many arrived destitute, having lost all their belongings, and had to be provided with all the necessities of life. Officials found themselves caught between two competing objectives. On the one hand they wanted to ensure that the basic needs of these distraught populations were met, but on the other, they wanted to prevent the majority from becoming so comfortable and well established that they settled in for the duration. It was already clear that they were going to have to make more long-term arrangements for those groups that the Germans refused to allow to be repatriated, so they wanted to ensure that those who were required to go home did so unless they were able to find employment, and thereby contribute to the local economy.[86] The presence of growing numbers of demobilized soldiers added to their concern to limit the number of refugees who would need to stay over the winter months. It seemed that problems of food supply could only be solved by their departure. Ridding their departments of refugees who qualified for repatriation but refused to return home became such a worry for some of the authorities that they resorted to revoking their benefits, a step which left those affected with little option but to return home.[87] On the other hand, many host families took it upon themselves to house refugees for longer, often expecting little or no payment, especially in cases where their tenants faced an uncomfortable or dangerous future if they were to return.

Understanding Repatriation

Despite German interference, the main bulk of repatriation had been achieved by 15 September 1940 and the Germans were determined to take as much credit for it as they could. On 6 September 1940 the German propaganda magazine *Le Moniteur* ran an article entitled 'German help for repatriation of refugees' which described in detail the significant role played by the Germans—just a small mention went to the French railways for its contribution to the process.[88] In the meantime, refugees remaining in the Unoccupied Zone were being carefully tracked by officials who collated monthly statistics of those present in each commune.[89] Repatriation continued throughout the summer and into the autumn. On 1 November 1940 repatriation was more or less suspended. By this time more than three million refugees had been returned to their homes. Nonetheless significant populations still remained displaced across the country. On 7 March 1941, it was reported that of the seven million displaced refugees, close to one million (972,000) had not been able to return to homes in both zones. Close to half of these (432,000) were still in the Occupied Zone with slightly more remaining in the Unoccupied Zone (540,000).[90] Repatriation was therefore a slow and incomplete process. Those who chose to stay included people whose economic needs were not directly linked to the Paris region, and who preferred to remain in the provinces, on the Basque coast, or near to Vichy. Others preferred to hang on where they were, believing themselves better off than at home. Those who had been able to find work were reluctant to give it up as they could not be sure of finding work when they got home. Some also stayed because they wanted to maintain as much distance from the Germans as they could.

Refugees from Alsace and Lorraine found themselves in a very particular situation. Gritou Vallotton worked among them for many months as a social worker in Périgueux, and noticed that by July, they were coming to understand the true nature of Hitler's ambitions towards their home departments. Non-Jewish Alsatians who were able to prove that their families had been resident there for three generations were under pressure to return to their homes, but by 5 August 1940

The Alsatians who were delighted after armistice at the idea that they could immediately return to Alsace whatever the conditions there, who had already buckled their suitcases and trunks, appear to be in less and less of a hurry and have been less demonstrative, even silent over the past two weeks. We no longer hear that eternal 'Wann wieder heim?' (When can we go home?). They are starting to realize what their return will be like. The German regime with all sorts of difficulties, separation of families, and stories of prisoners does not encourage them.[91]

Those from Lorraine were in a similar position. They articulated their agonizing dilemmas about whether or not to return home.

In general, 98 per cent of those from Lorraine don't want to go home. 'Advise us. What should we do? What would be for the best? I have my house, my fields, here I have nothing, just this room. There I have coal, here only wood, my family is there, but food supplies are limited and Hitler's regime makes people's lives difficult, and that is not acceptable! But if they suppress my refugee benefits, we will have to find some way of living. Why don't they wait until the peace to get us to go home?'[92]

Most would eventually find themselves forced to leave and did so despite their misgivings. If many of those refugees from Alsace and Lorraine tried to postpone their departure until the last possible moment, other populations including foreigners found the extended wait extremely frustrating. The Belgian populations in the Tarn-et-Garonne, for example, repeatedly visited local town halls, demanding to know when trains would be laid on for them.[93] Seen as less of a priority for the French authorities, many Belgians had to wait until the late summer before this was organized.

As the main thrust of repatriation came to an end, planning was now underway to put into place the necessary arrangements for those who were likely to remain for the longer term. For this purpose remaining refugees were classed into two main categories: those who were being *provisionally* prevented from returning home, whose homes were in the Forbidden Zone for example, and those who were likely to be *definitively* prevented from returning.[94] Refugees from the Forbidden Zone were forced to stay put and make the best of the situation, though many defied orders not to return, and ignored advice that they would not be allowed access to their homes. In

Rennes, for example, of ten thousand refugees from the Forbidden Zone, only just over a thousand remained in November 1940.[95] Many of those from the north who attempted to reach their homes found themselves stranded in places which could not ensure their comfort as well as the places they had left. The luckier among them gravitated to reception centres in Paris where they could take shelter.[96] The more comfortable choice was to wait. It was several long months before the German authorities agreed to allow these refugees to return home. Only in spring 1942 were convoys arranged for them and these continued from 24 April 1942 to 15 March 1943.[97] Jews, both French and foreign, along with other foreigners who were considered as 'undesirable' by the authorities, were the main target category of refugees who were definitively prevented from returning. They quickly found themselves in an extremely vulnerable position which soon became acutely dangerous.

Despite all the indications that the Germans were likely to persecute the Jews, approximately thirty thousand French Jews refused to be chased from their homes in the Occupied Zone by the Nazis. Like most other French refugees, they trekked back to their homes in the capital. Many succeeded in crossing the demarcation line before the Germans had established strict controls.[98] Their decision to return was certainly influenced by the 'correct' behaviour of the Germans which impressed them as it did other Parisians. Many would pay the consequences of this misplaced confidence in the goodwill of the Germans with their lives.[99] Other French Jews were more wary. Those who had sufficient money or contacts normally managed to escape internment, and many, like Robert Kahn, made arrangements to remain in the Unoccupied Zone, suspecting that returning to their homes would expose them to more serious danger. 'In August 1940 my father rented the Villa Benedicta in Saint-Just. Anxious to protect his family, but still wanting to remain close to society, he thought this lost hamlet, set against the fold of a dale of chestnut woods and cow fields would provide a safe and peaceful haven.'[100] Jewish women who had arrived in the southern departments during the exodus waited for news of their men who had been mobilized. After the armistice, if they were able to escape capture, these men, like other soldiers, attempted to join their families and demobilize. If the soldiers had withdrawn to the south with their military units, they immediately arranged for members of their families in the Occupied Zone to join them.[101]

Once Vichy took control, it soon became clear that the regime was totally unsympathetic to the plight of foreign Jews who had taken shelter in the Unoccupied Zone to escape German persecution. The Vichy authorities would far rather have repatriated or expelled foreign refugees, but in the circumstances this was impossible. On the contrary, Vichy soon discovered that the Nazis intended to use the Unoccupied Zone as a dumping ground for all their 'undesirables'. Outraged by this major violation of the armistice agreement, Vichy continued to implement its own policies of exclusion. Internment provided the authorities with the cheapest and easiest solution. Jewish refugees were particularly targeted as they were seen as a threat on a number of levels. Not only was it feared that they would join the ranks of the growing unemployed and become an added drain on resources, they were also perceived as a potential threat to law and order and as a group who might oppose Vichy policies. In this context, in spite of their contribution to the French war effort, the thirty to sixty thousand foreign Jewish soldiers who had joined the French army were demobilized, and most were sent directly to camps.[102]

While the Vichy authorities tended to be reluctant to intern French Jews in large numbers, they were targeted in other ways. First, a denaturalization law passed on 21 July 1940 rescinded the French nationality of many recently naturalized Jews. Then, on 3 October, the introduction of a Jewish statute prevented all Jews from working in several sectors including the officer corps, the media, and senior civil service positions. All this was justified on the grounds that Jews had contributed significantly to the defeat. This measure made life even harder for those Jews who had managed to escape detention. They struggled to find jobs to support their families, often in new homes surrounded by unknown populations. Most did their best to keep a low profile and stay out of sight of the authorities. Those who did not claim refugee benefits were more likely to miss the official radar and to pass unnoticed. A second Jewish statute became law in June 1941 and further reduced the position of Jews to second-class citizens. It extended prefects' powers of internment to allow them the discretion to detain French-born Jews. If the Vichy authorities still hesitated to intern French Jews, they hounded other foreigners, both Jewish and non-Jewish, whom they saw as 'useless mouths to feed', as one deputy prefect put it.[103]

In July 1940, of an estimated 180,000 Jews in the southern zone, nearly 40,000 were held in detention camps.[104] Others had sought refuge in large cities where they clustered together, a thousand at a time. Like most French people they believed that the armistice had brought the war to an end and hoped that if they obeyed orders, accepted their status as a discriminated minority, kept their heads down, and avoided any contact with the authorities, they would be able to ride the storm. Many of those in the Unoccupied Zone were able to survive in this manner for the first two years of the Vichy regime. Some were even able to escape to the US, Latin America, or Shanghai, but such escape attempts carried enormous risks.

Already entire families have emigrated to the United States, England, Switzerland, or Canada according to their means and the possibilities the countries had to accommodate them. This flow accelerates but at the same time these passages have become dangerous and very expensive if not terrible traps organized by murderous criminals. But who is to be believed and who is to be trusted? . . . Jews blinded by their panic are very easy prey. How many poor people are being assassinated by individuals who agree to help smuggle them out under false pretences and in fact strip them of their money and their tickets.[105]

Furthermore, while fostering a policy of Jewish emigration would appear consistent with Vichy's policies, administrative incompetence was such that many thousands of those who did have visas were not able to use them.[106]

After the closure of the Spanish border, Marseilles and the department of the Bouches-du-Rhône had become a central rallying point for all those who wanted to leave France. Foreign intellectuals who had been picked up by the authorities were held nearby in the transit camp of Les Milles, next to Aix-en-Provence. German intellectuals had gravitated to Canary-sur-Mer, just along the coast. Large numbers of them now waited for the necessary exit and departure visas which would make their journeys possible. Many lived in a cloud of uncertainty for several weeks, waiting for news of visas or possible escape. The tension was intense. These refugees who knew they were at risk from the Germans because of their political sympathies or their Jewish origins attempted to lie low and to pass unnoticed. Many were pushed into a position of illegality in their attempts to escape. Several structures, which included religious groups and American agencies, worked tirelessly to rescue Jews and German dissidents of all kinds, especially socialists and syndicalists. Their courageous efforts made it possible for many refugees successfully to leave the country.[107]

For thousands of families, Parisians among them, the uprooting caused by the exodus marked the beginning of a traumatic exile. Many of those who found themselves persecuted never returned home and perished at the hands of the Nazis. If they were able to find secure and comfortable shelter in hiding, they were more likely to survive. André Chamson, the writer, who remained in exile for the entire duration of the Occupation, wrote:

'I am writing these pages in one of the regions of France which until now I knew least. A few weeks have been enough for it to become a second home [*une seconde petite patrie*]. It is a place of asylum for me during my time of servitude.'[108] Many of those chased from their homes in 1940 only felt able to return years later, after the departure of the Germans from France in 1944. Among these individuals, one of the most symbolically important personalities to return to Paris after a prolonged period of exile was Charles de Gaulle. In his five years of exile abroad, his movement gained considerable support. While presence on French soil had contributed to Pétain's credibility in the early years of the Occupation, as the Vichy regime became increasingly dominated by the Nazis, de Gaulle's position of exile first in London and then in Algeria, played in his favour.[109] His success in uniting his movement with other Resistance movements across the country helped him to identify himself as the incarnation of liberated Republican France. In order to fulfil this role effectively, much was at stake on his return to Paris.

Anxious to reach the capital before the Allies, de Gaulle did not wait for the fighting to be over before he entered the city. On 25 August, at 8 p.m., arriving at the Hôtel de Ville, de Gaulle made the famous speech in which, in the interests of national unity, he claimed that Paris had been liberated by the efforts of the French army and the French people, sidelining the crucial role that had been played by the Allies.

> Paris, Paris abused, Paris broken, Paris martyred, but Paris liberated by her own people, with help of the armies of France, with the help and support of the whole of France, that is to say of fighting France, that is to say of the true France, the eternal France.[110]

He made a symbolic march from the Étoile to Notre-Dame the following day to popular acclaim. This proved sufficient for him to take control and replace the authorities which had been put into place under the Vichy regime. His provisional government soon gained international recognition and, while excluded from the Yalta conference, it was a co-signatory of the armistices in 1945 with both Nazi Germany and Japan.[111] Amidst the general perception that a strong France on the Continent was crucial for post-war reconstruction, de Gaulle succeeded in mobilizing national unity in the light of victory, in much the same way as Pétain had mobilized the defeat.[112]

However, the disruption and separation experienced by so many French families was not yet over. It was not until May/June 1945, almost exactly five years after the events of the spring and early summer 1940, that the

French men in German prison camps, the men working in factories in Germany, the Jews and political deportees who managed to survive the terrible conditions and the mass slaughter of the extermination camps, were finally to see their homes again. Depending on the nature of their experiences, their return and readaption to their situations was of varying difficulty. The most acute problems arose from the repatriation of those who had been deported to concentration camps, many of whom returned in the most appalling state. Some were close to death. The novelist Marguerite Duras described how she could barely recognize her husband Robert L. on his return from a German concentration camp:

> I don't recognise him. He looks at me. He smiles. Lets himself be looked at. There's a supernatural weariness in his smile, weariness from having managed to live til this moment. It's from this smile that I suddenly recognise him, but from a great distance, at the other end of a tunnel. It's a smile of embarrassment. He's apologizing for being here, reduced to such a wreck. And then the smile fades, and he becomes a stranger again.[113]

She goes on to express her anger that de Gaulle, whose symbolic return was so important to the people of France, made so little reference to the terrible suffering of these people in the camps.[114]

Let us now return to consider the situation of those who returned to their homes in the autumn 1940. As they settled back into familiar routines, they were able to contemplate what had happened to them and take stock of the consequences of the defeat and the changed circumstances of their lives under occupation by the Germans. Some underwent a difficult process of adjustment and were reluctant to accept the situation. The majority, however, numbed by their recent traumas and overwhelmed with relief, slipped back into a semblance of normality despite the deprivations, difficulties, and frustrations that the Occupation brought to their daily lives.

6

Back to 'Normal'?

Everyone returned to their homes, everyone went back to their affairs and the black market began its fruitful career. The Germans behaved correctly. 'What do you expect?' said the small shopkeepers to their clients who expressed astonishment at the sudden shortages, 'What do you expect? We have been defeated!'

J. Jean Cassou, *La Mémoire courte*

Refugees who returned to their homes were encouraged by the German and Vichy authorities to get on with their lives in an atmosphere of business as usual. Their exodus experience was evoked by Pétainist publicists as a just punishment for believing in the Republican regime which had brought disaster upon the country. People tended to go along with this in the immediate aftermath of the defeat as they slowly came to terms with the upheaval these events had brought to their lives. Gradually the French began to wake up to the reality of their situation and soon came to realize that returning to their 'homes' could not provide the return to their normal lives that they longed for. The majority found themselves obliged to make the best of the changed situation and adapted to it as best they could. A small minority began to question the policies of the Vichy government, to react against the Occupation, and started to find ways of expressing this.

Regaining Control

Worry about what they would find on their return was the main preoccupation for refugees who feared that their homes would have been pillaged and invaded, and that their possessions would be stolen or damaged.

During our flight we feared for our lives, on the way home we feared for our possessions. We saw so many refugees going by before we left that we knew our house was in danger. Luckily my father had already made some hiding places in the cellar and we used these for our most precious possessions. When we got home, the house was wide open and it was clear that it had been pillaged. People had been inside and used the house; they must have been other refugees. They had used our sheets and must have eaten as they had left food on the table. It was dirty.[1]

For this reason, many were quick to indicate their presence by chalking their residency on the doors in order to discourage any refugees still without shelter. On a visit to the suburbs of Paris, de Beauvoir noticed that front doors had *maison habitée* (house occupied) or more often *Bewohnt* written on them.[2]

People's first concern was for their families; women still waited obsessively for news about the fate of their men.[3] News was slow to come; it took the authorities a long time to publish details of casualties. The first official lists did not appear for more than a month after the armistice.[4] In spite of expectations to the contrary, there was certainly no suggestion that the men taken prisoner would be returning home in the near future. Simone de Beauvoir's thoughts were only for Sartre, a feeling she shared with the other women she came across:

'He has not written, but no one has written, don't worry.' It is the same refrain everywhere; women in the metro, women on the doorsteps. 'Have you heard anything? No, he has certainly been taken prisoner. When will the lists come through?' etc. No, none of them will be released before the peace, that is certain, but stories are continuing to circulate.[5]

The problems of trying to get news of separated loved ones were ongoing and were often not resolved immediately. Georges Adrey, for example, recalled that getting news of their son, who had been on the front, was a difficult process and slow to arrive.[6]

The next priority for people was to try and pick up their lives; financial concerns had become very pressing for many refugees. As we have seen, many had their benefits revoked by the authorities in order to oblige them to return home. Some continued to qualify for benefits for a two-week period after returning home. They had to present themselves at their local town halls immediately so that they could be classified as having 'officially' returned.[7] Although this measure was designed to tide the refugees over until they were able to find employment, two weeks was often too short a time for them to find work and this situation led to financial insecurity as refugees sometimes experienced extended periods of unemployment. Many were in a similar position to Georges Adrey, who had failed to rejoin his factory in retreat despite his best efforts, and the whole experience led to him losing his job. His wife had also lost hers since she had been forced to resign in order to flee with her husband.[8] Both eventually managed to find other jobs, but Madame Adrey lost her pay scale bonus points acquired through seniority. The presence of the occupier did, however, provide more employment opportunities as French industry was put to work for the German was effort.

First Impressions of the Germans

By the time Parisians returned to their city, the Germans were well established there. Aware that their presence was likely to impact significantly on returning refugees, the Germans redoubled their efforts to appear courteous and polite while maintaining a strong physical and visual presence. Maurice Sachs wrote of his first impressions of Occupied Paris:

> We arrived in Paris on 29 June 1940. It was four in the afternoon. Sandbags were obstructing the arteries of the entrances to the city at the gates of the capital . . . We were curious to have a wander around Paris. There were some people in the Latin quarter, some young women sitting at tables at the Capoulade restaurant with German officers, a few passers-by on the boulevard Saint-Germain, but the rue de Rivoli, Place de la Concorde was populated by only a few Germans and surprising at first sight were the large red standards with the Nazi cross on them in the centre of the city. It was a dead city, a rather lovely spectacle like that of a destroyed civilization.[9]

The young Flora Groult was anxious about how she would feel on finding her home city under occupation.

> I was as afraid of returning to Paris as if it was someone I had loved that I had not seen for ten years. It was a shock to discover it and then almost instantly we were used to it. The roads were not as empty as we had been told . . . It is ignoble to become accustomed to seeing the German cross flying over the Chamber of Deputies; nonetheless we did become used to it. The nightmare became perfectly familiar to us.[10]

Like Flora Groult, many were surprised that they were able to adapt to the German presence more easily than they had imagined. The reality was not as terrifying as most had feared and their own personal experience of the Germans they had encountered during their return seemed to reinforce this. Léautaud, who witnessed the arrival of the Germans, commented on their good manners and the excellent quality of the French spoken by many of them:[11] 'their politeness, their agreeable behaviour, their remarks to refugees has had their impact. People are celebrating all of that. We were told that they were so terrible! But they are so very nice.'[12]

De Beauvoir also noted the positive nature of reactions to the Germans. First she commented on the Germans as they arrived at her place of refuge:

> Quite a significant attachment of them installed themselves in the village. Towards nightfall, shyly the peasants returned to their homes, the cafés opened their doors. The Germans did not cut the children's hands off, they paid for the drinks they bought in the farms, they were polite, and all the shopkeepers smiled at them.[13]

Then, on her return to Paris, she hitched a lift one day after a walk in the suburbs of the city. On seeing German soldiers chatting happily with some young women, her driver commented,

> 'Some little Germans are certainly going to be made!' I heard this sentence ten times and never did it carry any blame. 'It's only natural', the chap said to me, 'you don't need to speak the same language for that to happen.' I had seen no evidence of hatred, only some fear among the villagers and, once this subsided, a surprised and grateful look.[14]

Germans soldiers were widely billeted in empty houses and did not hesitate to force the doors if no one appeared to be at home.[15] On returning to Paris in mid-July, one refugee, finding the city deserted, feared that her apartment might have been requisitioned. Fortunately her concierge had looked after her flat and refused to hand over her keys to the German soldiers. A soldier did subsequently come to her flat to check that it was indeed inhabited.[16] This was another reason why returning refugees were anxious to make their presence explicit by chalking evidence of it on their front doors.

The German occupation did, however, bring significant changes to the daily lives of Parisians. Curfew was introduced and clocks were moved forward an hour to German time, food supplies became unreliable and irregular, and in September 1940 rationing was introduced. Many Parisians became convinced that if they followed orders and appeared respectful, the Germans would do them no serious harm. After all the panic and disruption of the exodus, most French people just welcomed German friendliness with relief. They hoped that life under the Occupation would prove to be less of an ordeal than they had previously been led to believe.[17]

Staying Put in Paris

As refugees returned they exchanged notes with those who had stayed put and many soon came to the realization that leaving their homes in the capital had probably been a mistake. They learned that in their absence Paris had not been bombed, nor had it been the scene of extensive fighting, and that food supplies had been consistently ensured. The government's decision to leave the police force in control in Paris had prevented the possibility of the kind of population unrest so feared by Weygand. Pillaging was also kept to a minimum.[18] Simone de Beauvoir, in an effort to kill time while waiting for news of Sartre, decided to visit the suburbs as people were returning home. There she eavesdropped on the conversations of the returning refugees. ' "We've just got back from Montauban, if we had known, we would never have left!" I heard this all along my way,' she commented.[19] It transpired that staying at home would probably have been the safer and better choice. Among refugees who had returned, this knowledge contributed to a growing sense of resentment against the authorities who had taken no action at any stage to prevent them from taking to the roads and unnecessarily risking their lives.

Furthermore, throughout the summer of 1940, as the facts of the exodus gradually emerged, numerous stories circulated of the actions committed by individuals and communities in the absence of law and order. Once again the failure of the proper authorities to advise people during these difficult weeks only seemed to add to the perception that governing elites had behaved irresponsibly and further emphasized the true scale of their incompetence. For example, only in November did it come to light that the two hundred sick and injured who were in the hospital of Argenteuil had been abandoned by those in charge to the care of an externally recruited nurse. Many died and, in the absence of coffins, flour sacks were used for the burials.[20] The extent to which certain communities had taken the law into their own hands and introduced their own particular methods of justice only emerged in March 1941.[21] Revelations like these aggravated existing tensions in local communities. When those who had fled started to drift back to their homes, they were resented by those who had stayed behind.

The latter felt that they had managed to cope to the best of their abilities after being more or less abandoned by officials to face events and left without access to adequate means for them to assure their basic needs. In May/June 1940 a distinction had almost immediately been drawn between those who stayed and those who fled and this was to haunt relations between French people for some time to come. Mendès France had written in mid-June 1940 that

> The capital is emptying. An immense silence embraces the city. A general sadness descends upon its inhabitants. A rift starts to appear which will become more serious in time; a moral divorce begins to come into play between those who are leaving (or who will try to do so) and those who are staying put. The latter already feel lonely. Without the local authorities, the government, and the press, the capital gives the impression that it has been abandoned.[22]

The people who remained in Paris were predominantly the less affluent, or the elderly and the ill. They felt deserted, terrified not just that they would suffer some terrible fate at the hands of the German occupiers but also that they might be victims of complete social collapse in the absence of law and order and starve without adequate food supplies. Their worst fears were not realized. If there was a degree of serious pillaging, most localities found ways of assuring a minimum level of services for the short time before the arrival of the occupiers. On arrival, they too were less terrifying than Parisians had expected; the Germans were mostly on their best behaviour. However, the sense of abandonment experienced by those who remained long poisoned relations in many communities. In Versailles, for example, it was only in September 1940 that the conflicts between those who had stayed and those who had left were reported to have calmed.[23] The return of the elected officials throughout the summer of 1940 was the subject of acrimonious debate and the circumstances of their departure were subject to scrutiny. The Vichy government explicitly encouraged a judgemental approach which condemned those who had left, projecting them as having betrayed the trust of their charges, forcing them to face the occupiers without any protection. Pétain reinforced this position by sending messages of support to those who had stayed, affirming that they had demonstrated a serious devotion to duty, and they thereby gained the moral high ground.[24]

Most government officials had taken to the roads in the same panic as everyone else. Prefects often left at the last minute, influenced by the belief that as representatives of the government they should not allow themselves to be taken by the Germans. Few were given clear orders about what they should do and most followed their own judgement. Some left a representative as in the case of Robert Billecard, prefect of the Seine-et-Oise based in Versailles, who named his general secretary of police who was beyond mobilizable age to remain behind, unaware of the resentment this would cause.[25] More often than not, no one was present in the official buildings to receive the Germans at their arrival. Those who did choose to stay in place, like Jean Moulin, prefect of the Eure-et-Loire based in Chartres, were very much the exception. Moulin's attempts to maintain civilian structures were undermined by the disappearance of the mayor, accompanied by most of the municipal workers, as well as his own prefectoral staff who had also panicked and fled. The departure of firefighters and water workers whose help he needed in the wake of the bombing of the city seriously impaired his capacity to help the remaining population and the hordes of refugees who were passing through. It was only after visiting the commander of a regiment of soldiers who had made camp just outside Chartres that he realized that in staying he had taken an exceptional stance. The commander informed him that his regiment had come across no other prefects in the entire course of their retreat.[26]

Where Moulin, a prefect, was an exception in staying in his department, mayors, on the other hand, often felt that it was their duty to stay behind and care for those who could not flee. They were left to make their own decisions in the face of contradictory civilian and military orders which left them overwhelmed and confused. Many complained that they had been abandoned by the central administration and had to take decisions for themselves, trying to evaluate what would be the best course of action. The flight and departure of crucial services and administrations often made it difficult for them to see how they would manage to maintain normal services if the population were to stay put. Police and fire services were often the first to leave and in their absence there was no way of controlling pillaging or organizing population movements or of helping potential victims of bomb attacks. Jean Moulin explicitly complained that the police and fire service had left Chartres three full days before the Germans arrived in his department.[27] In this context, many mayors were relieved to be given orders to evacuate by the military.[28] Others looked to the prefectoral administration for a lead, and finding that they had already left, took this to mean that they too should leave and in turn urged their populations to evacuate. At Versailles on 13 June, a note was left on the town hall inviting the population to flee.[29] Other mayors, considering it their duty to follow those in their charge, decided to help take them to places of refuge.[30]

In the absence of the elected officials—mayors or local councillors, as well as prefects and their administration—civilian volunteers were left to receive the occupiers. In other cases, the remaining elected members of local and regional assemblies sometimes stepped in and attempted to maintain basic services. The events which took place in Viroflay, Versailles, and in the department of the Seine-et-Oise provide evidence of how these makeshift authorities attempted to cope and how the tensions towards those who were perceived to have abandoned them were played out.[31] Realizing that the mayor of Viroflay had disappeared, the remaining councillors convened a meeting on 13 June where they were urged to stay put but most of them were not prepared to give a firm commitment that they were prepared to do so.[32] As in Chartres, the local firefighters were determined to leave and after heated discussions they forced the issue and left in the municipal vehicles. This departure of all the elected officials whose names were known to the local people unsurprisingly led to panic among those who had remained behind and a crowd collected at the local town hall. The situation was calmed by one of the remaining local councillors, a certain Monsieur Polin, who volunteered to take on responsibility for addressing the problems of food supply, medical services, law and order, and to make contact with the Germans.[33] On 15 June, referring to himself as the 'communal administrator', he distributed a note designed to reassure the population, calling on them to return to their homes calmly and without provoking the German authorities. He invited volunteers to join him and put together a team to help oversee the local administration and especially to help deal with the problems of food supply.[34] Here we see explicit evidence of the secondment of individuals to positions of authority for which they had no electoral mandate.

Polin's team of self-appointed administrators managed to create a presence which reassured the locals by offering them a point of reference but they struggled to keep control and had considerable difficulty in ensuring the basic needs of the population. Foodstuffs were requisitioned and distributed and the population was advised how to manage in the absence of the normal services. On 21 June, for example, the people of Viroflay were asked to bury their rubbish at the bottom of their gardens until normal rubbish collection arrangements could be re-established.[35] Most significant, perhaps, was the hostile attitude taken by Polin and those around him towards those other members of the council who had left. When their return was under discussion, worries were voiced that those who returned would form a majority and take back power. It was felt that 80 per cent of the population were likely to take sides against the volunteers in support of the 'fugitives'.[36] The main fear was that the situation would degenerate into one of social disorder, that returning populations would find themselves unemployed as there would be no work, and demobilized soldiers would be angry if their arrival was not adequately planned. In order to avoid any such problems, Potin decided to set everyone to work. He arranged activities in the local school and set out a new curriculum in line with the current needs and certainly with an eye on the values of the occupier.[37]

In late June and early July the meetings of the local council of the department of the Seine echoed what was happening in Viroflay as discussions focused on the issue of who had left and when, and whether or not some or all of them should be allowed to remain on the various committees in consequence of their behaviour.[38] The General Council of the Seine met on 25 June 1940 to discuss the circumstances of the departure of the mayor of Villetaneuse, in the suburbs of Paris, and to decide whether he should be allowed to return to his position after an absence of a week in mid-June. A French general had given a written order to evacuate the town and the mayor had subsequently withdrawn to a commune (he could not supply the name) in the Étampes area and only returned on 21 June. The two remaining municipal councillors were left to offer guidance to those who had experienced a number of bomb attacks and to take over the administration of the town. The local council decided that the mayor's actions in leaving did not qualify him to be added to the list of those who had behaved appropriately and stayed at their post at the time of German occupation. One councillor wondered whether they had the power to oust those in elected positions, but was told that these were exceptional circumstances.[39]

The issue of whether government officials did their duty and whether they should have stayed or left was difficult and contentious and reflected many of the debates that had taken place on a national level as to whether the government should stay put or leave and continue the battle from elsewhere. Jean Moulin was taken prisoner by the German kommandant who found him in place at the prefecture of Chartres. Despite his arrest, he remained opposed to departure on the basis that it was unprincipled. He reflected on what he believed to be the duty of the civil servant to the populations in his charge: 'Run away? ... Wouldn't that be to act like all the others, like all those who have run away from responsibility, hunger, or danger?'[40] But once the exodus had begun, it was hard for those with or without authority to stem the tide of departures, as Moulin himself had found. He had struggled to prevent people from leaving but failed to persuade them, such was the compelling nature of the urge to flee. Yet, his insistence that it was his place to stay with his charges was well entrenched in Republican culture and this lay behind a refusal to accept exile.[41] Two key considerations came into play here. First, a sense of patriotism which echoed Danton's words: 'You cannot carry your homeland on the sole of your shoes [*On n'emporte pas la patrie à la semelle de ses souliers*]'. This idea originated during the French Revolution, when Danton was a key figure. The concept of the nation was intrinsically linked to the ideas of the Revolution, most especially that of the Republic. Opponents of the Republic—counter-revolutionaries—left the country and went into exile. Therefore, leaving the country was equated with an anti-republican and unpatriotic position. A second crucial concern for those in elected positions, and in particular those holding the post of mayor, was the desire to stay close to the electorate. During the First World War, the mayors of the Nord department had stayed with their populations during the German occupation and this had set an important precedent. The elected deputies, who had to choose whether or not to leave on the *Massilia* and accompany the government to North Africa to carry on the battle from there, based their decision on where they believed their duty lay. Those parliamentarians who were also mayors of large towns in the south which had become completely submerged with refugees and were struggling to cope or that were likely to be subject to German occupation, felt that their duty lay not with the government but with the needs of their charges. Vincent Auriol wrote in 1945 of his decision not to join the *Massilia*: 'Had I been a simple Deputy, I would have followed the offices of the Chambers and the Head of State, but I am a mayor. The region was to be occupied, my duty was to stay among those I administer and not leave my fellow citizens alone to face the Occupation.'[42]

Robert Billecard, prefect of the Seine-et-Oise who came under attack for leaving his post in Versailles and retreating south between 14 and 25 June 1940, drew a clear distinction between the position of a prefect—a non-elected representative of the government—and a mayor—an elected representative—when defending his decision to leave. He explained that, working on the basis of the precedent of the last war, he was of the view that prefects should not remain in occupied territory. He was critical of the government's affirmation that those prefects who had stayed had behaved appropriately. Billecard did not mince his words, describing such an action as idiotic because a prefect was a representative of the government who could do little but serve as hostage to the invader. Mayors on the other hand, he conceded, were locally elected officials whose mission was not to represent the government, thus naturally they should have stayed even if they were members of parliament. He continued thus:

> I knew that by leaving I would take the risk of being disowned or misunderstood. I knew that the risk I was taking in leaving was greater than that of staying . . .
>   I left, not because it was convenient for me to do so, but because I believed and I still do, that in the case of war, a government delegate should not remain with the invader . . . I returned only when my government had taken up peaceful relations with Germany and the invader, and I remain convinced that this was the best way forward.[43]

Mobilizing the Exodus Experience

Pétainist propagandists were keen to exploit these divisions to discredit the Republican order, its administrations and officials, and blame them for the defeat. The Vichy regime, emerging as it did from the disaster of the debacle, explicitly mobilized the exodus experience as a way of gaining the support of the population and justifying the need for a new regime. This experience, shared by so many, was an ideal propaganda vehicle, reaching a maximum number of people situated in both zones. Those who had stayed behind and felt abandoned were comforted by the discourse of betrayal and the blame directed at Republican officials for failing in their duty. Those who had taken flight also identified with the view that the authorities had failed them and this was reinforced by their own experiences on the road. Both Sadoul and Adrey repeatedly noted the absence of any authorities during their exodus. Many had taken flight without any help or guidance from officials and had met no one to advise them or offer guidance along the way. Host populations in the south who had witnessed the distress and experienced the chaos of the arrival of the fleeing people first hand could also identify with propaganda which emphasized the incompetence of officials and the way arrangements had been handled, especially later in June. Vichy propaganda sought to exploit these widespread feelings of resentment in the aftermath of the return, as populations looked for someone to blame for their misfortunes.

This process was already evident in Pétain's very first appeal on 17 June when he used the exodus to justify his authority and in particular his decision to ask for armistice. The exodus became a crucial symbol of the defeat, an image which was taken up and skilfully exploited by Vichy propagandists thereafter. The Pétainist explanation of the defeat set out in this first speech and made even more explicit in later ones, implied the following interpretation of events. Under the strength of the overwhelming German forces, the French front had fought bravely but collapsed against uneven odds and the government was forced to recognize that all was lost and ask for peace with the Germans in order to prevent the population from experiencing further loss of life, trauma, and misery. On 20 June Pétain clarified that it was indeed a question of armistice (having failed to actually mention this term in his earlier speech) which he personally had considered inevitable from 13 June. German military superiority and inadequate allies were stated as the main reasons for the defeat. 'Too few children, too little arms, and too few allies.' Thus, once again, blame for the defeat was shifted away from the military to that of the Republican politicians. Furthermore, the people of France were cast as being implicitly at fault for believing in the Third Republic and supporting its policies. The exodus was their punishment. Cast in this way, there was a certain logic in the idea that the military should not have to carry the burden of guilt when the entire nation, driven by the misguided beliefs of the civilian authorities, was in fact at fault. Everyone had played a part in the collapse of the regime even if it was just by giving it tacit support, and they were now destined to experience a period of suffering as a punishment for making the wrong choices. Taking on a tone as if admonishing children, Pétain preached that times would now be hard as the French people would have to suffer in order to rebuild their country and work their way through to forgiveness and redemption. Pétain made extensive use of the religious metaphors of suffering and redemption in relation to the moral and governmental collapse of the country. The only way to recovery, he explained, was for the French people to accept privations and expiate past sins. Scolding the French people in his speeches was to become another hallmark of Pétain's approach.

On 25 June, when Pétain communicated the terms of the armistice to the country, he conceded that they were indeed severe, but nevertheless stipulated that the fighting, even from the colonies (a reference to de Gaulle), had to come to an end. He advised that this was the price the people had to pay to be able to return to their homes, and they were more than anxious to do this. However, he reassured them, France would be rebuilt and they had to look to the future. It would not be easy, and the people would suffer, but there was no point keeping the truth from them as other governments had done: 'I hate these lies which have caused us so much harm', he stated, referring back to the propaganda of the previous regime which had promised everyone victory. Little further mention was made of the displaced refugees until his speech in August 1940 which was devoted to the recovery of the country. Here he set out his plans for repatriation to enable refugees to 'retrieve their normal conditions of existence' and described how this process was already under way.

> The arrangements made have already had important results. Between 1 and 10 August, half a million refugees and demobilized soldiers have been repatriated from all corners of the country. Similarly, more than fifty thousand cars have returned to the Occupied Zone. We are sparing no efforts to accelerate the pace of repatriation.[44]

This kind of assurance that life would return to normal gave refugees hope that their nightmare had now come to an end and was a recurrent theme in Vichy propaganda. It built up hopes among the refugees which would prove difficult to fulfil but which seduced them and certainly increased Pétain's support base.

Pétain's concern to aid a population whose main priority was to try and pick up their lives again was generally well received in the early summer months. Appearing to have the repatriation process in hand and to be prioritizing it, his speeches appealed to the traumatized nation of displaced refugees. There was a general perception that they had been victims of the resignation of the government and the collapse of a regime. Pétain's explanations for the causes of the defeat seemed plausible and most French people had little reason to doubt his word. As soon as the new regime took power, press articles appeared, seeking to discredit the old elites and explain to the public that the phenomenon not just of the defeat but also of exodus itself had come about because of the failure of the Republic and the unforgivable delinquency of the state officials. On 20 June 1940 Le Matin raged: 'Those in charge of administrating France did so with shameful flight, leaving several million of their charges without orders, without organization, and without news.'[45] Previous authorities had failed to protect them and therefore deserved to be swept away and replaced by a new one which promised to rebuild the country and create a better order. In the early days of the Vichy regime when the nation was still in a state of shock at the unexpected turn of events, the French people were particularly vulnerable to believing this kind of propaganda. The sense of trauma was considerably augmented by the fact that in line with all the propaganda leading up to May 1940 which had pointed to certain victory, no one had seriously contemplated the possibility of defeat. The discrepancy between the expected outcome of hostilities and the actual course of events discredited all the previous reassuring governmental discourses and undermined the credibility of all those who had been associated with them. Even the Germans, who had been portrayed as behaving like savages by government

16. This propaganda poster for Pétain's National Revolution was widely distributed in the Unoccupied Zone. In 1940, 510,000 copies were produced; a further 550,000 copies were circulated the following year.

17. The slogan on the poster reads, 'Work, The labour of the French people is the most important resource for the French homeland.' This montage included photos of the those working in an exclusively rural setting; a carpenter and a blacksmith can be clearly identified.

propagandists, did not correspond to the image people had been told to expect of them.[46]

Furthermore, Pétain's dogged refusal to leave the territory, which he repeated time after time at cabinet meetings, and his apparent determination to share his fate with the people chimed in with the strong attachment that the French have to their soil, their *patrimoine*, their physical heritage, and this was set against the position of those who were prepared to abandon the country and go to the colonies—or worse still other countries—albeit for the best possible reasons.[47] Gradually, through his speeches and the accompanying propaganda, the French people learnt of Pétain's plans for National Revolution with its triptych of *Travail, famille, patrie*, a slogan designed to replace the Republican *Liberté, égalité, fraternité*. The romanticism of rural France, a significant building block in this Vichy discourse, also resonated directly with the exodus experience. During their exile, Parisians, as well as other populations from the industrial north of Europe, had discovered a

18. Family values were at the centre of the National Revolution, and of all families, peasant families were best. This slogan reads, 'French families are the guardians of a long and honourable past.' Note that there are no young men in the picture, an elderly couple, a woman working in the field, and a group of women with children. Their husbands are doubtless prisoners-of-war.

rural world which they had not known still existed. While there had been vociferous complaints about the rudimentary, even primitive, nature of facilities, most had appreciated that their peasant hosts had been able to draw on the land to provide sustenance at a time when everything else had collapsed. Rural life had served them well at their time of utmost need. Pétain was determined to shape and exploit all the positive features of their understandings of this experience. He told the French people that, in the name of progress, those who lived in industrial areas of the north had become corrupted by moving too far away from the traditional, solid values of rural France. This was the reason for the collapse and the defeat. This had been clearly demonstrated to everyone by the way in which peasant communities had been able to come to the rescue of their misguided fellow

19. In this poster, the French homeland is equated with a rual village; no towns or factories are visible. The slogan reads, 'Follow me! And demonstrate your commitment to the eternal values of France'. Pétain himself appears here for he is the embodiment of the French *patrie*.

citizens at a time of national catastrophe. No one could deny that traditional rural values were the soundest ones in human life.[48]

In order to further reinforce this, Pétain's propagandists promoted an idealized picture of the peasant family, an iconic image which was now easily recognizable to the recently displaced refugee populations. By 'returning to the land', an expression adopted as a slogan in Vichy propaganda, French people had literally rediscovered their country, their heartland, and it had been their salvation. In line with Pétain's propensity to use religious imagery, progress was demonized and the primitive lives and methods of the peasants were held up as being good, righteous, and true. Pétain told the French people on 25 June 1940 that 'The land does not lie [*La terre ne ment pas*] and it is at the basis of the nation's identity.' Return to the land was therefore a policy intended to halt the progress of industrialization as Pétain declared to the American President on 22 August 1940:

"LA TERRE, ELLE, NE MENT PAS"

20. This slogan reads 'The land does not lie', the quote from Pétain's speech which was illustrated in many such posters. Pétain shakes the hand of the respectful peasant dressed appropriately in brown, for he is worthy of such a gesture. In the background are the young men at the Chantiers de Jeunesse, the youth camps organized by the Vichy government to occupy those due for military service. With military precision, they participated in scout-like activities while the key tenets of the National Revolution were instilled into them.

France will again become what she should never have ceased to be, an essentially agricultural nation. Like the giants in fairy stories, she will rediscover all her strength in making contact with the land.[49]

However, as the realities of the National Revolution became apparent, especially legislation like the Jewish statutes, public enthusiasm for these measures began to wane. Prefects' reports noted that French people in both the Occupied and Unoccupied areas were taking little interest in political matters, focusing rather on trying to put together their lives. 'The population is devastated and overwhelmed with its own worries', wrote the prefect of the Aude in his report on 28 July 1940; 'it discusses nothing'. In October the prefect of the Ain described the population as demonstrating 'intellectual and moral amnesia'. In the Seine-et-Oise, the population appeared 'sceptical, bitter, and disillusioned' and their lives were dominated by personal concerns.[50] In the light of reports like these, along with growing fears that Gaullist propaganda was gaining ground, the fact that the British

were still in the war, that Hitler's plans for the invasion of Britain did
not seem to have come to anything, and that the prisoners of war did not
seem likely to return in the near future, Vichy redoubled its propaganda
efforts.

One propaganda film is especially interesting for the use it makes of the
exodus, drawing on reconstructed visual material in an effort to mobilize
the population. Here, images of fleeing refugees are used to spur people to
donate to the Vichy charity 'Secours national'. The soundtrack urged, 'Give
to the Secours national, give, give! Marshal Pétain offered himself as a gift to
France, what have you done?' Later in the film, shots of people on the roads
as during the exodus were accompanied by the following voice-over:
'Think of those who wandered along the roads of the exodus with no
idea where they would end up, those who carried on walking without a
rest, abandoning everything in their lives; think of those who lost everything, those who found they could carry all their living possessions.'[51]

The anniversary of Pétain's armistice speech in June 1941 provided
another perfect propaganda opportunity. In an effort to rekindle support,
Pétain here drew directly on the exodus experience. After playing his entire
speech from 17 June 1940, aware that hearing this was bound to take those
who had been caught up in the exodus back to their circumstances of the
previous year, he went on to confront his critics:

> France is rising up again. But a good number of French people refuse to
> recognize it. Do they really believe that their lot is more tragic than it was a
> year ago?
> French people, you really have a short memory. Do you not remember the
> columns of escaping refugees composed of women, children, the elderly, all
> perched on vehicles of all kinds, advancing haphazardly, overwhelmed by fear
> and a desire to flee the enemy?

Visual versions of this speech were played in cinemas along with newsreels.
The film entitled *L'Anniversaire du Maréchal au pouvoir* (The Anniversary of a
Year in Office for the Marshal), shows him giving this speech from his office
on 17 June 1941. His words are juxtaposed with shots of refugees and battle.
He then explains to the camera that all has changed for the better. Things
may not yet be perfect, but they are improving. The visual contrasts
between defeat and exodus as opposed to the burgeoning agriculture of
the new France, symbol of renovation and renaissance, are intended to
demonstrate the success of the regime in rebuilding the country over the
previous twelve months.[52]

Attitudes to Pétain

It had been said that in 1940 France was dominated by forty million supporters of Pétain.[53] While the circumstances of peoples' situations at this time were extremely varied, everyone shared a desire for law and order

21. This propagandist photo-montage provides a portrait of Pétain, above another of the Vichy cabinet in September 1940. From left to right: General Huntziger, Alibert, Pétain, Baudouin, Darlan, Caziot, Peyrouton, Laval, Bouthillier, and Belin.

to be restored, and looked for ways of understanding what had happened to them. This need strongly predisposed them to greet Pétain's speeches and interpretations positively. Here was a respected figure who appeared to have some grasp of the nature of their distress and who seemed to be offering a way out of the situation. Pétain therefore emerged as an import-ant national rallying point with which a maximum number of people could identify. An unquestioned patriot, his enormous reputation meant that people believed sincerely that he could only have their best interests at heart.

> In my family there is tremendous fervour for Marshal Pétain and I share these sentiments. His past, his prestige, and his age are all guarantees of his courage and the rectitude of his behaviour at the head of the French state which, without being aware of it, has just been substituted for the Republic. 'Pétain' my mother says, 'is a father for France' and this is just how he appears to us.[54]

Their fear of disorder and the scenes of lawlessness that they had witnessed during the exodus predisposed many to accept the presence of the occupying forces and to accept some of the constraints on their lives which went along with them, like curfew for example. Here, accommodation or the adoption of a wait and see attitude was entirely logical in the circumstances. For many people, consciousness of the true state of events was often slow to dawn and most preferred to focus on their own more immediate family concerns. Once again, Henri Frenay's account gives a sense of the attitudes of those around him:

> The general climate of the population is profoundly disappointing. Other than friends we recruit, no sudden outburst, no revolt. The main preoccupation, sometimes the exclusive one, is food. It's true that foodstuffs are hard to come by ... Everyone is stocking up, some are hopeful, but almost all are convinced that the war will be over before the end of the year.[55]

Despite such hopes, the war was not to end for many months and it was not too long before people realized that repatriation would not mean a return to their normal lives. While Parisians found Paris changed under occupation, others who returned to homes in the Occupied Zone sometimes had an even greater shock. In areas which had been significantly bombed during the hosilities, their homes no longer existed. 'And when at last they returned to their town it was often only to discover that their house had disappeared. So, on these ruins, they planted a cross similar to those in churchyards, a sign which carried their name and their provisional address in some temporary shelter.'⁵⁶ Monsieur Fee was horrified by the state of Amiens when he returned there with his family. The town had been destroyed by German incendiary bombs. 'Arriving at the station in Amiens, what we saw, it was terrible—it was a disaster area, it looked like a desert.'⁵⁷ Unlike those who returned to Paris, many of those who attempted to return to homes in the north of the country were stranded in the capital for several weeks. Those from the departments of the north which had been the site of extensive bombing and fighting, or which were seen as crucial in the battle against England, were placed in holding refugee camps in Verneuil-l'Etang, Bré-tigny, and Versailles in the Paris suburbs.⁵⁸ At Ivry-la-Bataille for example, four thousand refugees were grouped together at the sugar factory where they were looked after by a French *médecin-commandant*, two lieutenant doctors, two German nurses, and sixteen French women.⁵⁹ Those who made it back to their department could be prevented from returning to their homes. On 27 July the prefect of the Somme, whose department was categorized as part of the Forbidden Zone, reported that refugees were being prevented from crossing over to the left bank of the river Somme. He indicated that those resident there should be discouraged from attempting to reach their homes as others who did so were being forced into nearby refugee camps to live in appalling conditions.⁶⁰ Some were not immediately allowed back to their homes. Those who were, found their houses in ruins, their homes pillaged, sometimes completely emptied, their property requisitioned or German soldiers billeted on them, and food shortages and rationing (often not yet very well organized).⁶¹ By contrast, those in the Unoccupied Zone under Vichy, were also subject to rationing, food shortages were frequent, but, generally speaking, apart from those in monocultural or coastal areas, they had an easier time.

Rejecting Vichy

In the weeks that followed their return, the population underwent a process of awakening. They were able to view the situation more rationally in the security of their own homes than they had been able to in lodgings separated from, and often without news of, their loved ones. For those who had believed that the armistice would mean the end of the war, the truth came as a disappointment. Even the closely censored news bulletins and the excessive German and Vichy propaganda, could not hide the fact that the British were managing to hold out against the Germans. Thus, it was inferred by many, as de Gaulle had pointed out, that the armistice had not necessarily been the best or only possible choice for the country. In the light of British success, many French people imagined that Pétain must also be protecting their interests and therefore be playing a double game, secretly waiting to see how things would turn out, maintaining contacts with the British as well as the Germans.[62]

As the weeks drew on, they were able to gain news of lost and separated family members. The total number of men transferred to camps in Germany was 1,580,000.[63] Realization dawned that these men would not be sent home to work in French industry but were likely to remain away for the duration of hostilities in Europe (940,000 were still in prisoner-of-war camps in 1944). The Vichy government had to work hard to prevent dissatisfaction and resentment by putting out extensive propaganda—particularly directed at women—in relation to prisoners.[64] The changed living conditions people found on their return exposed the empty promises made in the propaganda that they would get home and take up their lives again. Initial feelings of relief in relation to the occupying forces evaporated as they gradually discovered the true meaning of the German occupation. Rationing and the difficulties of survival became particularly acute during the winter of 1940–1 which was especially harsh. These troubles were compounded by the fact that finding work was hard, despite the need to rebuild and try to kick-start the economy. Many suffered periods (often prolonged) of unemployment, and working often meant gaining employment with the Germans. As the Occupation increasingly impinged on people's daily lives, they were forced to position themselves in relation to the changes it had brought.

Early forms of Resistance activity explicitly targeted confused Parisian populations. One pamphlet advised them not to be taken in by the friendly and helpful manner of the Germans. 'Don't be under any illusion: these people aren't tourists. Take your time, ignore what they say, shun their concerts and their parades.'[65] Traumatized populations who had been caught up in the exodus had hoped for a return to the security of their daily routines. Such a reaction is understandable for people whose lives had been affected by such significant disruption. Many now wanted to toe the line and practise what some commentators have referred to as the 'mentality of the conquered'. The challenge for the Resistance movement was to fight against this and maintain that the return home did not equate to a return to normality or peace, and that the state of war was an ongoing one. This task was facilitated by the fact that the initial correctness of the German troops changed in the face of growing resistance, meeting it with hostage-taking and reprisals. Such behaviour profoundly influenced French populations who came to see the true extent of German brutality.[66] November 1942 saw the German occupation moving into a much more serious repressive phase with the occupation of the whole country. Few French people, unless they were ideologically sympathetic to Nazism, could have illusions about German intentions towards the country.

By autumn 1941, active support for the Vichy regime was also beginning to wane in both zones. By the time the regime had been in power for a full year, the population had few misconceptions about the true nature of Pétainism. The armistice was not proving to be in the country's best interests. Vichy propaganda efforts had little impact in stemming the tide of support which was beginning to drift away. In spite of his enormous prestige, Pétain's persistent scolding and his insistence on their communal guilt proved irritating and counter-productive. Although people supported him and had enormous respect for his military persona, Vichy soon proved itself to be paradoxical in its aims, often racist and exclusionary in its policies which seemed to have little relevance in a country caught up in war. Historians acknowledge that from autumn 1940 to the summer of 1941, Vichy attempted to gain support for its policies by persuasion, but turned to more authoritarian methods thenceforth as they became aware that only a minority of French people were convinced by the National Revolution.[67] Pétain and his entourage probably also overestimated the extent of the backlash against the Republic. The complete failure of authority during the exodus had pointed up profound weaknesses within the institutions of the Republic. While the French were disgusted with the political establishment and believed that their elites had let them down, this did not necessarily mean that they were prepared to abandon the whole concept of republicanism on a permanent basis.[68] Irène Némirovsky, writing in 1942, puts it thus: 'The French grew tired of the Republic as if she were an old wife. For them, the dictatorship was a brief affair, adultery. But they intended to cheat on their wife, not to kill her. Now they realise that she is dead, their Republic, their freedom. They are mourning her.'[69] Many of those who had initially accepted the Vichy regime came to realize that its very existence, not to mention its policies, made it impossible for them to carry on as if nothing had changed.

Personal experiences of the exodus acted as a crucial variable. It motivated some people to accommodate themselves to the Germans and the Vichy regime; others were so disgusted at the outcome of events that they were persuaded from the early days that something had to be done. This was especially true for those who found themselves displaced in exile in the south. Few took a position of opposition publically against the armistice like de Gaulle, but other individuals were equally opposed to it. At first, there was little they could do. Henri Frenay, for example, was horrified by the complacency he found in the south. After Hitler's annexation of Alsace Lorraine in the autumn of 1940, the Germans expelled all those they considered not to be of German ethnic origin. Frenay railed against their treatment:

> Refugees from Alsace and Lorraine arrive in the region. They are still overwhelmed by the trials they have undergone. Tens upon tens of thousands of them, men, women, and children have been uprooted from their homes, obliged to leave within two hours, bringing only derisory sums of money, leaving everything else behind them including furniture, clothes, crops, and cattle. They relate how in the days following their departure, German families occupy their homes . . . And what is the government doing about it? What is the Marshal doing? This annexation is a violation of the Armistice Convention. It is not enough to offer these unhappy expelled people hot tea in the stations. Public opinion should be alerted, but our press remains quiet on all of this.[70]

These refugees from Alsace and Lorraine would give the later Resistance movement an important boost. Their experience of expulsion, and the treatment they had met at the hands of the Germans, made them natural recruits for anti-Nazi activity. Knots of activists soon realized this and in some areas of the southern zone efforts were made to group them together. Many joined the Resistance group Franc-Tireur.[71]

Certain foreign refugees immediately attempted to seek out those who shared their political allegiances. Others, found themselves isolated, and at first focused all their efforts on attempting to escape internment. In these circumstances, survival was their main priority and initially it was impossible for them to pursue any coherent political activity. As the concentration of foreign refugees grew in certain areas of the southern zone, their presence created a climate of intellectual ferment and discussion about what could be done. In Toulouse, for several years, the bookshop owned by the Italian socialist Silvio Trentin, who had himself come to France as a refugee in 1926, had been a well-known meeting point for political refugees from Italy and elsewhere. In 1940 intellectuals, university professors, and all those who rejected the situation congregated there, confident that they would encounter others with similar views. Two movements would later emerge from these contacts. The first was short-lived. In spring 1941 an escape route was established, known as the 'Réseau Bertaux', one of the first in the region to have a direct link with London. It was dismantled by the Germans in November 1941. Libérér et Fédérer was the name of the subsequent movement to be formed. With an active left-wing political agenda, the first edition of its journal was published in July 1942.[72]

Milieux dominated by refugees became breeding grounds for those opposed to Vichy and collaboration policies. Working on the premiss that they had already lost everything, they no longer had anything to risk, especially if they considered that their lives were already in danger. For some it was their only prospect for survival.[73] French intellectuals like Roland Dorgelès and André Chamson, who had taken temporary refuge in the south, soon found their situation of prolonged exile brought them into contact with such individuals. Through these contacts, they too found themselves drawn into a position of dissidence. That French refugees might have the potential to create unrest was recognized by the authorities who observed their activities closely. In Toulouse, for example, an 'Association of Refugees and those who have withdrawn from the Paris region' was noted by the prefectoral authorities as a group to keep an eye on because of their Gaullist persuasion.[74]

First gestures of resistance were also born of helping distressed refugees. During the exodus, reception communities had been shocked by what they saw. One woman explained:

I saw the Belgians and other refugees during the exodus in 1940. It was my first contact with political life. Several families had been placed in the main square. When you see things like that you discover a world you did not know about before. You can't accept things like that when you are young. People brought on to the main square who have nothing, no home, no country, no nothing. So I offered accommodation to a couple and a young girl. It was something which raised my consciousness of events, it made me think.[75]

Women like this one who sheltered refugees in 1940 were poised to help other political and Jewish refugees later on. With the roads to exile closed and conditions in the camps in the southern zone leaving many of those interned close to starvation, several groups—religious or otherwise—came to their aid. Many of these humanitarian organizations had already helped

Spanish refugees in previous months. The same structures were revitalized during the exodus and now again came into play. The activities of the Protestant movement CIMADE (Comité inter-mouvements auprès des évacués) had first mobilized to help the Protestant refugees evacuated from Alsace who found themselves in difficult circumstances. Its activists, including Madeleine Barot in particular, saw intervention in the internment camps as a natural progression for the movement. After managing to gain access to the internment camp at Gurs, near Toulouse, she realized that the movement could not have much impact alone. She successfully lobbied other local groups, including the Quakers and the Red Cross, to participate. By the end of 1940, she had succeeded in implanting substantial relief structures in Gurs and from there went on to tackle other camps of the southern zone. Shelters for those who were able to escape the camps were soon opened in Toulouse and Marseilles and the logical next step was to establish escape lines to smuggle those most at risk to safety in Switzerland. These were soon in place.[76] In this way, providing humanitarian aid led to illegal activity and later resistance.

Other organizations were also drawn into participating in this kind of early form of resistance, but it was not conceptualized in those terms at the time. In Marseilles, for example, under the aegis of the Emergency Rescue Committee, Varian Fry worked to help refugees trapped in exile. It has been estimated that he saved 1,200 refugees, among them intellectuals and artists like Heinrich Mann, Marc Chagall, André Breton, and Max Ernst.[77] As escape became more difficult, relief also took the form of helping them to survive. Fry's organization helped four thousand people, six hundred financially.[78] He managed to find successful clandestine routes across the Pyrenees at Bandol and by boat, and Fry's organization grew. As efforts to save refugees became impossible by legal means, Fry and his team moved almost seamlessly into illicit activities to achieve their goals. Fry's work was summarized by Victor Serge in the following way: 'Your tenaciousness allowed you to achieve dangerous work and many people (of whom I am one) probably owe you their lives. In fact, this was the very first form of resistance well before this word appeared.'[79] Ultimately, those involved in the process of helping those fleeing Nazi oppression found that they in turn became targets of persecution by the authorities.

> In Toulouse, certain groups of people endeavoured to relieve the misery, to rescue and give shelter to a small number of sad refugees from the camps . . . It is interesting that these same people would be among those who would

later help anti-Nazi Germans or Jews, and they, in their turn, would find themselves hunted down.[80]

Understanding the Exodus

The exodus was a prolonged ordeal for many families, one which defined the Occupation for most communities and which did not pass in any sense once they again found themselves in their familiar surroundings. Could it have been avoided? Many commentators posit the exodus as a symptom of France's lack of preparation for the war and the result of a widespread misconception of what modern warfare would entail. The mass departure of the French people from their homes was predominantly the result of the failure of government and the authorities to predict and organize for the war. Even once it started to become clear that France could not prevent invasion, officials remained blinded to the roles they should play. They failed to improvise or put the needs of those they were theoretically serving above their personal concerns, and this was to have disastrous consequences. It is, of course, impossible to speculate as to whether better preparation, more detailed evacuation plans, and clearer instructions to officials and civilians could have reduced the degree of collapse that took place.

Diary accounts, both at the time and since, present the civilian retreat and exodus as a major contributory factor in the defeat of France. The columns of escaping refugees are cast as having clogged roads and thereby hindered the capacity of the military to organize a concerted defence against the Germans. Many military figures who were caught up in the events of May 1940 were persuaded that the fleeing refugees had a very serious impact on limiting the possibility of troop movement. It seems likely that the presence of civilians caught up in the retreat had some bearing on the capacity of the army to organize any defence to slow down the German advance. Sadoul reported on 14 June:

> That afternoon our general staff tried to organize a defence of the Orge valley. Artillery was placed in the northern direction where the Germans were expected to arrive, but the roads being targeted were black with refugees and to shoot would have been to massacre them . . . Thankfully this order was countermanded and the batteries were withdrawn without shooting.[81]

French High Command also probably bombed fewer bridges in retreat to leave the way free for fleeing refugees. On an individual level, soldiers were compromised by the presence of refugees, especially if they had taken some under their wing. E. M. Guibert decided to hand himself over to the Germans in order to prevent the continuing battles which threatened refugees. 'I then thought things over, and realized that it was all over. I had all these people on my hands, I had to think of them, and not expose them to unnecessary risks.'[82]

However, historians now concur that while evacuation was certainly mismanaged and the presence of refugees added to the general confusion, the exodus itself probably had little bearing on the failure of the Allied military to handle the situation in strategic terms. As the Second World War specialist Jean-Pierre Azéma puts it:

> Some operations relating to food supplies were upset by this flow of civilians, but the defeat was already decided well before civilians came pouring out of their homes on to the roads. In most cases, the flight of the civilians followed the retreat of the French armies and did not precede it.[83]

The exodus was so overwhelming and its proportions so enormous that eyewitnesses naturally imagined that the chaos around them could only have significant wider consequences. This was their war and their capacity to survive would mark their reactions to what they had to face later with the occupation of the country by the Germans.

The Exodus Read as a Warning in Britain

As Hitler's armies stormed their way across the Continent, the British had observed events with horror. They looked to their own situation and wondered what lessons they could draw from the experience. They were aware that the collapse of France would leave them open to Nazi invasion and that Hitler would now turn his attentions to the island. As Churchill had put it, the fall of France put England into straits not known since the Armada.[84] The possibility of a German attack with a view to invasion had already been evoked in discussions between the British and the French in the run-up to the fall of France, and it was clear that both Pétain and Weygand did not rate Britain's chances of resisting attack very highly. Nonetheless, when Churchill answered Weygand's question about how he intended to tackle such an eventuality, Churchill explained that his technical advisers were of the opinion that they should 'drown as many as possible on the way over and knock the others on the head as they crawled ashore'. At which point Weygand dryly conceded, 'I must admit you have a very good anti-tank ditch'.[85] It was anticipated that Hitler would first paralyse the country by air attack and then launch an invasion by sea. Indeed, within ten days of the French accepting the German terms, the Luftwaffe had begun their air raids and the Battle of Britain was underway. On 16 July 1940 Hitler ordered his forces to prepare for Operation Sea Lion and the invasion of Britain. Throughout the late summer and early autumn of 1940, danger of invasion dominated British government concerns. Only with the coming of winter did the prospect of invasion appear less likely.

French civilians were perceived to have succumbed to panic and disobeyed the orders of the authorities. In its reports on events in France, the British press immediately pointed to the dangers of uncontrolled civilian movement. On Tuesday 18 June, for example, in an article in *The Times* entitled 'Refugees and Strategy', the author warned:

> Civilians must not be allowed to mar the mobility of the troops. The lesson for this country, which may any day now see fighting on its roads and its open places, is that those who will take no part in it, especially women and children, must establish themselves as soon as they can in or near the place they propose to occupy when bombing or fighting has begun. Above all, when that happens, they must avoid crowding all the roads and the railways.

Churchill's personal analysis of the collapse of Western Europe focused on the power of the blitzkrieg and he also noted the activities of civilian refugees who had clogged the roads and prevented defensive military movements. This interpretation was doubtless inspired by dispatches from the British ambassador to France, Ronald Campbell, who reported on 21 June:

> to make matters worse the hordes of panic-stricken civilian refugees . . . not only had a shattering effect on French troops but seriously interfered with their operations. I cannot insist too strongly on this point for it played a big part and there is moreover a lesson to be learnt from it.[86]

Throughout these months, as the people of Britain daily believed the invasion might begin, they were reminded of the instructions they had been given about how they should behave. Believing that the civilian disaster in France had been brought about by the lack of a coherent policy, leaving people to improvise in the absence of clear instructions, strategists were determined that the British population should know exactly what they were expected to do in the event of invasion. Instructions were distributed and the populations were reassured that detailed plans for home defence had been drawn up ready for implementation should it prove necessary. As events reinforced the urgency of the situation, the government stepped up its efforts to educate the public. On Wednesday 19 June *The Times* carried the government's official instructions to civilians entitled 'If Britain is Invaded' issued by the Ministry of Information, in cooperation with the War Office and the Ministry of Home Security.

> Hitler's invasions ... were greatly helped by the fact that the civilian population was taken by surprise. They did not know what to do when the moment came. You must not be taken by surprise. This leaflet tells you what general line you should take. More detailed instructions will be given to you when the danger comes nearer. Meanwhile, read these instructions carefully and be prepared to carry them out.

Civilians were urged first and foremost to 'Stay put': unless they were given orders to leave, they should stay where they were. Ignoring this advice would expose them to far greater danger, the risk of machine-gunning from the air, as well as blocking roads along which the armies would need to advance to tackle the invasion. Secondly, people were advised not to believe rumours or spread them. As in France, fifth column anxiety was intense and it was widely held that the Germans had adopted the method of spreading false rumours and issuing false instructions as a means of creating panic and confusion in the civilian population. People were instructed to report anything suspicious and in the event of invasion to refrain from giving the Germans anything or helping them in any way. Conversely, they should be ready to help the British military, organize systems in factories and shops to resist a sudden attack, and, most importantly, 'Think before you act. But think always of your country before you think of yourself.'

The following day the paper announced that every member of the public would receive a copy of the leaflet 'When the Invader comes' and the Ministry of Home Security again reiterated:

> The duty of the public in the event of invasion is to remain where they are unless they are instructed to leave.
> Recent experience in the Low Countries and still more recently in France, has shown how military plans to repel invasion may be dangerously hampered if roads are blocked by refugees.[87]

In another leaflet, headed 'Beating the Invader', Churchill assigned two orders and duties to the nation: 'First: STAND FIRM, and then, after battle, CARRY ON.'[88] Another lesson of the French experience which was taken to heart by the strategists, was the need for strong local leadership. The War Cabinet ordered every community to set up an invasion committee whose role was to plan for the worst. Their considerable powers ranged across the various arms of local government, civil defence, police, ambulance and hospital services. Their task was to set about assuring local services in the aftermath of invasion or air attack: they also had to plan for coping with heavy casualties and disposing of the dead.[89] Anything that might help the invader was taken away or locked up. Maps vanished from the shops, signposts, placenames, and milestones disappeared in an effort to baffle the invader.[90] 'Stop-lines' with pillboxes placed along them were designed to protect against a German advance. Many of them survive to this day.

Millions responded to Foreign Secretary Anthony Eden's call on 14 May 1940, for men aged between 17 and 65 to be members of the Local Defence Volunteers.[91] Renamed the Home Guard in July 1940, more affectionately referred to in recent decades as Dad's Army, its role was to provide preliminary defence in the event of invasion.[92] Less well known was the associated network of resistance cells established by the Secret Service MI6, designed to be activated in the event of invasion with a mission to implement sabotage in enemy-occupied territory.[93]

Whether or not these efforts to plan for possible invasion would have prevented the kind of collapse experienced in France, is difficult to surmise. However, the British public was certainly more prepared for the eventuality. British observers and fleeing British soldiers—since not all were evacuated at Dunkirk and there were many who had to head south where they were often able to board ships on the Atlantic coast—carried back their exodus experiences with them to Britain. They fed a general perception that refugees had contributed to the fall of France. By the time a booklet entitled *Panic* appeared in 1941, acute anxiety of invasion had passed. This collection of extracts from *The Road to Bordeaux* by C. Denis Freeman and Douglas Cooper, relating their experiences during the battle of France, was designed to illuminate British readers and demonstrate to them what had happened there. Few British readers could fail to draw the desired conclusion from this account whose last sentences left no doubts about the importance civilians had played in contributing to the catastrophe.

Only those in the Army knew the awful truth... The Army of France had been defeated by panic among the civilian population which it was fighting to defend. It was the civilians who had met the enemy face to face and, in their fright, taken to the road, sweeping back with them the troops who were advancing to protect them.[94]

The following caution by Harold Nicolson, the then Minister for Information, was reproduced on the front cover:

In the event of invasion of this Island it is the duty of ordinary men and women to 'Stay Put' and not to block the roads. These extracts from *The Road to Bordeaux* will give a vivid picture of what happens to a population which disregards these instructions.

The invasion of Britain did not occur, but had it done so, the British would doubtless have benefited from the experience of the French who had had no such immediate precedent on which to draw.

Afterword

Forgetting and Remembering the Exodus

Un peuple ne porte pas le souvenir des humiliations qu'il a subies comme
le fait un homme.

(A people does not carry the memory of its humiliations as an individual
does.)

André Chamson, *Écrit en 1940*

A recent headline in a broadsheet suggested that the British should
be cautious and less judgemental of their continental neighbours,
emphatically arguing that 'We would have done the same under Nazi
Occupation'.[1] Having escaped invasion and occupation, it is difficult for
foreigners to fully appreciate the delicate and contested nature of the legacy
it left for the French people. For some of those who find these memories
painful, attempting to forget and draw a veil over this difficult period has
been a way of dealing with it. As far as the exodus is concerned, it touched
the majority of French people's lives either because they were actively
involved through their own flight, because they were left behind, or
because they came into contact with the refugees. It was a defining moment
for many. Yet, collective memory appears to have retained little of these
events. By comparison with the extent of debate and cultural production in
relation to the French experience of the war in general, work devoted
explicitly to the exodus is very thin on the ground. The experience is
acknowledged in television documentaries which show clips of contemporary newsreels but often only as an introduction to what followed. In the
1980s and 1990s the trials of some very high profile individuals in France,
including the German Klaus Barbie and the collaborators Paul Touvier and

Maurice Papon, focused interest instead on those who had collaborated with the Germans and this dominated the concerns of historians and the media alike.[2] The national debates and discussions which accompanied these events centred around the previous taboos on the French participation in the Holocaust rather than the apparently less controversial issues of the defeat and the exodus.[3]

It is certainly the case that one gets little sense of the significance of the events of the spring and summer of 1940 close to seventy years ago. Efforts to collect such accounts for this study were often frustrated. In cases where people did agree to discuss it, their exodus is normally reduced to a few sentences which could be summarized as follows: 'We learnt that the Germans were coming. We left. It was terrible on the road, we were shot at. There were all sorts of people there with us, travelling in all sorts of vehicles. Cars often had mattresses on top of them. And then we came home.' Most have no detailed memory of these events, especially if they came home almost immediately and did not remain in exile. Others even demonstrate confusion about when the exodus took place. One witness related a story of leaving Paris to escape the Nazi round-ups of the Jews in 1942 as 'the' exodus, and of course it was also an exodus of sorts. On the other hand, if their accounts of the exodus seem somewhat truncated, as they move into talking about their experiences of the Occupation they need little encouragement before they are offering detailed descriptions of food shortages, their understandings of the Resistance and their own contact with it, however tenuous this may have been. It soon becomes clear to anyone attempting to solicit personal testimonies of the period that the Occupation, rather than the exodus, dominates memory of the Second World War in France. The same is often true of many diary and personal journal wartime accounts. Authors dwell relatively little on their experience of the exodus, preferring to focus on the difficulties of life under the Occupation and the strategies they were able to develop in order to be able to cope with them. The experience of flight is often merely used to introduce what comes later in a relatively cursory way. The return home is often more or less completely absent, or not explicitly mentioned, and many accounts start only after the defeat with an explanation of daily life under the Germans.[4] It seems that the exodus and especially the return home is absent from the historical record.

Why is this so? Part of the reason may appear obvious. No one wants to remember a humiliating, frightening, and unexpected defeat and routing of the population. Such uncomfortable, difficult, and traumatic memories might understandably be pushed to the back of one's mind and this might go some way to explaining why memories of the exodus seem to have been so effectively repressed. Nonetheless, other aspects of the war—memories which show the French in their wartime experience in both positive and at times extremely negative lights—are much more present in the collective consciousness, and are even the subject of public debate. What is of interest to me here, is to try and understand why it is that other difficult and uncomfortable memories of the war, which probably concerned a relatively limited number of French people, have been remembered whereas the exodus which touched the lives of most French people to a greater or lesser degree has been virtually erased from the record of public memory. To understand why this has happened and to explore the dynamics at work, it is necessary to return to the Liberation and see how and where the exodus fits into evolving understandings of the Second World War in collective memory.

Evolving Memories

Some of the battles that took place during the Liberation of France in 1944–5, especially those in the wake of the Normandy landings, provoked similar scenes of civilian exodus to those which had taken place some years before. Many of the civilians who were caught up in the fighting or hiding in the countryside were the same individuals who had fled four years previously.[5] This time, however, the routed soldiers were German rather than French. Martine Rouchard, a young woman who had participated in the exodus in 1940, recorded the following in her diary after seeing some German soldiers heading towards Paris, pushing one of their group in a pram. 'All the faces fade . . . It is French women and children streaming along the road. Some are dying, others cry out in fear or moaning from hunger. I see again the little pale-faced girl with solemn eyes among our refugees.'[6] At this time, memory of the exodus was still very much alive. Indeed, its consequences were still being directly felt for those who had chosen or had been forced into prolonged exile in the summer of 1940 and who were now at last able to return home.

In this context, de Gaulle's priority once he had secured power was not to dwell on the misfortunes brought to the country by defeat and exodus.

His pressing concern was to set out to rebuild the country and, in the interests of national unity, it was convenient to 'assume' that everyone had been working to the same end and that in its way the entire nation had contributed to the Resistance. This convenient glossing over reality was later labelled as the Gaullist myth. However inaccurate as a representation of real events, it was pragmatic and had an important role to play in the reconstruction of the country. In addition to general celebration, the departure of the Germans had brought a wave of dramatic and violent outbursts in communities which sought to punish the perpetrators of collaboration. De Gaulle's concern was to bring these purges under control and establish his administration across the country. An acrimonious dissection of the reasons for the defeat and its consequences could only serve to fuel what was an already potentially explosive situation of French people turning against each other. The time had come for the French people to unite and move forward in an attempt to re-establish their place in the world, not to tear themselves to pieces.

If the reasons for the Gaullist myth are understandable, its success in the late 1940s and 1950s was phenomenal. It tapped into a need to focus on positive memories of events and this assumption of widespread male resistance gave the country a basis upon which to resolve wartime differences. It legitimized and encouraged a certain memory and interpretation of events and gave a powerful mouthpiece to many of those who had been involved in the Resistance and who now needed to regularize their position. It was not easy to give a heroic meaning to the exodus which could contribute to this narrative in a significant way. The public memory of the phoney war, the defeat and its consequences thus became separated from the memory of the dark years which followed. The earlier events were cast as uncomplicated and in a sense resolved whereas the legacy of the Occupation emerged as contentious and difficult. The competing positions taken by French people in relation to collaboration and resistance dominated public consciousness in the post-war period far more than the events of 1939–40. In this way, memories of 1940–4 have had a dominating influence on shaping the memory of the French experience of the Second World War.

The nature and widespread adoption of the Gaullist myth until the late 1950s shows how memory can be manipulated and officially sanctioned in the interests of political convenience. Public memories can often evolve from the desire on the part of some social group to select and organize representations of the past so that these will be embraced by individuals as their own.[7] Individual memories cannot compete and do not have the same status as representations of the past. By the same token, therefore, if there are no social groups which seek to target given events in the past to exploit them for their own ends, this also means that these events can be overlooked and forgotten. Sometimes this is convenient and deliberate, in other cases it is simply an oversight. Sacrifice, suffering, death, and starvation on the roads of France could not be glamorized. They offered little mileage for any political interest group. Furthermore, it was difficult to find any heroism in what could essentially be qualified as 'running away'. It may well be that Vidalenc's masterful book on the exodus which appeared in 1958 was an attempt to make it fit into this heroic resistance narrative. His argument that fleeing Hitler's armies during the exodus was in reality a demonstration of a first form of resistance is a difficult argument to accept in the face of the numerous examples of terrified departures. Perhaps his work should be read as an attempt to render the exodus experience more acceptable and to create a space for people to remember it within the resistance paradigm. The fact that this failed is perhaps a demonstration that the argument itself did not correspond closely enough to survivors' perceptions of their own experiences.

Active involvement in the Resistance only concerned a small minority of French people, so the majority could not contribute to the heroic discourse of memory of resistance. But there was also a parallel memory where the focus was on victimhood and martyrdom. This more inclusive metaphor of victimhood was convenient on many levels. It united the nation as one that had collectively suffered at the hands of the Germans and it allowed the population to avoid taking any responsibility for other choices they may have made, including their possible involvement in collaboration, thereby enabling them to avoid historical responsibility. Even as the interest in the Gaullist myth started to recede, memory of the defeat was still eclipsed by the images of sacrifice and deprivation that accompanied it.

It could be argued that as the memory of victimhood gained public currency it should also have encompassed memories of the exodus. This period could be represented as a time when people had no control over their fate; they were driven from their homes by the German invaders and the failure of their government and administrations to protect their interests. However, the exodus memory barely emerged within the images of victimhood. The reason for this may be related to the sense of disappointment experienced by many who believed that, after the armistice, peace would soon be agreed and their lives would return to normal. The shock of returning home to the changed circumstances of the Occupation and the years of repression and deprivation which followed, thus suppressed the importance of the exodus experience.[8] This may perhaps go some way to explaining why the memories of the Occupation itself served to overwhelm and render less significant the often more traumatic experiences of the exodus. Furthermore, it could also have been because the return home included an element of choice—though limited—for many families. The implication that they may have made the wrong choice, that they allowed themselves to be duped into believing that their lives would now return to some sort of normality, that they moved into a situation of accommodating themselves to the Germans, may explain why they do not want to explore in depth the moment at which they settled on this path.

The town of Oradour-sur-Glane clearly symbolizes the way in which victimhood came to be a central aspect of post-war memory. This town, which was the scene of appalling German atrocity, has been preserved as it was at the time, as a permanent reminder of the horrors of the Occupation.[9] At first an exclusively French place of commemoration, since 1999, it has become a 'global' Centre de la Mémoire which encompasses all victims of occupation, totalitarianism, and genocide. Commemoration of this kind represents another important way in which memories can be kept alive in the local and national consciousness.[10] Deciding who, what, and when commemoration should take place falls both to the state and to the localities. In the context of the exodus, the issue of commemorating a defeat raises obvious difficulties and it is perhaps not surprising that neither authority ever chose to do this. Those killed in the campaign of 1939–40 have simply been added to the lengthy lists of those who lost their lives on the war memorials of the 1914–18 war which are a central feature of every village, town, and city in France. In line with traditional expectations that memorials should concern those who die in battle, nothing equivalent exists to commemorate the civilian experience of the exodus. The tremendous sacrifices made by numerous French civilians along with the soldiers, the remarkable courage that many displayed in the face of defeat, had no bearing on the final outcome. People leaving home, being separated from their family, taking risks, being attacked, living dangerously, even losing loved ones did not change the fact that the Germans won and occupied.[11]

Furthermore, trying to commemorate the exodus, assuming there was a will to do so, would prove a difficult task, for when would such a commemoration be held? The dates of flight of populations were spread across weeks starting as early as 10 May 1940, and people were still leaving their homes further south well over a month later. While 11 November provided a memorable and symbolic date for the purposes of commemoration of the First World War, it was more difficult to find an appropriate date to commemorate the Liberation which took place throughout August 1944. However, different regions, towns, even the capital have mostly fixed their own dates to celebrate the Liberation and tend to do so regularly each year. No such local consensus has sprung up about the exodus. The recent grandiose commemorations of the sixtieth anniversary of the Liberation in France directed the focus for these ceremonies very much towards the events of 1944 and did not move beyond them. Once again, the exodus experience was left out of the picture.

Discomfort with the events surrounding the defeat is also reflected in French commemorative culture such as war museums which have also tended to overlook the exodus. Writing in 1995, Marie-Hélène Joly, an employee of the Ministry of Culture in France, noted that the memorial legacy of the Second World War is one of division and conflict and that there is no consensus in relation to the fall of France and the armistice as well as the position adopted by the Vichy regime and collaboration.[12] In the early post-war years, in reaction to the absence of a coherent national position on the commemoration of the period, a number of groups who rejected the political consensus associated with the Gaullist myth set up their own war museums. Most of these museums emphasize a duty to remember and many now seek to explain the Resistance along with deportation and the Holocaust.

The exodus clearly holds an ambiguous place in French collective memory. Its apparent absence from official commemorations may go a long way towards explaining why people find it difficult to talk about it and why they have not cultivated detailed memories of these events. Dori Laub, the psychologist, discussed the traumatic processes inherent in 'Bearing Witness' to the memory of difficult events in the past. She explored how the 'act of telling' can itself become extremely traumatizing. Furthermore, if you relate an experience without being properly heard or listened to, the telling of it might be lived as a return of the trauma, a re-experiencing of the event itself.[13] Having an audience is therefore crucial in the process of recounting difficult experiences. Madame Perrot confirmed her own experience that few people had expressed any interest in hearing about these events. She explains:

We don't talk about the war much and when we do, it's more about the Resistance as the exodus is not a very glorious time to explore. I did tell my children but they were more interested in the Resistance. It is strange that the Resistance which touched so few people is talked about so much, yet this experience which touched so many is obscured. At the time we were so glad to get home and to get on with our lives we just wanted to forget about it. We wanted not to talk about it. We were home safe and sound and that was the end of it. This is the first time I've talked about it for as long as I can remember.[14]

Personal Narratives of the Exodus

Nonetheless, if the exodus experience is often overlooked in post-war accounts, it is by no means completely absent from French collective memory. The numerous personal narratives this study has drawn on in order to reconstruct the exodus is evidence of the richness of the testimony available. The works cited here, as well as other numerous fictional novels and films which allude to the exodus, demonstrate that it does have a presence in popular memories of the war, if a relatively limited one. This study has preferred to draw on contemporary diaries or journals where possible as these tend to have more immediacy and describe vivid personal involvement. While women were more likely to be caught up in the exodus than men who were mobilized on the front, few of them left detailed accounts of this experience. It may well be that many women recorded their exodus in diaries and journals but since these were less likely to be published and therefore did not often reach the public domain, perhaps remaining hidden in family archives or tucked away in trunks and attics, this study has mainly drawn on accounts by men. Women's experiences are, however, very well represented and female narratives have been introduced wherever possible.

Those accounts which were published during the war itself clearly have to be treated with care. Indeed, some of the earliest wartime accounts were politically engaged and many were labelled as dishonest because of a deliberate attempt to use them to legitimize discourses of collaboration. Lucien Rebatet's *Les Décombres*, for example, which became a best-seller in 1942, repeatedly emphasizes the disastrous nature of the old regime in order to put the new one in a better light. In this context, *Les Lettres françaises*, the Resistance journal, celebrated the appearance of Antoine de Saint-Exupéry's

Pilote de guerre, an account of his experiences in 1940 which appeared in 1942. The clandestine publication described Saint-Exupéry's work as a book which the French 'could read without blushing' in contrast to 'shameful war books' like Rebatet's *Les Décombres*. 'For three years the complicity of the enemy cultivates the memory of June 1940. Those who remind people of the defeat, and comment on it, celebrate it because it is their justification and their comfort.'[15]

Concern that their accounts may seem biased in some way might also explain why other narrators were sometimes emphatic about their attempts to offer an honest account of their experiences. Léon Werth asserted, 'I am relating what I saw and what I felt. I am not attempting a historical reconstruction, or a coherent and critical recital of military activity after the event.'[16] And again, 'I am relating detached episodes, separated one from another. A bit more topography and it may perhaps be clearer, but this would make it more of a report and slow it down, a process which is more likely to falsify this account.'[17] Later in the book he qualified his description of a particularly obnoxious collaborator and explained, 'I would like to apologize to the reader for reporting this speech but I am not writing a novel and I do not choose my characters.'[18]

Visual records of the exodus have survived along with such personal testimonies. News film and photos of the exodus were taken and widely circulated both during and after the war: some photos have been reproduced as illustrations in this book. Photographers sought to conform to a manner of presentation which would be considered acceptable to those who would see them. They attempted to capture scenes which emphasized the disastrous proportions of the catastrophe, which would arouse pity for the plight of those involved or admiration for their endurance.[19] 'Many images of refugees circulated within a framework of shared understanding that on an individual level the exodus meant loss of possessions and a way of life, and that loss and impediment could be symbolized metonymically by the farm-wagon in Paris, the dead horse at the roadside or by shoes impossible to walk in and bundles too heavy to carry.'[20] However, some contemporary commentators felt that the scale of events was such that neither visual representations nor words could communicate what they had witnessed. André Morize wrote in 1941 that 'No printed words or photos have ever succeeded in exactly recreating the atmosphere of the nightmarish scenes of desolation.'[21] Similarly, Camille Bourniquel wrote in his diary on 11 June 1940: 'Hell is on the roads and at the entrance to the bridges of the Loire.

No films from the cinematographic service of the army, no reporter who was there could give the slightest idea of the shuffling flow of humanity under the beating sun!'[22]

It is impossible to judge how representative an impression the surviving accounts and images can offer. What is noticeable, however, is that most accounts of the exodus seem to be punctuated by certain key iconic moments whether they were written at the time or since. Most make reference to hordes of refugees of all kinds using all manner of transport and clogging roads in rural settings. Many accounts describe the refugees as a heterogeneous mixture of people from all walks of life. Accounts are also often framed in terms of their narrators being one of the last to leave Paris or having been one of the lucky few to manage to take the last train south from the capital or to cross the Loire to safety before the bridges were detonated by the French army in retreat. Another crucial moment described is that of hearing Pétain's speech. Few claim to have heard de Gaulle. Many of these 'moments' have now assumed symbolic status, and as such tend to emerge regularly in other cultural representations of this experience.

Cultural Representations of the Exodus

Fiction has offered many of those who experienced these events a means of expressing what happened to them. Richard Cobb, for example, has insisted on the boost that the exodus brought to literary production. He remarked on the fact that people were forced to walk, obliging them to discover or rediscover the landscape and thereby providing authors with new material.[23] Others have noted that the exodus did not stimulate a body of creative literature comparable to that of the Occupation.[24] Yet, those interested in memory have emphasized the importance of the link between cultural production and the cultivation of certain collective memories. In this way, an overview of the exodus, an exploration of its place in cultural production can help us to understand better some of the dynamics involved in how people remember these events. For example, while the exodus appears to be relatively absent from the collective consciousness of the wartime experience, it has nonetheless had a widespread symbolic presence in films, many of which have shaped iconic visual memories of these events. One of the earliest of these was *Casablanca* (1942) for which the exodus was a backdrop. The opening sequences portray recognizable scenes of civilians fleeing and maps chart the refugee trail which went from Paris to Marseilles and thence to Vichyite Casablanca where the often well-to-do refugees waited anxiously for papers which would gain them passage to Lisbon and promised freedom. Designed as a propaganda film to educate American audiences about the nature of Vichy and the situation in France, it tends to be remembered more for its romantic storyline.

The French feature film *Les Jeux interdits* (Forbidden Games, 1952) by René Clement, based on a novel by François Boyer which appeared in 1947, had an important role in shaping retrospective views of the exodus in the early post-war years.[25] The film was especially popular in the US and UK where it collected numerous accolades including an Academy award for best foreign language film and a BAFTA. Its reputation is mainly for being one of the first films to show the horrors of war through the eyes of children who become caught up in an obsession with death. The opening scenes of the film show queues of terrified refugees under attack from the air by machine-gunners, and these images have become the key iconic representation of the exodus in French collective memory. Paulette, a young girl, is sheltered from the air attack by her mother's dead body. She emerges to chase after her dog, only then realizing that both her parents have been killed and that she has been left completely alone. The child subsequently meets and befriends a young peasant lad, Michel, who takes her home to his family. The children indulge in necromantic fantasies and conduct obsessive death rituals in an animal cemetery they create. Some commentators have seen the film as a critique of war. The beautiful Paulette is a symbol of purity soiled by the terrible 'war games' of the adults. War erupts into the lives of children and steals their innocence. This idea is expressed most clearly when the little boy, Michel, kills a cockroach with a penholder. After having drawn spirals above it and imitated the noise of a plane, he brutally pierces the creature. When Paulette protests against the murder of the insect, Michel replies, 'it was not me, it was a bomb'.[26] The film also alludes to the military defeat. When the soldier in the family reaches home, he explains his experience to his father: 'There ain't no bosses . . . no more English . . . no more nothing . . . So? I says to myself, it ain't worth walking along like this fore'er, is it? So I legged it. And 'ere I am.'[27] *Les Jeux interdits* successfully lifted the taboo of representing descriptions of the military collapse of 1940, but it was short-lived. The conflict in Algeria erupted soon after the film's appearance and it was a long time before any other film-maker attempted a detailed exploration of these events.[28]

In the plethora of cultural production that has emerged about the Second World War experience since the 1960s, literature has been the main vector. In line with the dominant memories discussed earlier, the experience of the Occupation rather than the exodus itself has been the main focus of this body of work. A gradual uncovering of women's experience also emerged through this literature post-1968 and the Jewish experience of persecution and deportation dominated accounts from the 1980s onwards.[29] For those who did choose to write about the exodus, as in *Iron in the Soul*, one of the volumes of Sartre's *Chemins de la Liberté* (Roads to Freedom), the exodus provides a marvellous fictional tool, a perfect plot device enabling authors to contrive meetings between the most unlikely individuals. Fictional accounts made much of the difficult travelling conditions, dramatic scenes of separation from children, and unlikely meetings along the road. The frequency of extraordinary sexual encounters in Gabriel Danzou's novel *L'Exode* (1960) is the only feature which betrays that it is fiction; in almost every other way, the detailed descriptions so convincingly capture the atmosphere of the exodus, they must certainly reflect a considerable measure of first-hand personal experience. His story of a lost child is particularly poignant.

> 'Mum has left in the train, Mum has left in the train', he wept. His mother, carrying a newborn baby, someone remembered noticing her, had got on the train without him, certainly intending to find a place and then come back to get him. The unfortunate woman never imagined that once inside the compartment she would not be able to move again or ask for help from others on the train who were all completely immersed in their own worries![30]

The first volume of Regine Desforge's popular wartime series of novels, *La Bicyclette bleue* (1986), also uses the roads of the exodus to engineer a chance meeting for her key protagonists.

Recent developments suggest a significant renewed interest in this period of the war. In particular, two films—*Les Égarés* (2002) and *Bon Voyage* (2003)—have appeared which attempt to represent explicitly the civilian experience of the period. Both draw on children's exodus memories and use them as a backdrop to recount extraordinary stories emanating from the situations and events of the time. *Les Égarés*, directed by André Téchiné, is based on a novel entitled *Le Garçon aux yeux gris* (Fayard, 2001) by Gilles Perrault. Perrault used the exodus as a situational ploy which allows two extremely unlikely characters to meet. He was himself 'a mature 9-year-old during the exodus', as he put it, where 'we met such unexpected people'.[31] *Bon Voyage* takes on much more serious subject matter. Its director, Jean-Paul

Rappeneau, also described himself as 'a little boy of the exodus [*un petit garçon de l'exode*]'.[32] Dramatizing the last days of the Third Republic in Bordeaux, the somewhat convoluted and complicated storylines are set against a wonderful reconstruction of events. Again we see many iconic and familiar images of the exodus, including the last train to Bordeaux and scenes of streams of refugees flooding into the city. Most recently, Irène Némirovsky's best-selling book *Suite française* met enormous success on both sides of the Channel and captured popular imagination about the period. The extraordinary and tragic circumstances of its origins have certainly added to its appeal.[33]

An immigrant from Kiev, Irène Némirovsky arrived in Paris in 1919 where she quickly established herself as a best-selling writer. At the time of the outbreak of the war, she was married with two daughters, Denise and Elisabeth. The children, then aged 5 and 13, were sent away from Paris to the care of their nanny's mother at Issy-l'Evêque in the Sâone-et-Loire, south of Dijon. In June 1940 the Némirovskys joined their children and they all soon found themselves under German occupation. Classified as Jews by the Vichy authorities and obliged to wear the yellow star, Némirovsky, not unaware of the dangers she was facing, refused to flee or contemplate exile. She embarked upon *Suite française*, a major work along the lines of Tolstoy's *War and Peace*. The French police soon came for her and she died on 17 August 1942 after being deported to Auschwitz. Her husband soon suffered a similar fate. The two children survived the war after spending the last two years of the occupation in hiding. Denise had fled with Némirovsky's precious manuscript but had never had the courage to open her mother's notebook. Years later, before handing it over to a library, Denise decided to transcribe the miniscule handwriting which filled it. She discovered

A vivid snapshot of France and the French—spineless, defeated and occupied: here was the exodus from Paris; villages invaded by exhausted hungry women and children battling to find a place to sleep, if only a chair in a country inn; cars piled high with furniture, mattresses, pots and pans, running out of petrol and left abandoned in the roads; the rich trying to save their precious jewels; a German soldier falling in love with a French woman under the watchful eye of her mother-in-law; the simple dignity of a modest couple searching amidst the chaos of the convoys fleeing Paris for a trace of their wounded son.[34]

Published in France in 2004 to enormous critical acclaim, described by *Le Monde* newspaper as 'a masterpiece', it was awarded the prestigious French literary Renaudot prize.

The first part of the book, entitled 'Storm', is a valuable account of the exodus and written in 1941-2, it is almost contemporary with the events it describes. The narrative tells the interweaving stories of several key characters. Their various trajectories powerfully depict the diversity of experiences during the exodus. Of her characters, it is the description of the Michauds, 'the only ones who are truly noble', who come closest to those in the memoirs that have survived.[35] Unable to get a lift from their employer at the bank, they make for the train station.

> They would never manage to get inside the large departure area; it was closed, locked, blocked off by soldiers and by the jostling crowd crushed against the barriers. They stayed until the evening, struggling in vain. All around them people were saying. 'Too bad. We'll have to walk.'
>
> Everyone spoke with a kind of devastated astonishment. They clearly didn't believe what they were saying. The looked around and expected some miracle: a car, a truck, anything that would take them. But nothing came. So they headed out of Paris on foot, past the city gates, dragging their bags behind them in the dust, then on into the suburbs, all the while thinking, 'This can't be happening! I must be dreaming!'[36]

This couple, like Georges Adrey and his wife, spend their exodus mostly on foot. Madame Michaud peers at all the soldiers she meets in her heart-rending search for her beloved son Jean-Marie.

> Madame Michaud kept thinking she saw her son among them. Not once did she see his regiment's number, but a kind of hallucination took hold of her. Every unfamiliar young face or voice caused her to tremble so fiercely that she had to stop dead in her tracks, clutching her heart and softly muttering, 'Oh, Maurice, isn't that...'[37]

It is this kind of evocative detail with a certain eyewitness quality about it which so convincingly brings the period alive. Némirovsky's intention that the novel should 'unfold like a film' successfully adds to its vividness and apparent realism.[38] This is doubtless the main reason for its popularity. The various strands of the narrative are at times confusing to follow, but perhaps no more so than other similar styles of books upon which she modelled its structure. There are, however, some flaws. While the story is masterfully told, her cynicism towards the privileged classes is very apparent, and the satire sometimes interferes. The acts of violence she describes, the horrific murder of the priest Philippe by the orphans he evacuates, is possibly intended to symbolize the complete collapse of social structures, but it does not ring true. The book is also curiously lacking in ideology. Although

Némirovsky writes at length of the politics of her situation in her notes, and appears aware that her life is under threat, the narrative makes little mention or critique of Nazism. Perhaps her notes explain why:

> Never forget that the war will be over and the entire historical side will fade away. Try to create as much as possible: things, debates . . . that will interest people in 1952 or 2052.[39]

This decision to adopt such a neutral position is a serious shortcoming, but does not diminish the moving evocation of 1940 that this work achieves.

Teaching the History of the Exodus

While representations of the exodus can be tentatively traced in literary and filmic representations of the period, since the work of Vidalenc in the late 1950s, traditional historians have tended to avoid writing about it. This is largely because of the lack of 'official' sources and archives. This has made it impossible to put together the kind of formal 'scientific' history of the period which is especially favoured in France. The very nature of the event, with everyone—including most officials—fleeing from their posts, meant that the archives upon which professional historians normally depend, such as prefects' reports, are either not available or incomplete. So the historian is largely dependent on journals, memories, oral accounts, and novels to piece together the collective experience of this event. In 1970 Nicole Ollier produced a moving personalized account which was cross-referenced in as scholarly a way as possible and evoked the experience very convincingly.[40] Today there is a growing realization that this episode in French history has been largely overlooked and some studies have started to appear which draw on the existing archives, especially those in the departments which received the most refugees, for example. In 2000 the town of Montauban held a conference which explored many of the issues faced by the host departments in 1940. This research was later published as a book.[41] A 450-page description of the exodus appeared in 2003, by Pierre Miquel.[42] This rather vulgarized account attempts to offer a detailed exploration of the various trajectories taken by those caught up in it, but offers very little analysis and is rather difficult to digest. It does, however, signal increased interest in these events. Further work by more serious scholars is in the pipeline and there are a growing number of doctoral theses on the subject.[43]

These signs of burgeoning uptake are also evident in the French school system. In 2002 Éditions Maynard published a version of Léon Werth's moving account of his *33 jours* with full commentary—some of this account has been quoted here.[44] Recommended as a school history text for pupils in the equivalent of the sixth form in France, it provides a powerful and accessible first-hand account. Similarly, a novel by Philippe Bardeau entitled *Juin 40: Peur sur la route* (June 1940: Fear on the Roads), is also designed for teaching purposes. This fictional reconstruction of events of the exodus follows the adventures of 14-year-old Georges and thereby taps into a Republican pedagogical tradition in education of using the experience of children as key protagonists in history. This project, sponsored by the Ministry of Defence, states its intention as being that of 'using rigorous historical methods' and 'placing the reader at the heart of difficult periods of our history'.[45] The inclusion of such texts on school syllabuses points to a growing awareness of the importance of these events.

Finally, cross-cultural and cross-national perspectives on these events appear to be opening up. Journalist and historian Max Lagarrigue has recently published a history of the exodus experience of the people of Charleroi in Belgium who found themselves in the department of the Tarn-et-Garonne in 1940.[46] Heavily based on oral sources, Senator Jean Baylet introduces the book as 'giving witnesses the chance to express themselves for the first time about these tragic moments which nonetheless bore witness to great human solidarity'. Baylet goes on to note:

> What is unknown is that the Tarn-et-Garonne was therefore during the period of the Second World War one of the most important crossroads of clandestine Belgian immigration for England via Spain. This is further proof that the history of the Tarn-et-Garonne, an ancestral land of refuge and hospitality, is inextricably linked to that of our Belgian friends.[47]

This joint effort at historical research instigated by both communities demonstrates that there are ways for this kind of work to be successfully carried out 'from below'. The Charleroi authorities organized a call for witnesses in the local press in both Charleroi and the Tarn-et-Garonne. In 2001 refugees and their hosts were brought together at an event sponsored by both of the authorities concerned. The resulting book, *1940: La Belgique du repli* (2005), marked 'the birth of long-lasting exchanges between the families of those who were in retreat and those who provided them with shelter, sometimes even marriage, and mutual support'. Those involved celebrated that fact that they had brought to light 'issues, rarely tackled by traditional historical scholarship, which were at the heart of this project and the work that grew from it'.[48]

Such developments, combined with the enormous surge of interest in the exodus that has been brought about by Némirovsky's *Suite française*, seem to pave the way for a more informed and open discussion. It may well be that there is now an audience for the few survivors who will be encouraged to speak about those weeks which were, for many, among the most traumatic of their lives. The attraction of such memory work has been the marked individualism that is attached to it. Each person can define their own relationship with the past and each narrative is as valid as any other. Some commentators have therefore expressed concern that the current shift to memory has meant that historical facts become of secondary importance.[49] This shift from history to memory may even lay the basis for the abandonment of history altogether. The fear that memory may replace history has led Henry Rousso to comment, 'How can we remember what we do not know?'[50] The developments explored here suggest that if history and memory work together, the forgotten popular experiences of the defeat of 1940 could be more openly explored and acknowledged. It is to be hoped that this book will contribute to the process and add to understandings of these events. The seventy-year commemorations of the defeat and the exodus loom large for 2010. It may be that this anniversary will serve as an ideal opportunity for a rethinking of the dramatic events which surround this defining moment in the history of France in the twentieth century.

Notes

INTRODUCTION

1. C. Bourniquel, 'Printemps 40', *Esprit* (1960), 1556.
2. Quoted in H. R. Kedward, 'Patriots and Patriotism in Vichy France', *Transactions of the Royal Historical Society* (1981), 181.
3. L. Rebatet, *Les Décombres 1938/1940: Les Mémoires d'un fasciste*, i (Paris: Pauvert, 1976), 498.
4. A. Lunel, *Par d'étranges chemins* (Monaco: L. Jaspard, 1946), 52.
5. N. Ollier, *L'Exode: Sur les routes de l'an 40* (Paris: Laffont, 1969), 126.
6. G. Sadoul, *Journal de guerre* (Paris: Harmattan, 1994), 323.
7. Ibid. 316–17.
8. Ibid. 317.
9. Ibid. 323.
10. L. Werth, *33 jours* (Paris: Magnard, 2002), 14.
11. R. Dorgelès, *Vacances forcés* (Paris: Albin Michel, 1985), 11-12.
12. G. Adrey, *Journal d'un replié: Notes et impressions d'un métallo Parisien pendant l'exode (11 juin–26 juin 1940)* (Paris: René Débresse, 1941), 36-7.
13. R. Downing, *If I Laugh* (London: Harrap, 1941), 7.
14. G. Adrey, *Journal d'un replié*, 16.
15. W. H. Halls, *The Youth of Vichy France* (Oxford: OUP, 1981), 5.
16. See discussion in conclusion about those who wrote about the Exodus experience.
17. S. de Beauvoir, *La Force de l'âge*, ii (Paris: Gallimard, 1960), 502.
18. Ibid. 300.
19. S. Hoffmann, 'Témoignage', in M. Lagarrigue (ed.), *1940: La France du repli, L'Europe de la défaite* (Toulouse: Éditions Privat, 2001), 16.
20. R. Rémond, 'L'Opinion française des années 1930 aux années 1940: Poids de l'événement, permanence des mentalités', in J.-P. Azéma, and F. Bédarida (eds.), *Vichy et les Français* (Paris: Fayard, 1990), 483.
21. A. Papillon, 'L'Exode à Paris en juin 40: Causes, déroulement, mémoire', Maîtrise (Paris, June 1990), 28.
22. L. Werth, *33 jours*, 11.
23. Unpublished diary of Georgette Guillot held in the Archives nationales (henceforth AN) 72 AJ/2277 J.
24. J. Vidalenc, *L'Exode de mai–juin 40* (Paris: PUF, 1957), 252.

25. M. Bloch, *L'Étrange Défaite* (1946; Paris: Gallimard, 1990), 162.
26. G. Guillot, Unpublished diary, 5.
27. M. Perrot, interview with the author (Paris, Apr. 2005).
28. M. Darrow, *French Women and the First World War* (Oxford: Berg, 2000), 115.
29. J. Horne, and A. Kramer, *German Atrocities 1914: A History of Denial* (New York: Yale University Press, 2001).
30. Ibid.
31. P. Nivet, *Les Réfugiés français de la Grande Guerre 1914–1920: Les 'Boches du Nord'* (Paris: Economica, 2004), 555.
32. Ibid.

CHAPTER I

1. J.-L. Crémieux-Brilhac, *Les Français de l'an 40*, i (Paris: Gallimard, 1990), 456.
2. H. Diamond, *Women and the Second World War in France: Choices and Constraints, 1939–1948* (London: Longman, 1999).
3. G. Sadoul, *Journal de guerre*, 17.
4. J.-L. Crémieux-Brilhac, *Les Français de l'an 40*, i. 456–65.
5. See J. Jackson, *The Fall of France: The Nazi Invasion of 1940* (Oxford: OUP, 2003), 27 for a detailed description of these defence plans.
6. P. Vaillaud, *L'Exode, mai–juin 1940* (Paris: Perrin, 2000), 11.
7. See J. Jackson, *Fall of France* and A. Shennan, *The Fall of France 1940* (Harlow: Longman, 2000), whose work complicates this picture somewhat and shows that confidence in the capacity of the armies to defeat the Germans was not present in all quarters.
8. Table adapted from P. Vaillaud, *L'Exode*, 14.
9. A. Papillon, 'L'Exode à Paris en juin 40', 14.
10. Table put together from J. Vidalenc, *L'Exode*, 23–4.
11. P. Vaillaud, *L'Exode*, 13.
12. P. Miquel, *L'Exode, 10 mai–20 juin 1940* (Paris: Plon, 2003), 410.
13. N. Ollier, *L'Exode: Sur les routes de l'an 40* (Paris: Laffont, 1969), 32.
14. N. A. Dombrowski, 'Beyond the Battlefield: The French Civilian Exodus of May–June 1940', Ph.D. thesis (Ann Arbor: UMI, 1996), 26.
15. Ibid. 40.
16. L. L. Downs, 'Milieu Social or Milieu Familial? Theories and Practices of Childrearing among the Popular Classes in 20th-Century France and Britain: The Case of Evacuation (1939–1945)', *Family and Community History* (2005), 57.
17. Ibid.
18. F. Trabacca, 'L'Enfance en mouvement de l'evacuation à l'exode: Les Enfants de Paris et de la Région parisienne en déplacement pendant la Deuxième Guerre mondiale, 1939–1940', DEA (Paris, Oct. 2004).
19. N. A. Dombrowski, 'Beyond the Battlefield', 48.

20. A. Meynier, 'Les Déplacements de la population vers la Bretagne en 1940–1941', *Les Annales de Bretagne* (1948), 87.

21. N. Ollier, *L'Exode: Sur les routes de l'an 40*, 30.

22. A. Papillon, 'L'Exode à Paris en juin 40', 73.

23. Hoffman refers to this departure in Sept. 1939 as 'the first exodus' although that term is more commonly used to denote the first wave of departures from north and eastern France in May 1940.

24. S. Hoffman, 'Témoignage', in Lagarrigue (ed.), *1940: La France du repli*, 15.

25. G. Guillot, Unpublished diary, 1.

26. P. Mendès France, *Liberté, liberté, chérie* (Paris: Fayard, 1977), 11.

27. N. Ollier, *L'Exode: sur les routes de l'an 40*, 31.

28. Ibid.

29. N. A. Dombrowski, 'Beyond the Battlefield', 39.

30. A. Papillon, 'L'Exode à Paris en juin 40', 13; N. A. Dombrowski, 'Beyond the Battlefield', 67.

31. AN F23 225, quoted in A. Papillon, 'L'Exode à Paris en juin 40', 14.

32. For a fuller discussion of these debates see N. A. Dombrowski, 'Beyond the Battlefield', 39; A. Papillon, 'L'Exode à Paris en juin 40', 14.

33. N. A. Dombrowski, 'Beyond the Battlefield', 57.

34. Ibid. 60.

35. A. Papillon, 'L'Exode à Paris en juin 40', 14.

36. See C. Delporte, 'The Image and Myth of the "Fifth Column" during the Two World Wars', in V. Holman and K. Keppy (eds.), *France at War in the Twentieth Century* (Oxford: Berghahn, 2000), 50–61.

37. N. Ollier, *L'Exode: Sur les routes de l'an 40*, 35.

38. J.-L. Crémieux-Brilhac, *Les Français de l'an 40*, 541.

39. In Mar. 1940 reports were sent to the French government by the Parliamentary Army Committee that there were 'grave insufficiencies' at Sedan and that this was a 'weak point' in the French defences. Huntziger replied that he believed that 'no urgent measures are necessary to reinforce the Sedan front'. J. Jackson, *Fall of France,* 35 ff, for a superb account of this military defeat.

40. P. Miquel, *L'Exode*, 96.

41. Ibid. 83.

42. Ibid. 109.

43. Ibid. 114.

44. J. Vidalenc, *L'Exode de mai–juin 1940,* 107.

45. Mme Asquin, interview with the author (Amiens, April 2005).

46. P. Miquel, *L'Exode*, 413.

47. P. Mendès France, *Liberté, liberté, chérie*, 21.

48. H. Amouroux, *La Grande Histoire des Français sons l'Occupation*, i. *Le Peuple du désastre 1939–1940* (Paris: Laffont, 1976), 389.

49. B. and F. Groult, *Journal à quatre mains* (Paris: Denoël, 1962), 24.

50. Ibid. 26.

51. J. Vidalenc, *L'Exode de mai–juin 40*, 123.
52. P. Baudouin, *The Private Diaries (March 1940–January 1941) of Paul Baudouin* (London: Eyre & Spottiswood, 1948), 31.
53. P. Mendès France, *Liberté, liberté, chérie*, 15.
54. P. Baudouin, *Private Diaries*, 31.
55. W. Churchill, *The Second World War*, ii. *Their Finest Hour* (1949; London: Cassell, 1967), 42.
56. J.-L. Crémieux-Brilhac, *Les Français de l'an 40*, i. 545.
57. Those Belgians who did not make it to France simply waited in whatever shelters they could reach, often in the open air, until the fighting calmed. Many then returned home to find complete destruction. Most then had to survive as best they could for several days until the Wehrmacht finally occupied the whole of the country and re-established essential services.
58. P. Miquel, *L'Exode*, 408.
59. A. Fabre-Luce, *Journal de France 1939–1944* (Geneva: Éditions du Cheval Ailé, 1946), 204–5.
60. D. Léca, *La Rupture de 40* (Paris: Fayard, 1975), 142.
61. J. Vidalenc, *L'Exode de mai–juin 40*, 124.
62. E. Dépigny, 'Juin 40 à l'Hôtel de Ville', Unpublished diary kept by the Director of Finance at Paris Town Hall, 1943–4, 5.
63. M. Gilbert, *Winston Churchill*, vi. *1939–1941* (London: Heinemann, 1983), 369.
64. H. Amouroux, *Le Peuple du désastre*, 357.
65. I. Ousby, *Occupation: The Ordeal of France* (London: Pimlico, 1997), 23.
66. General M. Weygand, *Recalled to Service* (London: Heinemann, 1952), 47.
67. P. Baudouin, *Private Diaries*, 35.
68. J.-L. Crémieux-Brilhac, *Les Français de l'an 40*, i. 580.
69. A. Werth, *The Last Days of Paris: A Journalist's Diary* (London: Hamish Hamilton, 1940), 65.
70. J. Vidalenc, *L'Exode de mai–juin 40*, 162. For the full text of this which appeared in *Le Temps* on 19 May 1940, also reproduced in a telegram sent by Campbell to London, see Foreign Office papers (henceforth FO), 37124310, 20 May.
71. Radio Stuttgart also set out explicitly to frighten people and to encourage them to flee.
72. P. Baudouin, *Private Diaries*, 39–40.
73. J. Vidalenc, *L'Exode de mai–juin 40*, 160–1.
74. G. Sadoul, *Journal de guerre*, 220.
75. Camps were constituted in Colombes, Maisons Laffitte, and Massy-Palaiseau. See Colonel G. A. Groussard, *Chemins secrets*, i (Paris: Bades-Dufour, 1948), 17.
76. E. Dépigny, 'Juin 40 à l'Hôtel de Ville', p. 6.
77. R. Dorgelès, *La Drôle de guerre* (Paris: Albin Michel, 1973), 265.
78. A. Papillon, 'L'Exode à Paris en juin 40', 22.
79. FO 371 24310, Campbell, 6 June 1940; J. Vidalenc, *Exode de mai–juin 40*, 252.
80. A. Werth, *Last Days of Paris*, 143.

81. W. Churchill, *Their Finest Hour*, 142 (11 June).
82. P. Mendès France, *Liberté, liberté, chérie*, 18.
83. P. Léautaud, *Journal littéraire*, xiii. *Février 1940–juin 1941* (Paris: Mercure de France, 1962), 54.
84. J.-L. Crémieux-Brilhac, *Les Français de l'an 40*, i. 565.
85. G. Guillot, Diary, 1–7.
86. E. Dépigny, 'Juin 40 à l'Hôtel de Ville', 9.
87. G. A. Groussard, *Chemins secrets*, 24.
88. J.-L. Crémieux-Brilhac, *Les Français de l'an 40*, i. 566.
89. Ibid. 567.
90. G. A. Groussard, *Chemins secrets*, 22.
91. J. Vidalenc, *L'Exode de mai–juin 40*, 406.
92. A. Papillon, 'L'Exode à Paris en juin 40', 43.
93. P. Léautaud, *Journal littéraire*, xiii. 71–3.
94. Ibid. 8.
95. Ibid. 79.
96. Friday 14 June.
97. G. A. Groussard, *Chemins secrets*, 22.

CHAPTER 2

1. R. Downing, *If I Laugh*, 10.
2. G.-A. Pros, *Sans tambour ni trompette* (Paris: Harmattan, 2001), 8.
3. Mme Leclercq, interview with the author (Paris, Apr. 2005).
4. J. Charpentier, *Au service de la liberté*, quoted in Vidalenc, *L'Exode de mai–juin 40*, 167 dated 6 June.
5. M.-M. Fourcade, *L'Arche de Noé: Réseau 'Alliance' 1940–1945* (1968; Paris: Plon, 1989), 19.
6. G. Sadoul, *Journal de guerre*, 313–14.
7. Ibid. 313.
8. A. Arenstram, *Tapestry of a Debacle* (London: Constable and Co., 1942), 40.
9. E. Dépigny, 'Juin 40 à l'Hôtel de Ville', 9.
10. R. Downing, *If I Laugh*, 17–18.
11. R. Dorgelès, *La Drôle de guerre*, 275.
12. G. Sadoul, *Journal de guerre*, 319–20.
13. G. Adrey, *Journal d'un replié*, 31.
14. N. Ollier, *L'Exode: Sur les routes de l'an 40*, 168–9.
15. R. Downing, *If I Laugh*, 61.
16. G. Sadoul, *Journal de guerre*, 335–6.
17. Ibid.
18. Mme Pierrat, interview with the author (Paris, Apr. 2005).
19. J. Moulin, *Premier Combat (Journal posthume)* (Paris: Éditions de Minuit, 1947), 45.

20. I. A. Fabre, 'Les Réfugiés de l'exode, mai–juin 1940, en Languedoc méditer-ranéen', Ph.D. thesis (Montpellier, Dec. 1995), 175.
21. R. Dorgelès, *Vacances forcés*, 12.
22. Ibid. 16.
23. L. Werth, *33 jours*, 41.
24. Ibid. 20.
25. A. Papillon, 'L'Exode à Paris en juin 40', 84.
26. R. Dorgelès, *Vacances forcés*, 13.
27. Ibid. 16.
28. Mme Thouvenot, interview with the author (Paris, Apr. 2005).
29. J. Vidalenc, *L'Exode de mai–juin 40*, 269.
30. Ibid.
31. Imperial War Museum, 99/581, Guibert, Unpublished diary.
32. G. Sadoul, *Journal de guerre*, 351.
33. J. Moulin, *Premier Combat*, 43.
34. Ibid.
35. R. Dorgelès, *La Drôle de guerre*, 277.
36. A. Morize, *France: Été 40* (New York: Éditions de la Maison Française, 1941), 42.
37. E. d'Astier, *Sept fois, sept jours* (Paris: Gallimard, 1961), 8.
38. A. Fabre-Luce, *Journal de France*, 215.
39. L. Werth, *33 jours*, 26–8.
40. G. Sadoul, *Journal de guerre*, 343.
41. L. Werth, *33 jours*, 37.
42. F. Trabacca, 'L'Enfance en mouvement', 49.
43. A. Morize, *Été 40*, 40.
44. I. A. Fabre, 'Les Réfugiés de l'exode, mai–juin 1940', 180.
45. L. Werth, *33 jours*, 29.
46. Ibid. 21.
47. R. Downing, *If I Laugh*, 28.
48. G. Sadoul, *Journal de guerre*, 320.
49. A. Fabre-Luce, *Journal de France*, 196.
50. Ibid. 217.
51. J.-P. Sartre, *Iron in the Soul: The Roads to Freedom* (London: Penguin, 1975), 16.
52. G. Adrey, *Journal d'un replié*, 10–11.
53. G. Sadoul, *Journal de guerre*, 373.
54. I. A. Fabre, 'Les Réfugiés de l'exode, mai–juin 1940', 188.
55. A. Fabre-Luce, *Journal de France*, 215–16.
56. G. Adrey, *Journal d'un replié*, 36.
57. G. Sadoul, *Journal de guerre*, 267.
58. Ibid. 235.
59. N. Ollier, *L'Exode: sur les routes de l'an 40*, 185.
60. J. Moulin, *Premier Combat*, 45.

61. G. Guillot, Unpublished diary, 15–16.
62. See incidents recounted by Dombrowski, 'Beyond the Battlefield', 210–11.
63. DVD *Les Égarés*, interview with Gilles Perrault.
64. J.-M. Guillon, 'Talk which was not Idle: Rumours in Wartime France', in H. Diamond and S. Kitson, *Vichy, Resistance, Liberation*, (Oxford: Berg, 2005), 77.
65. L. Werth, *33 jours*, 53.
66. M.-M. Fourcade, *L'Arche de Noé*, 15.
67. H. R. Kedward, 'Patriots and Patriotism in Vichy France', 175–92, and see also N.A. Dombrowski, 'Beyond the Battlefield', 196–7.
68. N.A. Dombrowski, 'Beyond the Battlefield', 197.
69. L. Werth, *33 jours*, 31.
70. N. Ollier, *L'Exode: Sur les routes de l'an 40*, 234.
71. Emilieu Delannoy barely escaped being lynched after being taken for a German by the population of a village in the Pas-de-Calais. He was obliged to show the crowd pictures of his family before they were satisfied that he was a French non-commissioned officer. Imperial War Museum, 92/34/1, Collection M. El Baze.
72. R. Downing, *If I Laugh*, 32.
73. P. Baudouin, *Private Diaries*, 78.
74. M. Ferro, *Pétain* (Paris: Fayard, 1987), 33.
75. Quoted in A. Shennan, *Fall of France*, 12.
76. E. Spears, *Assignment to Catastrophe*, ii (New York, A. A. Wyn, 1955), 43.
77. Comte de Guell, *Journal d'un expatrié catalan*, 80 quoted in J. Vidalenc, *L'Exode de mai–juin 40*, 395.
78. J. Vidalenc, *L'Exode de mai–juin 1940*, 397.
79. A. Morize, *France: Été 1940*, 40.
80. E. Spears, *Assignment to Catastrophe*, ii. 44.
81. J. Vidalenc, *L'Exode de mai–juin 1940*, 415–16.
82. H. Amouroux, *Le 18 juin 1940* (Paris: Fayard, 1964), 186.
83. M.-M. Fourcade, *L'Arche de Noé*, 18.
84. R. Dorgèles, *Vacances forcés*, 11.
85. H. R. Kedward, 'La Résistance et le discours d'exile', in *Matériaux pour l'histoire de notre temps*, Bibliothèque de documentation internationale contemporaine, (henceforth BDIC) (July–Sept. 2002), 51–60.
86. R. Downing, *If I Laugh*, 16.
87. G. Adrey, *Journal d'un replié*, 57.
88. Ibid. 62–3.
89. A. Morize, *France: Été 1940*, 40.
90. L. Werth, *33 jours*, 33.
91. R. Gildea, *Marianne in Chains* (Oxford: Macmillan, 2002), 44.
92. N. Ollier, *L'Exode: Sur les routes de l'an 40*, 179.
93. G. Sadoul, *Journal de guerre*, 376.
94. Ibid. 354–5.

CHAPTER 3

1. G. Guillot, Unpublished diary, 11.
2. P. Baudouin, *Private Diaries*, 95.
3. FO371 24311, Report of 27 June 1940, Right Honourable Viscount Halifax.
4. P. Baudouin, *Private Diaries*, 88.
5. E. Spears, *Assignment to Catastrophe*, ii. 143; M. Gilbert, *Winston Churchill*, 502.
6. E. Spears, *Assignment to Catastrophe*, ii. 151.
7. Spears had expressed astonishment at this, ibid. 205–9.
8. P. Baudouin, *Private Diaries*, 98.
9. Ibid.
10. Ibid. 99.
11. Ibid. 114.
12. M. Ferro, *Pétain*, 60.
13. P. Baudouin, *Private Diaries*, 76.
14. J.-P. Azéma, *1940: L'Année terrible* (Paris: Seuil, 1990), 96.
15. M. Gilbert, *Winston Churchill*, 507.
16. Ibid. 529.
17. De Gaulle informed Spears that Baudouin 'was putting it about to all and sundry . . . the Churchill had shown complete comprehension of the French situation and would understand if France concluded an armistice and a separate peace . . . I asserted that . . . he had clearly indicated the contrary. What he had said in French, when the idea was indicated by Reynaud, was "Je comprends" (I understand) in the sense of "I understand what you say," not in the sense of "I agree" '. And to further clarify this, Spears added in a note that 'Several times while Reynaud was speaking the Prime Minister had nodded or said "Je comprends," indicating his understanding of the words before they were translated.' Spears, *Assignment to Catastrophe*, ii. 218–19. This incident is also quoted in Gilbert, *Winston Churchill*, 536.
18. M. Gilbert, *Winston Churchill*, 533.
19. W. Churchill, *Their Finest Hour*, 62.
20. E. Spears, *Assignment to Catastrophe*, 227.
21. Ibid. 229.
22. Text read by Marshal Pétain on 13 June 1940, cited in Ferro, *Pétain*, 76.
23. J.-L. Crémieux-Brilhac, *Les Français de l'an 40*, i. 597.
24. A. Fabre-Luce, *Journal de France*, 225.
25. N. Ollier, *L'Exode: Sur les routes de l'an 40*, 182.
26. G. Guillot, Unpublished diary, 11.
27. J. Vidalenc, *L'Exode de mai–juin 1940*, 301.
28. E. Spears, *Assignment to Catastrophe*, 249.
29. A. Fabre-Luce, *Journal de France*, 238.
30. P. Mendès-France, *Liberté, liberté, chérie*, 31.
31. Quoted in J. Vidalenc, *L'Exode de mai–juin 1940*, 349.
32. J.-L. Crémieux-Brilhac, *Les Français de l'an 40*, i. 585.

33. M. Gilbert, *Winston Churchill*, 520.

34. P. Baudouin, *Private Diaries*, 113.

35. FO 371 24311, text of Franco-British Union.

36. W. Churchill, *Their Finest Hour*, 182.

37. M. Ferro, *Pétain*, 84.

38. I. Ousby, *Occupation*, 40.

39. W. Churchill, *Their Finest Hour*, 186.

40. M. Junot, *1940: Tel que je l'ai vécu* (Paris: France Empire, 1998), 90; P. Baudouin, *Private Diaries*, 116.

41. J.-P. Azéma, *1940: L'Année terrible*, 151.

42. M. Ferro, *Pétain*, 85.

43. D. Léca, *La Rupture de 1940* (Paris: Fayard, 1978), 236–7.

44. W. Churchill, *Their Finest Hour*, 141; M. Gilbert, *Winston Churchill*, 520.

45. J.-P. Azéma, *1940: L'Année terrible*, 152.

46. P. Baudouin, *Private Diaries*, 123.

47. Ibid. 129.

48. M. Ferro, *Pétain*, 91.

49. Ibid. 96.

50. P. Mendès-France, *Liberté, liberté, chérie*, 50.

51. Ibid. 52.

52. C. de Gaulle, *Mémoires de guerre: L'Appel, 1940–1942* (Paris, Plon, 1954), 67; E. Spears, *Assignment to Catastrophe*, ii. 322.

53. J. S. Ambler, *The French Army in Politics 1945–1962* (Ohio: Ohio State University Press, 1966), 65.

54. J.-P. Azéma, *1940: L'Année terrible*, 162.

55. E. Spears, *Assignment to Catastrophe*, ii. 120.

56. J.-L. Crémieux-Brilhac, *La France Libre: De l'appel du 18 juin à la Libération* (Paris: Gallimard, 1996), 52.

57. P. Mendès-France, *Liberté, liberté, chérie*, 55–6.

58. J.-L. Crémieux-Brilhac, *La France Libre*, 47. This notion of taboo is also discussed in Ch. 6.

59. J. S. Ambler, *French Army in Politics*, 66.

60. Quoted in A. Horne, *The French Army and Politics 1870–1970* (London: Macmillan, 1984), 68.

61. P. Baudouin, *Private Diaries*, 133.

62. B. Vormeier, 'La Pratique du droit d'asile à l'égard des réfugiés en provenance d'Allemagne et d'Autriche en France', in Lagarrigue (ed.), *1940: La France du repli*, 110.

63. P. Baudouin, *Private Diaries*, 149.

64. Ibid. 153.

65. I. Ousby, *Occupation*, 84.

66. L. Rebatet, *Les Décombres*, i. 523.

CHAPTER 4

1. J. Lacouture, *Le Témoignage est au combat: Une biographie de Germaine Tillon* (Paris: Seuil, 2000), 62.
2. Interview, Mme Perrot.
3. A. Fabre-Luce, *Journal de France*, 221.
4. G. Adrey, *Journal d'un replié*, 68.
5. S. de Beauvoir, *La Force de l'âge*, ii. 510.
6. J. Vidalenc, *L'Exode de mai–juin 40*, 304.
7. G. Adrey, *Journal d'un replié*, 69.
8. Ibid. 71.
9. P. Léautaud, *Journal littéraire*, xiii. 88.
10. R. Langeron, *Paris, juin 40* (Paris: Flammarion, 1946), 80.
11. Ibid.
12. Ibid. 98.
13. G. Adrey, *Journal d'un replié*, 70.
14. C. Pomaret, *Le Dernier Témoin: Fin d'une guerre, fin d'une république, juin et juillet 1940* (Paris: Presses de la Cité, 1968), 133.
15. G. Sadoul, *Journal de guerre*, 374.
16. A. Meynier, 'Les Déplacements de la population', 129.
17. A. Morize, *France: Été 40*, 69.
18. R. Aron, *Mémoires* (Paris: Julliard, 1983), 164.
19. L. Rebatet, *Les Décombres*, 499.
20. J.-L. Crémieux-Brilhac, *Les Français de l'an 40*, ii. 688.
21. R. Gildea, *Marianne in Chains*, 44–6.
22. G. Sadoul, *Journal de guerre*, 354.
23. J.-L. Crémieux-Brilhac, *Les Français de l'an 40*, 693.
24. P. Miquel, *L'Exode*, 389.
25. Y. Durand, *Les Prisonniers de guerre français* (Paris: Hachette, 1987), 39.
26. H. Frenay, *La Nuit finira* (Paris: Laffont, 1973), 18.
27. J.-L. Crémieux-Brilhac, *Les Français de l'an 40*, ii. 693.
28. P. Miquel, *L'Exode*, 390.
29. E. M. Guibert, Unpublished diary.
30. Y. Durand, *Les Prisonniers de guerre français*, 42.
31. R. Brasillach, quoted in J-L. Crémieux-Brilhac, *Les Français de l'an 40*, ii. 693.
32. M. Fee, Interview with the author (Amiens, Apr. 2005).
33. N. Ollier, *L'Exode: Sur les routes de l'an 40*, 185.
34. Colonel J. Vernet, 'Le Replie des armées françaises, juin 1940', in M. Lagarrigue (ed.), *1940: La France du repli*, 21–33.
35. AN 72AJ1271, Compagne de France. E. Spears, *Assignment to Catastrophe*, i. 192.
36. M. Ferro, *Pétain*, 75.
37. E. Alary, *La Ligne de démarcation 1940–1944* (Paris: Perrin, 2003), 24.
38. G. Sadoul, *Journal de guerre*, 385.

39. R. Downing, *If I Laugh*, 156.

40. R. Dorgelès, *Vacances forcés*, 27.

41. S. Hoffman, 'Témoignage', 18.

42. A. Meynier, 'Les Déplacements de la population', 140.

43. J. Vidalenc, *L'Exode de 40*, 354.

44. A. Meynier, 'Les Déplacements de la population', 140.

45. R. Dorgelès, *Vacances forcés*, 19.

46. M.-M. Fourcade, *L'Arche de Noé*, 24.

47. E. Alary, *La Ligne de démarcation*, 50.

48. Ibid. 157–60.

49. M.-J. Vielcazat-Petitcol, 'De la drôle de guerre au régime de Vichy: Itinéraires de réfugiés juifs en Lot-et-Garonne', in M. Lagarrigue (ed.), *1940: La France du repli*, 94.

50. V. Caron, *Uneasy Asylum: France and the Jewish Refugee Crisis, 1933–1942* (Stanford: Stanford University Press, 1999), 261.

51. N. Ollier, *L'Exode: Sur les routes de l'an 40*, 234.

52. Ibid. 232.

53. Ibid. 235.

54. V. Caron, *Uneasy Asylum*, 262.

55. M.-J. Vielcazat-Petitcol, 'De la drôle de guerre au régime de Vichy', 94.

56. N. Ollier, *L'Exode: Sur les routes de l'an 40*, 237.

57. A. Fabre-Luce, *Journal de France*, 245.

58. R. Downing, *If I Laugh*, 183.

59. A. Werth, *Last Days of Paris*, 208–9.

60. A. Shennan, *Fall of France*, 15.

61. R. Aron, *Mémoires*, 165.

62. G. Sadoul, *Journal de guerre*, 378.

63. H. Amouroux, *Le 18 juin 1940* (Paris: Fayard, 1964). 187.

64. M.-M. Fourcade, *L'Arche de Noé*, 25.

65. J.-L. Crémieux-Brilhac, *La France libre*, 97.

66. A. Shennan, *Fall of France*, 17.

67. N. Atkin, *The Forgotten French: Exiles in the British Isles, 1940–1944* (Manchester: Manchester University Press, 2003), 49.

68. M. Junot, *1940: Tel que je l'ai vécu*, 80.

69. Quoted in Atkin, *Forgotten French*, 5.

70. E. de Miribel, *La Liberté souffre violence* (1981; Paris: Plon, 1989), 38. See also N. Atkin, *Forgotten French*, which is extremely illuminating about the activities of the French community in London during the Second World War.

71. J. S. Ambler, *French Army in Politics 1945–1962*, 65.

72. N. A. Dombrowski, 'Beyond the Battlefield', 31.

73. ADTG 37W30, Circular, 1 June 1940.

74. N. A. Dombrowski, 'Beyond the Battlefield', 81.

75. ADTG AM546, Réfugiés civils, Instructions vaccinations. The fear that the presence of refugees in Montauban could be a health hazard is substantiated by the volume of documentation to this effect which survives in the archives.
76. I. A. Fabre, 'Les Réfugiés de l'exode, mai–juin 1940', 255.
77. ADTG 37 W 30, Refugiés guerre 1939–45, 17 May 1940.
78. R. Dorgelès, Vacances forcés, 28.
79. A. Morize, France: Été 40, 69.
80. I. A. Fabre, 'Les Réfugiés de l'exode, mai–juin 1940', 257.
81. ADTG 37W30, 3 Sept. 1940.
82. R. Dorgelès, Vacances forcés, 29–30.
83. B. Vormeier, 'La Pratique du droit d'asile à l'égard des réfugiés', 110.
84. ADTG 37W30, 30 Aug. 1940, Report from the Sub-Prefect of Castelsarrasin to the Prefect of the Tarn-et-Garonne.
85. H. R. Kedward, Resistance in Vichy France (Oxford: OUP, 1978), 13.
86. Ibid.

CHAPTER 5

1. Lamalou in the department of the Hérault saw its population increase by 50%. H. Chauvin, 'Une micro-Europe des défaites: Le Refuge héraultais de 1940', in M. Lagarrigue (ed.), 1940: La France du repli, 129.
2. AN 72AJ623, Vidalenc papers, Letter from Trie-sur-Baise, 13 Apr. 1953.
3. J. Vidalenc, L'Exode de mai–juin 1940, 381–2.
4. R. de Chambrun, La Vie de la France sous l'Occupation (1940–4) (Hoover Institute, 1957), 305.
5. Ibid. 307.
6. ADTG 37W30.
7. J. Vidalenc, L'Exode de mai–juin 1940, 382; N. Ollier, L'Exode: Sur les routes de l'an 40, 270.
8. S. de Beauvoir, La Force de l'âge, ii. 510.
9. M. Junot, 1940: Tel que je l'ai vécu, 94.
10. See Colonel J. Vernet, 'Le Repli des armées françaises, juin 1940', in M. Lagarrigue (ed.), 1940: La France du repli, 21–33.
11. Interview, M. Fee.
12. P. Miquel, L'Exode, 427.
13. E. Alary, La Ligne de démarcation, p. 50.
14. S. de Beauvoir, La Force de l'âge, ii. 511.
15. A. Morize, France: Été 1940, 69.
16. Interview, Mme Perrot.
17. S. de Beauvoir, La Force de l'âge, ii. 511.
18. Ibid.
19. J. Horne and A. Kramer, German Atrocities 1914, 401.
20. Ibid. 402.

21. M. Junot, *1940: Tel que je l'ai vécu*, 126.
22. J. Lagrange, 'Le Rapatriement des réfugiés après l'exode', *Revue d'histoire de la Deuxième Guerre mondiale* (1977), 43.
23. This point will be further explored in Ch. 6.
24. ADTG 37W30. The sub-prefect of Castelsarrasin, for example, pointed out in a report to the prefect on 30 August that the refugee question had become alarming for a time from the point of view of food supplies and that the situation had improved after the departure of significant numbers of refugees.
25. ADTG 37W30. They were asked to provide figures according to the following four categories: government officials and employees from the 'Free Zone', government officials and employees from the 'Occupied Zone', 'ordinary refugees' from the 'Free Zone' or from the 'Occupied Zone', and finally those who were from Alsace and Lorraine, Belgium, Holland, and Luxembourg.
26. J. Vidalenc, *L'Exode de mai–juin 1940*, 5.
27. Sous-secrétariat aux réfugiés, SHAT 1P9, compte-rendu de la réunion, quoted in I. A. Fabre, 'Les Réfugiés de l'exode, mai–juin 1940', 297. These figures were confirmed a year later in Mar. 1941 by the armistice services in answer to to a request made by the German embassy relative to the number of people who left their homes during the exodus. This information numbered these at 7,000,000 French and foreigners residing in France and 1,200,000 Belgians, Luxembourgers, and Dutch. Thus the number of refugees was estimated at 8,200,000, AN F60 1507, Note à l'ambassade d'Allemagne du service de l'Armistice, Délégation générale du gouvernement français dans les territoires occupés, 7 Mar. 41.
28. J. Lagrange, 'Le Rapatriement des réfugiés', 49.
29. P. Miquel, *L'Exode*, 423.
30. *La Vie de la France sous l'Occupation*, 326.
31. However, these priorities tended to be changed according to dates and needs. I. A. Fabre, 'Les Réfugiés de l'exode, mai–juin 1940', 499–500.
32. H. Amouroux, *La Grande Histoire des Français, sous l'Occupation*, ii. *Quarante millions de Pétainistes* (Paris: Éditions Robert Laffort, 1976), 161.
33. E. Alary, *La Ligne de démarcation*, 57.
34. G. and A. Vallotton, *C'était au jour le jour: Carnets (1939–1944)* (Paris: Payot, 1995), 99. This concentration of trapped refugees is also mentioned in M. Lagarrigue (ed.), *1940: La Belgique du repli* (Charleroi: Imprimerie provinciale du Hainaut, 2005), 203.
35. *Paris Soir*, 4 July 1940, Minister of Interior at Vichy, Marquet, 'Refugees should stay where they are.'
36. The Germans took control of allocating this documentation in the autumn. I. A. Fabre, 'Les Réfugiés de l'exode, mai–juin 1940', 494.
37. In Mar. 1941 the SNCF (French railways) put together a list of 13,000 owners who had not claimed their possessions. H. Amouroux, *Quarante millions de Pétainistes*, 161.

38. AN F60 395, Note du General Koeltz, General du Division Directeur des Services de l'Armistice, au Secretariat General du Conseil Superieur de la Defense Nationale, Vichy, 20 July 1940.

39. AN 72 AJ 473, Rapport de M. Tuja, Chef de Service de l'Exploitation au Directeur de l'Exploitation pour l'Exercice 1940.

40. Late July and early Aug. saw large numbers of refugees flood into Paris and pass through the three main stations: 5,000–6,000 refugees arrived at the Gare de Lyon daily, 22,000–23,000 at the Gare d'Austerlitz, and 17,000–18,000 a day at Montparnasse. Resultats du recensement de la Seine, N. Ollier, *L'Exode: Sur les routes de l'an 40*, 264.

41. ADTG 37W30.

42. A. Meynier, 'Les Déplacements de la population', 282.

43. N. Ollier, *L'Exode: Sur les routes de l'an 40*, 262.

44. H. Amouroux, *Quarante million de Pétainistes*, 160.

45. I. A. Fabre, 'Les Réfugiés de l'exode, mai–juin 1940', 495–7.

46. Ibid.

47. G. Adrey, *Journal d'un replié*, 93–5.

48. J.-P. Marcy, and F. Jarrige, 'L'Aveyron et les réfugiés en 1940', in M. Lagarrigue (ed.), *1940: La France du repli*, 166. ADTG 37W30, the prefect of the Tarn and Garonne made a similar complaint.

49. ADTG 37W30, 19 July 1940, note from repatriation services in Toulouse to Prefect of Tarn and Garonne.

50. Ibid.

51. Ibid.

52. ADTG 37W31. There were, however, concerns that those travelling by car might take more than their fair share of food with them and on 24 July 1940 the repatriation services warned that all French and Belgian cars heading for the Occupied Zone were to be prevented from taking stocks of petrol and other food products including sugar, coffee, chocolate, and olive oil. All vehicles were to undergo vigorous inspection to prevent this.

53. A. Meynier, 'Les Déplacements de la population', 280.

54. A. Kahn, *Robert et Jeanne à Lyon sous l'Occupation* (Paris: Payot, 1990), 45.

55. A. Morize, *France: Été 1940*, 167.

56. J. Lagrange 'Le Rapatriement des réfugiés', 48.

57. A. Morize, *France: Été 1940*, 168.

58. ADTG 37W30. Certain local authorities complained that arrangements could have been more consistent.

59. AN FC111 1192, Rapport de Préfet, Somme, 14 and 27 July 1940.

60. E. Alary, *La Ligne de démarcation*, 60.

61. G. & A. Valloton, *C'était au jour le jour*, 111.

62. ADTG, 37W30, Letter from the Sub-Prefect of Castelsarrasin to the Prefect of Tarn-et-Garonne, 30 Aug. 1940.

63. N. A. Dombrowski, 'Beyond the Battlefield', 369.

64. The department had benefited from supplies sent from the US but the prefect was evidently overwhelmed, J. P. Marcy and F. Jarrige, 'L'Aveyron et les réfugiés en 1940', 164.

65. A. Meynier, 'Les Déplacements de la population', *Les Annales de Bretagne* (1949), 276.

66. Mme Bulli, interview with the author (Paris, Apr. 2005). In Dordogne this was well organized and efficient.

67. I. A. Fabre, 'Les Réfugiés de l'éxode, mai–juin 1940', 27.

68. A. Meynier, 'Les Déplacements de la population', 277.

69. Mme Conrad, interview with the author (Paris, Apr. 2005).

70. I. A. Fabre 'Les Réfugiés de l'exode, mai–juin 1940', 405.

71. Interview, Mme Perrot.

72. I. A. Fabre, 'Les Réfugiés de l'exode, mai–juin 1940', 454.

73. R. Cobb, *A Historian's Appreciation of Modern French Literature* (Oxford: OUP, 1980), 53.

74. Paid holidays were part of the legislation passed in 1936 by the Popular Front government.

75. G. Danjou, *Exode 1940* (Paris: Éditions du Scorpion, 1960), 303.

76. A. Meynier, 'Les Déplacements de la population', 276.

77. I. A. Fabre, 'Les Réfugiés de l'exode, mai–juin 1940', 223.

78. A. Meynier, 'Les Déplacements de la population', 276.

79. I. A. Fabre, 'Les Réfugiés de l'exode, mai–juin 1940', 430.

80. A. Meynier, 'Les Déplacements de la population', 275.

81. See ibid. 274–7; M. Fee helped the winegrowers in Charente harvest the grapes in the autumn, only returning home in Oct.

82. See the epigraph to this chapter.

83. A. Meynier, 'Les Déplacements de la population', 278.

84. J.-P. Marcy and F. Jarrige, 'L'Aveyron et les réfugiés en 1940', 168.

85. F. Trabacca, 'L'Enfance en mouvement', 51.

86. A. Meynier, 'Les Déplacements de la population', 277; J.-P. Marcy and F. Jarrige, 'L'Aveyron et les réfugiés en 1940', 168 and 171.

87. N. A. Dombrowski, 'Beyond the Battlefield', 338.

88. Quoted in J. Lagrange, 'Le Rapatriement des réfugiés', 49.

89. See e.g. in the Tarn and Garonne.

90. J. Lagrange, 'Le Rapatriement des réfugiés', 49. By this time, countless other displaced individuals would have taken refuge in the Unoccupied Zone, but would not have appeared in the figures as they deliberately sought to escape the notice of the authorities.

91. G. & A. Vallotton, *C'était au jour le jour*, 106.

92. Ibid. 111: 19 Aug. 1940.

93. C. Collomb and B. Groppo, 'Le *Jewish Labor Committee* et les réfugiés en France 1940–1941', in M. Lagarrigue (ed.), *1940: La Belgique du repli*, 211.

94. See ADTG archives.

95. A. Meynier, 'Les Déplacements de la population', 283: 1,100 remained.

96. J. Lagrange, 'Le Rapatriement des réfugiés', 50; see also Ch. 6.

97. A. Laurens, 'Populations réfugiées et déplacées en Ariège de 1939 à 1945', *Revue d'histoire de la Deuxième Guerre mondiale*, 119 (1980), 50.

98. Bringing the number of Jews present in Paris in Oct. 1940 to close to 150,000, L. Lazare, *Rescue as Resistance: How Jewish Organizations fought the Holocaust in France* (Columbia: Columbia University Press, 1996), 36.

99. P. Hyman, *The Jews of Modern France* (Berkeley and Los Angeles: University of California Press, 1998), 164.

100. A. Kahn, *Robert et Jeanne*, 47.

101. M.-J. Vielcazat-Petitcol, 'De la drole de guerre au régime de Vichy: Itinéraires de refugiés juifs en Lot-et-Garonne', in M. Lagarrigue (ed.), *1940: La France du repli*, 97.

102. M. R. Marrus and R. Paxton, *Vichy et les Juifs* (Paris: Calmann Lévy, 1981), 74.

103. J.-P. Marcy and F. Jarrige, 'L'Aveyron et les Refugiés en 1940', in M. Lagarrigue (ed.), *1940: La France du repli*, 169.

104. L. Lazare, *Rescue as Resistance*, 37.

105. A. Kahn, *Robert et Jeanne*, 46.

106. M. R. Marrus and R. Paxton, *Vichy et les Juifs*, 153; L. Lazare, *Rescue as Resistance*, 83–4.

107. See Ch. 6 for a wider discussion of this.

108. A. Chamson, *Écrit en 1940...* (Paris: Gallimard, 1944), 16.

109. A. Shennan, *Fall of France*, 59.

110. I. Ousby, *Occupation*, 295.

111. J.-L, Crémieux-Brilhac, *La France Libre*, 911.

112. Ibid.

113. M. Duras, *La Douleur* (London: Flamingo, 1987), 54.

114. Ibid. 33.

CHAPTER 6

1. Interview, Mme Perrot.

2. S. de Beauvoir, *La Force de l'âge*, ii. 520.

3. S. Fishman, *We will wait: Wives of French Prisoners of War* (London: Yale University Press, 1991).

4. I. Ousby, *Occupation*, 111.

5. S. de Beauvoir, *La Force de l'âge*, ii. 519, 1 July 1940. Georges Adrey also noticed that inhabitants on their return to Orléans had chalked evidence of their occupation of their homes on their doors to prevent other refugees from forcing entry. G. Adrey, *Journal d'un replié*, 84.

6. G. Adrey, *Journal d'un replié*, 98.

7. AN F23 234, Circulaires et notes concernant les réfugiés, Paris, 2 Aug. 1940, Notes concerning payment to refugees on returning to their homes.

8. G. Adrey, *Journal d'un replié*, 99.

9. H. Amouroux, *Quarante millions de Pétainistes*, 162.
10. B. and F. Groult, *Journal à quatre mains*, 19 July 1940, pp. 68 and 73.
11. P. Léautard, *Journal littéraire*, xiii. 83.
12. Ibid. 101.
13. S. de Beauvoir, *La Force de l'âge*, ii. 509.
14. Ibid. 520, 1 July 1940.
15. P. Léautard, *Journal littéraire*, xiii. 83.
16. S. Parvane-Bourrin, *Exode d'une Parisienne (juin–juillet 1940)* (Hanoi: Imprimerie de G. Taupin, 1942), 91.
17. I. Ousby, *Occupation*, 58.
18. Roger Langeron, and Colonel Groussard, who under Dentz had no illusions about the role they were expected to play to prevent any insurrection: Groussard, *Chemins Secrets*, 28.
19. S. de Beauvoir, *La Force de l'âge*, ii. 520.
20. H. Amouroux, *Quarante millions de Pétainistes*, 173.
21. Ibid.
22. P. Mendès-France, *Liberté, liberté chérie*, 28–9: 11 June 1940.
23. It was only in his prefect's report of 9 Sept. that Billecard was able to report that the conflicts between those who stayed and those who left had generally calmed down. M. Junot, *1940: Tel que je l'ai vécu*, 225.
24. BDIC, F delta 22 Res, Dossier Conseil Municipal de Paris, June–July 1940, Letter from Pétain telling members of the Paris municipal council that those who stayed in place acted appropriately.
25. M. Junot, *1940: Tel que je l'ai vécu*, 214.
26. J. Moulin, *Premier Combat*, 58.
27. Ibid.
28. P. Miquel, *L'Exode*, 403.
29. H. R. Kedward, 'French Resistance: A Few Home Truths', in William Lamont (ed.), *Historical Controversies and Historians* (1998; London, UCL, 2001) 4.
30. This was the case related by Mme Perrot who was urged by her mayor to leave.
31. Although most archives of meetings of local and regional councils for the second half of June have not survived, remarkably the BDIC holds the notes of the meetings held by these reconstituted councils throughout the months of June and July which provide invaluable insights into the debates and issues of concern.
32. BDIC Q Res 37, Gestion de la commune de Viroflay depuis le 13 juin 1940: 13 June 1940.
33. Ibid., 14 June 1940.
34. Ibid., 15 June 1940.
35. Ibid., 21 June 1940.
36. Ibid., 24 June 1940.
37. Ibid.
38. BDIC, F delta 22 Res, Conseil Municipal de Paris, June–July 1940.

39. Ibid., notes of 25 June 1940.
40. Although Moulin and Pétain were to transmute this position into rather different courses of action, it is interesting that they should have shared it in the early days.
41. G. Morin, 'Les Socialistes du Midi en 1940 entre refus, accommodements ou collaboration', in M. Lagarrigue (ed.), *1940: La France du repli*, 305.
42. Quoted in G. Morin, 'Les Socialistes du Midi', 305.
43. Letter addressed by M. Robert Billecard, prefect of the Seine-et-Oise to M. Henry-Haye, Senator and Mayor of Versailles, 1 Aug. 1940, quoted in Junot, *1940: Tel que je l'ai vécu*, 215–18.
44. Pétain's speech, 13 Aug. 1940.
45. Lettres de lecteurs, p. 2, quoted in Papillon, 'L'Exode à Paris en juin 40', 119.
46. R. Rémond, 'L'Opinion française des années 1930–1940', 483.
47. The sense of attachment to the land did not extend to the empire.
48. See H. R. Kedward, 'Patriots and Patriotism in Vichy France', 175–92. In this brilliant article Kedward shows how the images of rural France were also mobilized by France Libre in their publications and that rural imagery was eventually won over to the cause of the Resistance.
49. Quoted in G. Miller, *Les Pousse-au-jouir du Maréchal Pétain* (Paris: Seuil, 1975), 132.
50. Excerpts from prefects' reports quoted in Marrus and Paxton, *Vichy et les Juifs*, 29.
51. S. Wharton, *Screening Reality: French Documentary Film during the German Occupation* (London: Peter Lang, 2006), 70–2.
52. Ibid. 69–70.
53. Title of book by H. Amouroux.
54. H. Frenay, *La Nuit finira*, 26.
55. Ibid. 36.
56. A. Fabre-Luce, *Journal de France*, 255.
57. Interview, M. Fee.
58. H. Amouroux, *Quarante millions de Pétainistes*, 158–9.
59. Ibid.
60. AN F1/cIII/1192, Rapport de Préfet, Somme.
61. P. Vaillaud, *L'Exode*, 83.
62. H. R. Kedward, *Resistance in Vichy France*, 33–4.
63. S. Fishman, *We will wait*, p. xv.
64. See H. Diamond *Women and the Second World War in France*, and S. Fishman, *We will wait*, for detailed discussions of these issues.
65. Quoted in I. Ousby, *Occupation*, 57.
66. J. Horne and A. Kramer, *German Atrocities 1914*, 407.
67. Quoted in J. F. Sweets, *Choices in Vichy France: The French under Nazi Occupation* (Oxford: Oxford University Press, 1986) 158.
68. A. Shennan, *Fall of France*, 54.
69. I. Némirovsky, *Suite Française* (London: Chatto and Windus, 2006), 350.

70. H. Frenay, *La Nuit finira*, 33.

71. H. R. Kedward, *Resistance in Vichy France*, 234.

72. M. Goubet and P. Debauges, *Histoire de la Résistance dans la Haute-Garonne* (Cahors: Milan, 1986), 18 and 38–9.

73. R. Mencherini, 'Exode et exil, survie et engagement: Itinéraires de réfugiés artistes et intellectuels à Marseille (1940–1942)', in M. Lagarrigue (ed.), *1940: La France du Repli*, 133–8; J-P. Marcy and F. Jarrigue, 'L'Aveyron et les réfugiés en 1940', 171–2.

74. M. Goubet, *Toulouse et la Haute-Garonne dans la Guerre 1939–1945* (Saint-Étienne: Horvath, 1987), 18.

75. Interview with Mme Fontanier, in H. Diamond, 'Women's Experience during and after World War Two in the Toulouse Area 1939–1948: Choices and Constraints', Ph.D. thesis (University of Sussex, 1992), 164.

76. See J. Pujol, 'Les Protestants français en 1940 et les débuts de l'aide aux réfugiés et aux internés', in M. Lagarrigue (ed.), *1940: La France du repli*, 247–61.

77. C. Collomp B. Groppo, 'Le *Jewish Labor Committee*', 211.

78. Fifteen thousand came to ask for aid. See J.-M. Guillon, 'La Provence refuge et piège: Autour de Varian Fry et de la filière américaine', in M. Lagarrigue (ed.), *1940: La France du repli*, 282.

79. Ibid. 282–4.

80. M. Goubet, P. Debauges, *Histoire de la Résistance dans la Haute-Garonne*, 10–11.

81. G. Sadoul, *Journal de guerre*, 331.

82. Imperial War Museum, 99/581, E. M. Guibert, Unpublished diary.

83. J.-P. Azéma, *1940: L'Année terrible*, 128.

84. S. Lawlor, *Churchill and the Politics of War, 1940–1941* (Cambridge: Cambridge University Press, 1994), 61.

85. E. Spears, *Assignment to Catastrophe*, ii. 158.

86. FO 371 24311, 21 June 1940.

87. *The Times*, Thursday 20 June 1940, 'If the Invader Comes'.

88. D. Brown, *Somerset v Hitler, Secret Operations in the Mendips 1939–1945* (Reading: Countryside Books, 1999), 15.

89. Ibid.

90. D. Brown, *Somerset v Hitler*, 33.

91. Ibid. 38; see also N. Longmate, *The Real Dad's Army* (London: Arrow, 1974).

92. After a successful TV comedy show which teasingly satirized the activites of this home militia.

93. D. Brown, *Somerset v Hitler*, 64–5.

94. C. D. Freeman and D. Cooper, *Panic* (London: Ministry of Information, 1941).

AFTERWORD

1. M. Hastings, *Guardian*, 25 Apr. 2006.

2. N. Wood, *Vectors of Memory: Legacies of Trauma in Postwar Europe* (Oxford: Berg, 1999); E. Conan and H. Rousso, *Un passé qui ne passe pas* (Paris: Fayard, 1994).

3. According to the eminent memory specialist Henry Rousso, the defeat is no longer problematic for the French people. He cites a poll published in *Le Figaro Magazine* in 1980 which claimed that 'the defeat of 1940 does not divide France anymore' according to the statistical data. Most French people approved of the armistice, 53% believed that the government was right to sign it and remain in the country, 10% believed it was a very good thing, and 52% believed it was a good thing. H. Rousso, *Le Syndrome de Vichy de 1944 à nos jours* (Paris: Seuil, 1990), 322.

4. N. A. Dombrowski, 'Beyond the Battlefield' also acknowledges this.

5. V. Holman, 'Representing Refugees: Migration in France 1940–1944', *Journal of Romance Studies* (2002), 63.

6. M. Rouchaud, *Journal d'une petite fille, 1940–1944* (Paris: Gallimard, 1945), 254–5 quoted in A. Shennan, *Fall of France*, 88.

7. N. Wood, *Vectors of Memory*, 2.

8. N. A. Dombrowski, 'Beyond the Battlefield', 526.

9. S. Farmer, *Martyred Village: Commemorating the 1944 Massacre at Oradour-sur-Glane* (Berkeley and Los Angeles: University of California Press, 1999).

10. P. Nora (ed.), *Les Lieux de mémoire*, 7 vols. (Paris: Gallimard, 1984–92), trans. as *Realms of Memory: The Construction of the French Past*, 3 vols. (New York: Columbia University Press, 1997).

11. A. Shennan, *The Fall of France*, 159–60.

12. M. H. Joly, 'War Museums in France', in S. Blowen, M. Demossier, and J. Picard, *Recollections of France* (Oxford: Berghahn, 1998), 35.

13. D. Laub, 'Bearing Witness or the Vicissitudes of Listening', in S. Felman, and D. Laub, *Testimony: Crises of Witnesses in Literature, Psychoanalysis and History* (London: Routledge 1993), 57–74.

14. Interview, Mme Perrot.

15. Founded in 1941 by Jean Paulhan and Jacques Decœur, quoted in M. Atack, 'Narratives of Disruption', *French Cultural Studies* (1990), 235.

16. L. Werth, *33 jours*, 51.

17. Ibid. 53.

18. Ibid. 117.

19. V. Holman, 'Representing Refugees: Migration in France 1940–1944', 59.

20. Ibid. 62.

21. A. Morize, *France en 1940*, 35–6.

22. C. Bourniquel, 'Printemps 40', 1555.

23. R. Cobb, *Promenades*, 53.

24. S. Hoffman, quoted in A. Shennan, *Fall of France*, 160.

25. Ibid. 161.
26. S. Lindeberg, *La Seconde Guerre mondiale dans le cinéma français (1944–1969)*, (Paris: CNRS Éditions, 1997), 277.
27. Ibid. 265.
28. Ibid. 400.
29. See C. Gorrara, *Women's Representations of the Occupation in Post-'68 France* (London: Macmillan, 1998).
30. G. Danjou, *L'Exode*, 137.
31. *Les Égarés*, directors' cut.
32. *Bon Voyage*, directors' cut.
33. I. Némirovsky, *Suite française* (Paris: Éditions Denoël, 2004); trans. into English by Sandra Smith (London: Chatto and Windus, 2006).
34. I. Némirovsky, *Suite Française* (Eng.), 402.
35. Ibid. 348.
36. Ibid. 39–40.
37. Ibid. 51.
38. Ibid. 350.
39. Ibid. 356.
40. N. Ollier, *L'Exode: sur les routes de l'an 40*.
41. M. Lagarrigue (ed.), *1940: La France du repli*.
42. P. Miquel, *L'Exode*.
43. N. Dombrowski, 'Beyond the Battlefield'; I. A. Fabre, 'Les Refugiés de l'exode de mai–juin 1940'; and F. Trabacca, 'Les Enfants de l'exode' (forthcoming).
44. L. Werth, *33 jours*.
45. P. Nardeau, *Juin 40: Peur sur la route* (Paris: Nathan & Ministère de la Defense, 2003).
46. M. Lagarrigue, *1940: La Belgique du Repli*.
47. Ibid. pref.
48. Ibid. 18.
49. H. Diamond and C. Gorrara, 'The Aubrac Controversy', *History Today* (2001), 2–3; J.-M. Guillon, 'L'Affaire Aubrac, ou la dérive d'une certaine façon de faire l'histoire', *Modern and Contemporary France* (1999), 89–93.
50. C. Bickerton, 'France's History Wars', *Le Monde diplomatique*, (Feb. 2006).

Further Reading

THE DEFEAT

It is difficult to understand the exodus without some grasp of the defeat. A number of excellent books have now appeared on this. I found J. Jackson, *The Fall of France: The Nazi Invasion of 1940* (Oxford: OUP, 2003) to be especially illuminating. A. Shennan, *The Fall of France 1940* (Harlow: Longman, 2000) gives a marvellous sense of the long-term consequences. In French, M. Bloch, *L'Étrange Défaite* (1946; Paris: Gallimard, 1990) remains a crucial text. J.-L. Crémieux-Brilhac, *Les Français de l'an 40*, 2 vols. (Paris: Gallimard, 1990) is superb and provides remarkable detail and background. J.-P. Azéma, *1940: L'Année terrible* (Paris: Seuil, 1990) thematically situates various aspects of the defeat.

For a rather less scholarly approach, there are a number of books in English on the fall of Paris which provide considerable insights into the atmosphere of the time. The best is the memoirs of A. Werth, *The Last Days of Paris: A Journalist's Diary* (London: Hamish Hamilton, 1940). H. Lottman, *The Fall of Paris, June 1940* (New York: Sinclair Stevenson, 1992) provides some vivid description.

THE EXODUS

On the exodus, there is virtually nothing in English. R. Vinen, *The Forgotten French* (London: Allen Lane, 2006) has a chapter which situates the key issues well. A detailed overview of the failure of evacuation plans and reactions of the authorities to the refugees in the reception departments is provided in N. A. Dombrowski, 'Beyond the Battlefield: The French Civilian Exodus of May–June 1940', Ph.D. thesis (Ann Arbor: UMI, 1996). H. R. Kedward, 'Patriots and Patriotism in Vichy France', *Transactions of the Royal Historical Society* (1981), 175–92, is a crucial text on the importance of the rural symbolism relating to the exodus both to Pétainism and later to the France Libre movement. *Resistance in Vichy France* (Oxford: OUP, 1978), by the same author, highlights the importance played by displacements brought about by the exodus in contributing to later resistance.

More is available on the exodus in French. For general background, H. Amouroux, *Le 18 juin 1940* (Paris: Fayard, 1964); *La Grande Histoire des Français sous l'Occupation*, i. *Le Peuple du désastre, 1939–1940*, ii. *Quarante millions de Pétainistes* (Paris: Éditions Robert Laffont, 1976) provide some evocative details.

Of the books that deal exclusively with the exodus, J. Vidalenc, *L'Exode de mai–juin 40* (Paris: PUF, 1957) remains the most complete and most authoritative book on the topic. This is closely followed by N. Ollier, *L'Exode: Sur les routes de l'an 40* (Paris: Laffont, 1969), an interesting mix of personal testimony and historical narration. P. Vaillaud, *L'Exode, mai–juin 1940* (Paris: Perrin, 2000) gives a short accessible account and reproduces a remarkable number of documents and photos from the period. The more recent P. Miquel, *L'Exode, 10 mai–20 juin 1940* (Paris: Plon, 2003) is a popularized account. This voluminous work collects together much valuable material but the excessive detail can make difficult reading.

Two unpublished theses in French are especially helpful. A. Papillon, 'L'Exode à Paris en juin 40: Causes, déroulement, mémoire', Maîtrise (Paris, June 1990) and I. A. Fabre, 'Les Réfugiés de l'exode, mai–juin 1940, en Languedoc méditerranéen', Ph.D. thesis (Montpellier, Dec. 1995).

RECEPTION OF REFUGEES

For a magnificent collection of invaluable case studies of the reception of refugees in the south, see M. Lagarrigue (ed.), *1940: La France du repli, L'Europe de la défaite* (Toulouse: Éditions Privat, 2001). Lagarrigue has also recently published a detailed account of the Belgian exodus to south-west France, *1940: La Belgique du repli* (Charleroi: Imprimerie provinciale du Hainaut, 2005). A. Meynier, 'Les Déplacements de la population vers la Bretagne en 1940–1941', *Les Annales de Bretagne* (1948), 86–155 and (1949) 249–80, provides a detailed regional study of the refugees who reached Brittany. A further useful regional study is provided by A. Laurens, 'Populations réfugiées et déplacées en Ariège de 1939 à 1945', *Revue d'histoire de la Deuxième Guerre mondiale*, 119 (1980), 45–59.

REPATRIATION

There is very little published research which deals explicitly with repatriation. J. Lagrange, 'Le Rapatriement des réfugiés après l'exode', *Revue d'histoire de la Deuxième Guerre mondiale* (1977), 39–52 is a helpful, if dated article. E. Alary, *La Ligne de demarcation 1940–1944* (Paris: Perrin, 2003) is interesting on the early days of the demarcation line and the problems refugees faced crossing it.

JEWS AND THE EXODUS

There are no specific works on this but the following works give some helpful context. V. Caron, *Uneasy Asylum: France and the Jewish Refugee Crisis, 1933–1942* (Stanford: Stanford University Press, 1999); P. Hyman, *The Jews of Modern France* (Berkeley and Los Angeles: University of California Press, 1998); L. Lazare, *Rescue as Resistance: How Jewish Organisations fought the Holocaust in France*

(Columbia: Columbia University Press, 1966); M. R. Marrus, *The Unwanted.*
European Refugees in the Twentieth Century (Oxford: OUP, 1985); M. R. Marrus
and R. Paxton, *Vichy et les Juifs* (Paris: Calmann Lévy, 1981), translated as *Vichy
France and the Jews* (Stanford: Stanford University Press, 1995).

DIARIES AND MEMOIRS

Numerous diaries and memoirs of the period provide vivid and poignant detail of
the exodus experience. Those I found most useful are listed below. Few of them
have been translated into English.

Politicians and Government Officials

Paul Badouin, *Neuf mois au gouvernment (avril-decembre 1940)* (Paris: Éditions de la
Table ronde, 1948) available in English as *The Private Diaries (March 1940–January
1941) of Paul Baudouin* (London: Eyre & Spottiswood, 1948); W. Churchill, *The
Second World War*, ii. *Their Finest Hour* (1949; London: Cassell & Co, 1967); M.
Junot, *1940: Tel que je l'ai vécu* (Paris: France Empire, 1998); R. Langeron, *Paris, juin
1940* (Paris: Flammarion, 1946); D. Léca, *La Rupture de 1940* (Paris: Fayard, 1978); P.
Mendès France, *Liberté, liberté, chérie* (Paris: Fayard, 1977); A. Morize, *France: Été
1940* (New York: Éditions de la Maison française, 1941); J. Moulin, *Premier Combat
(Journal posthume)* (Paris: Éditions de Minuit, 1947); C. Pomaret, *Le Dernier Témoin:
Fin d'une guerre, fin d'une république, juin et juillet 1940* (Paris: Presses de la Cité, 1968).

Members of the armed forces

E. d'Astier, *Sept fois, sept jours* (Paris: Gallimard, 1961); R. Dorgelès, *La Drôle de guerre*
(Paris: Albin Michel, 1973); H. Frenay, *La Nuit finira* (Paris: Laffont, 1973); Col.
G. A. Groussard, *Chemins secrets*, i (Paris: Bades-Dufour, 1948); A. Lunel, *Par
d'étranges chemins* (Monaco: L. Jaspard, 1946); G. Sadoul, *Journal de guerre* (Paris:
Harmattan, 1994); L. Rebatet, *Les Décombres 1938/1940: Les Mémoires d'un fasciste*, i
(Paris: Pauvert, 1976); for a remarkable and gripping read, E. Spears, *Assignment to
Catastrophe*, vols. i and ii (New York: A. A. Wyn, 1954–5).

Journalists and writers

S. de Beauvoir, *La Force de l'âge*, ii (Paris: Gallimard, 1960); A. Chamson, *Écrit en
1940 ...* (Paris: Gallimard, 1944); R. Dorgelès, *Vacances forcés* (Paris: Albin Michel,
1985); R. Downing, *If I Laugh* (London: Harrap, 1941); P. Léautaud, *Journal
littéraire*, xiii.: *Février 1940–juin 1941* (Paris: Mercure de France, 1962); L. Werth,
33 jours (Paris: Magnard, 2002).

For a moving account of her husband's return, having survived deportation,
M. Duras, *La Douleur* (Paris: POL, 1985), trans. as *La Douleur* (London: Flamingo,
1987).

Civilians from popular and middle classes

G. Adrey, *Journal d'un replié: Notes et impressions d'un métallo Parisien pendant l'exode
(11 juin–26 juin 1940)* (Paris: René Débresse, 1941); A. Arenstam, *Tapestry of a*

Debacle (London: Constable and Co., 1942); P. Fontaine, *Last to Leave Paris* (London: Chaterson Ltd, 1942); M.-M. Fourcade, *L'Arche de Noé: Réseau 'Alliance' 1940–1945* (1968; Paris: Plon, 1989); B. and F. Groult, *Journal à quatre mains* (Paris: Denoël, 1962); A. Jacques, *Pitié pour les hommes* (Paris: Éditions du Seuil, 1943); A. Kahn, *Robert et Jeanne à Lyon sous l'Occupation* (Paris: Payot, 1990); S. Parvane-Bourrin, *Exode d'une Parisienne (juin–juillet 1940)* (Hanoi: Imprimerie de G. Taupin, 1942); G. and A. Vallotton, *C'était au jour le jour: Carnets (1939–1944)* (Paris: Payot, 1995).

FICTIONAL ACCOUNTS OF THE EXODUS

F. Boyer, *Jeux interdits* (Paris: Denoël, 1968); G. Danjou, *Exode 1940* (Paris: Éditions du Scorpion, 1960); R. Desforges, *La Bicyclette bleue* (Paris: Fayard, 1983); I. Némirovsky, *Suite française* (Paris: Denoël, 2004) trans. into English by S. Smith as *Suite française* (London: Chatto and Windus, 2006); F. Sagan, *Les Faux-Fuyants* (Paris: Julliard, 1991); J.-P. Sartre, *La Mort dans l'âme* (Paris: Gallimard, 1972), trans. as *Iron in the Soul* (London: Penguin, 1975).

FILMS SET DURING THE EXODUS

Casablanca (1942); *Les Jeux interdits* (1952); *Les Égarés* (2002); *Bon voyage* (2003).

For a discussion of French films produced during the war see S. Lindeberg, *Les Écrans de l'ombre: La Seconde Guerre mondiale dans le cinéma français (1944–1969)* (Paris: CNRS Éditions, 1997). On documentary film see S. Wharton, *Screening Reality: French Documentary Film during the German Occupation* (London: Peter Lang, 2006).

MEMORY AND REMEMBERING

In order to fully grasp the importance of repercussions from the First World War, refer to the fascinating book by J. Horne and A. Kramer, *German Atrocities 1914: A History of Denial* (New York: Yale University Press, 2001) and P. Nivet, *Les Réfugiés français de la Grande Guerre 1914–1920: Les 'Boches du Nord'* (Paris: Economica, 2004). For memories of the Second World War, H. Rousso, *Le Syndrome de Vichy de 1944 à nos jours* (Paris: Seuil, 1990) remains the most authoritative text. N. Wood, *Vectors of Memory: Legacies of Trauma in Postwar Europe* (Oxford: Berg, 1999) is also very helpful. A. Confino, 'Remembering the Second World War, 1945–1965: Narratives of Victimhood and Genocide', *Cultural Analysis*, 4 (2005) gives a more succinct overview.

DE GAULLE

On de Gaulle's France Libre movement, J.-L. Crémieux-Brilhac, *La France Libre: De l'appel du 18 juin à la Libération* (Paris: Gallimard, 1996). The position of French residents and refugees in London is explained in N. Atkin, *The Forgotten French: Exiles in the British Isles, 1940–1944* (Manchester: Manchester University Press, 2003). The memoirs of E. de Miribel, *La Liberté souffre violence* (1981; Paris: Plon, 1989) evoke her experiences working with de Gaulle.

Acknowledgements

Acknowledgement is made to the following for permission to reproduce illustrations: Bibliothèque de Documentation internationale contemporaine et Musée d'histoire contemporaine, Nanterre, Figs. 3, 4, 5, 14, 16, 17, 18, 19, 20, 21; ECPAD (rights reserved), Fig. 15; Hulton Archive/Getty Images, Figs. 6, 8; Keystone, France/Camera Press, London, Figs. 2, 9, 13; LAPI-Viollet/TopFoto. co.uk, Figs. 7, 10; Roger-Viollet/TopFoto.co.uk, Figs. 1, 11.

In a few instances we have been unable to trace the copyright owner prior to publication. If notified, the publishers will be pleased to amend the acknowledgements in any future edition.

Index